THE NEWS FROM ARKANSAS

SENSE OF HUMOR REQUIRED

VALERIE KATZ

The News From Arkansas: Sense of Humor Required
This book is written to provide information and motivation to readers. Its purpose is not to render any type of psychological, legal, or professional advice of any kind. The content is the sole opinion and expression of the author, and not necessarily that of the publisher.

Copyright © 2020 by Valerie Katz

All rights reserved. No part of this book may be reproduced, transmitted, or distributed in any form by any means, including, but not limited to, recording, photocopying, or taking screenshots of parts of the book, without prior written permission from the author or the publisher. Brief quotations for noncommercial purposes, such as book reviews, permitted by Fair Use of the U.S. Copyright Law, are allowed without written permissions, as long as such quotations do not cause damage to the book's commercial value. For permissions, write to the publisher, whose address is stated below.

Printed in the United States of America.

ISBN 978-1-951913-91-5 (Paperback)
ISBN 978-1-951913-92-2 (Digital)
ISBN 978-1-951913-93-9 (Hardback)

Lettra Press books may be ordered through booksellers or by contacting:

Lettra Press LLC
30 N Gould St. Suite 4753
Sheridan, WY 82801, USA
1 307-200-3414 | info@lettrapress.com
www.lettrapress.com

CHAPTER 1

Sunny Southern California, 2007

I was getting ready for work and my boyfriend David, who was *not* getting ready for work, as he was already *retired*, hollered at me from his warm cozy bed. "Honey, Eric Estrada is inviting us to Arkansas for the weekend. Come look at this beautiful place. We haven't been anywhere in a while and it's free, let's go! You know, just to look around."

Eric Estrada? The actor?

David... The first time I met David was at a country-western bar. We were taking a group dance lesson. You would dance with one guy and then every few minutes you would shift to the next one. When David came around for the second time I was so proud of myself. I actually remembered his name! I looked up and said "Hi, its Dave isn't it?" Now he is a full foot taller than I am. He looked down his nose at me and said, "My name *is David*." Well, I thought, *"La Dee Da"*.

I certainly remembered him! However, I didn't speak to him for 15 years. I even went to a party at his home with a friend of mine and didn't speak to him then. He was "That Snotty David" He, of course, had absolutely *no* idea who I was.

I wanted to learn how to do the West Coast swing, so I was out in a club one night where I ran into Richard, a friend of David's. He said if I wanted to learn how to do the West Coast swing I should take the lessons from his roommate. When he pointed his roommate out to me, it was David Katz! "Well", I thought to myself "When my feet are cold because *HELL* is freezing over, *that's* when I'll take a lesson from *David Katz.*"

But Richard said David was the best teacher for beginners and I really wanted to learn so I started taking lessons from David.

One Friday night I was in a club where David was giving lessons and D.J.ing. He came up and asked me if I would like to go dancing up in Ventura on Sunday. I was taken completely by surprise and stammered "Yes". The next day I called my friend Charlotte and said, "You won't believe it, but I think I have a date with that snotty David on Sunday" she said "What do you mean you *think* you have a date? You sound like a 12-year-old!"

David called later in the day and asked if we were still on for dancing. When I asked if this was an outing for the class he said no, it was not a class trip, and did I still want to go. When I said yes he said he would pick me up. But his house was 1/2 way between my house and Ventura, so I said I would meet him there.

We went to Ventura, danced all afternoon and had a wonderful time. He was so warm and friendly. I completely change my mind about him. I had mentioned that the Hungry Hunter was my absolute favorite restaurant and on the way home nothing would do but that we stop there for dinner.

When we got back to David's house, and my car, it was about 9 PM and I thought I really should be getting home. David asked me to come in and when I said no he gave me the sweetest little kiss and helped me into my car.

After that I saw him at my regular dance classes, but our day of dancing was not mentioned. I figured he wasn't interested in dating me. About three weeks later I was again at the Friday night dance and he came up behind me and said, "It's too bad I don't play golf." When I asked him why he said, "If I did then maybe I'd have a chance with you." I answered, "You probably would if you just picked up the phone and gave me a call." I said it ever so sweetly and with a smile. ;)

We fell in love and decided I should move in with him. Now I had been single for over 30 years, raising my family and not budging from my home. This was a very big change! There were some very surprised reactions from family and friends when I sent out "We are moving" notes.

The "We" was me and a 70 lb. Rottweiler named Hoover. You should have seen the look on his face when I said, "Love me, love my dog". My son Larry and his family were set to move into my home and David wanted to know why Larry wasn't going to keep the dog. I informed him, in no uncertain terms, that Larry would love to, but Hoover was *my* dog.

He said he would have to think about that and headed for home. When he arrived there, a whole 15 min. later, he said he had it all worked out. He would put in a doggie door from the laundry room to the garage and another one from the garage to the back yard. Hoover was welcome.

There had never been a dog in his house. When an old roommate of his found out about the dog she said she would give us 3 months. Things are going great so I hope we can get an extension :) He and Hoover are mad for each other. I told him I was going to have to sue for alienation of affection. As I said, he is retired so he takes her everywhere. To the dog park for walks, and even the to the bank. When he leaves to go someplace without her, she sits at the door and cries until I holler at her. Hey, I'm still here! Ungrateful wench! Anyway, he is a love and wants to make me happy. My Mom and the kids all like him so I guess we are ahead of the game.

David had taken me too many places to look for a better place to retire. Los Angeles was out of the question, he advised. My answer was always the same. "*NO!*" It was set in stone. When he asked me just what I did want, that answer was always the same also. "When I look out my windows, I want to see green." He finally realized his thoughts of Palm Springs or Vegas were never going to fly. When asked what he wanted, his answer was always the same too. A three-car garage, my man has tools, and, of course, a room big enough for his dance studio. He wanted to continue giving his lessons.

Bella Vista was as beautiful as advertised, lush and green, set in the Ozark Mountains with golf courses and lakes all over the place. It was a 3-hour flight to get there and I hadn't a clue where we had landed. We met a nice couple in the bar and I asked, "Where is Arkansas? Where are we?" Their answer… "About halfway across the country and little bit south" I knew all I needed to know. I fell in love with Bella Vista Village.

Gone was the girl who had announced loud and long, "I'm not moving! I will always live right here." My four children, six grandchildren, my Mom, who was almost 90, my two sisters and my brother were all within an hour and a half of me. My children had been unofficially forbidden to move *more* than an hour and a half from their Mother! I wasn't going anywhere.

After our tour of the area… "Honey" I said to David "I've always wanted to live in a place just like this". "Really!" He then asked, with more than a little skepticism, "Should I call a real estate agent?" Now as much to his surprise as mine, I said "Yes!" We looked at homes and picked one out. It had the three-car garage David wanted and I could see nothing but trees out of every window. Sold!

That was all well and good, but I did have one little concern. David and I were living together but had no plans to get married. It was necessary... I had to tell him... I was not moving all the way to Arkansas without a piece of paper that said he was legally bound to stick by me once we got there! It was, after all, a little out of my comfort zone. "Okay" he said, "Let's go home and plan a wedding."

Giving the good news to my family went something like this. It was Easter Sunday and the gang was all there. We lined them all up on the stairs for the usual round of picture taking, and I told them we had a few announcements to make. I had already gotten one new cornea and I needed the other one, so we started there with our news. A date had been set for the next cornea. That's wonderful they said and started to get up. Waving my hands in the air, I said "NO, NO, there's more! "

The next good news was that we were getting married, so I announced with a flourish, "I would like to introduce you to my fiancée!" Then they were really excited! "Mom that's wonderful!" was being expressed so loudly the grandkids, who had been sent upstairs when their round of pictures had been taken, all started to come down to see what in the world was going on! Loud cheering started, and they started to get up again. I started waving again "NO, NO, there's still more!"

"We have one more announcement. We have decided to sell both of our homes and buy one together." That was greeted with more excitement and the question "Where?" When my answer was Arkansas, there was dead silence. Then the girls started to cry, and boys look like they wanted to. I wanted to remember this day, so David was making a video. My oldest grandgirl, Kirsten, looked right in the lens and said "*YOU CAN'T GO!* But, in the end, they all gave us big hugs and said what they wanted most was for us to be happy.

It was time to make plans! A date was set for the wedding and a honeymoon cruise to Alaska was booked. My friend

Charlotte was to be my Maid of Honor. She asked if she could wear a red dress that was a favorite of hers. Her friends had told her *NO. NOT* a good choice for the Maid of Honor. But when I informed David of the idea, he said "Honey, that's a great idea. I have a red bow tie and red cummerbund. Red will be the color! We'll get them for the boys too!" My David was never one to hide his light under a bushel! Our grandsons, Alex (mine) and Ryan (his), were chosen to be ring bearers and they got their red bow ties and red cummerbunds. They just looked adorable! So, did the groom.

There was a hitch. David's daughter, Marcy and grandson Ryan, were living in Toronto and there was something wrong with the passport situation. They couldn't get here in time for the wedding! So, we did the only thing we could possibly do...we delayed the wedding. We were having it in our Rose Garden, so it could easily be delayed, but the honeymoon, which was already paid for, could not! As my sister Martha likes to say "Life is short. Eat dessert first!" We went on the honeymoon, came back, got married, and started making plans to move.

The die was cast... We had no idea what we were getting in to...

The real estate market in California had really tanked, so for a year we couldn't sell the house. We had to settle for visits to Bella Vista. I would get there all ramped up, in my California rush, rush, mode. I would go to the store, people would be chatting me up, and in my mind, I would be thinking "Oh please, please, just give me my change let me be on my way!" It would take me three or four days to calm down, a *little*, and start to relax. Then it would be back to California and the rush was on!

Since we couldn't move to Arkansas we decided to make long weekend trips to our new home. Some went smoothly, some did not. On one of the trips we had trouble with flights and delays and ended up spending the night in Texas. We got a call,

4am Texas time, 2 am California time. A neighbor of ours, in California, said he just rescued our other dog, Cricket. When he came home and pulled in the driveway a very tired Cricket came running up to him. There were coyotes following her! Apparently, Cricket had jumped out of the back yard and decided to run and frolic with the coyotes. She was getting tired and they were moving in. She had figured out her error and was so happy to find someone to rescue her!

David called home and when he got our roommate Richard on the phone he asked where the dog was, Richard, just having been awakened, was understandably confused and wanted to know what in the heck David was calling about. The dog was probably asleep! David said no, she's been out frolicking with coyotes. She is across the street with the neighbors; would he please go and get her? Cricket is a smart dog, she had learned her lesson. She *did not* go play with the coyotes again.

On our visits to Arkansas we didn't have our computers and David hadn't, as yet, met the iPhone. His "business" in California needed his monitoring. So, we went to the library and got library cards. Their technology wasn't up to speed. It took forever, to find, read, or send anything, but David was happy. He was in contact with California! We were moving to a new world and we needed to keep in touch with civilization.

On another visit my sister Martha came with us. We had sent a half truck of furniture to our new home so that when we got there, we wouldn't have to sleep on the blowup mattress and we would have a refrigerator and some furniture. She came with us on that trip, so she could see our beautiful new world. Washing windows and screens had not been mentioned to her *before* the trip but she joined in, with smiles?!

David went out to run errands. When he came home he had found a house for sale on the next cul-de-sac and nothing would do but for Martha and I to come see it. He usually returned home with information on a new place to eat! This is not California my friends. The house had an Open House sign on it, was unlocked, and no one was there minding the store! David had become quite smitten with the house and thought maybe we should be moving. Again! I told him no way! His but honey, it has a mud room and a backyard and another bedroom downstairs, fell on *my* deaf ears. My replied? We don't need a backyard or another bedroom downstairs, I love the house we are moving into! That did not fall on deaf ears. He could hear just fine! We went back to Bella Lane.

In July we went to visit our now semi-furnished home. No flight problems! Showers! David made us drinks, we sat down in our rockers and started to unwind, me in my Tinkerbell PJ's and David in his underwear and socks. He hooked up the VHS and we watched Law and Order. Good Times!

CHAPTER 2

Arkansas News, 2008

Notes to the kids. July. Our trip to Arkansas was uneventful. No delays and no bumpy air. David is really not feeling well so we are spending a lot of time at home, which is lovely for me. I like just being here. We spent all afternoon and evening watching the whole season of Damages. (Thanks Denise!) We would like to see a couple of movies, something we never find time to do in CA, but David is not sure he can sit in a movie that long.

We had our first BBQ. David bought some filets and we had that and salad our first night here. I am sending this from the library and this computer is 3 to 10 words behind my typing so don't be dismayed if the whole thing sounds a little off. David went to the golf etc. club this morning and went in the Jacuzzi. I stayed home and read. There is nothing very exciting to write about. Just so you all know we got here safe and are enjoying. —*Love, Mom.*

We were here for a week when David produced a fever of 102. He had had a bad night the night before and I was in a panic! Who to call! Shall I call California and talk to Kaiser? Feverish heads prevailed. "No honey. Look in my wallet for my

V.A. card. There will be a number on the back to call." Thank God for the V.A. Hospital here. It is rated 3rd in the nation and they treated David wonderfully, like he was a General! Tonsillitis AND pneumonia!

I wrote home... If I told you I would think of you all often and write every day, I lied! We are enjoying good weather, no rain. Our deck is so surrounded by trees it looks like we are actually sitting in a tree house, and I am sleeping in every day.

If you are all gathering rocks to throw at me upon my return, let me add this: My Mom is back in the hospital; David has had tonsillitis and pneumonia since we got here, and to add insult to injury, the weather hates my hair! David has been on so many meds he can't join me for the cocktail hour. I'm sure it will surprise no one when I say that has not slowed me down one bit!

We are supposed to break out of the house tomorrow for dinner for our anniversary which David would not have lived to see if he wasn't such a good patient! *See you all soon, Mom.*

We have received GOOD NEWS!! Our Real Estate lady from California called. She has someone who wants to rent our house for 2 years!! Check in hand! As soon as we stopped jumping up and down we divided up the bathroom drawers and cabinets and organized the kitchen drawers. We are going home to pack! I have made a mental note to learn how to slow and down and be friendly when we move here. —*Love, Mom.*

August. Well my darlings, I guess we are really going. Yesterday David signed a 2-year lease on this house and they will be moving in on Sept. 26. We will be very busy packing now. If there is anything in this house you have ever coveted, please let us know now. We are not going to take all this stuff with us. So, no matter how big or small, if you want something let me know and we can tell you if it is going with us or not. If you just want to come, look and maybe shop around, do it soon. We will be packing, and you may want to save us the time packing some little thing or 2. Don't be bashful! —*I love you all, Mom.*

I had been a single mom for 33 years and had worked at the same job for 34. My claim to fame was, "If you are looking for me, call my home or office. You'll always find me." WOW! Had that changed! New phone numbers, new time zone, new zip code! A new world...

That's when the "News" started. Arkansas was almost a foreign country to us. I found such humor in all we encountered. The subject line on my e-mails was "The News from Arkansas." I could tell my family about all the fun we were having, all the new customs, and all the nice people. Then David wanted his family added to the "News" list and soon many of our friends also wanted to know what we were up to. No one would be able to say, "David and Valerie moved away, and we never heard a word from them." I sent the "News"!

SO... Here's the "News"

September 2017. We are here! Arkansas is now officially our home. We arrived with wine, scotch and Daughter-in-law, Debbie's homemade biscuits. Now the "Where are we going to put it all" tour begins.

October. It took the movers 2 days to unload all our stuff. One of our new neighbors drove the men with the moving van down to the house so they could decide how to get that huge truck here at the end of our very crooked street. We have been packing for months so unpacking is a real treasure hunt. I have spent most of the past 3 days unloading the kitchen and deciding where everything should go, very *daunting* to say the least. I'm someone who needs a whole week just to figure out how to load a new dishwasher for crying out loud!

VALERIE KATZ

The people here amaze us every day. We went out for pizza with Lee and Becky, the real estate couple who sold us this house. Becky asked if we *liked* to play cards or games. Get together for pot luck and games! Am I in heaven or what!

Some neighbors came over today with cookies and brownies and said they would like to have all the new folks over for some treats and a slide show they have made about all the fun and beautiful things to do around here. I'm thinking of having the neighbors over for dinner when we get most of the stuff put away. Anyone still standing after that last sentence? I'll try. I really will! —*We are home, love Valerie.*

I woke up today to wonderful thunder and lightning. I've been feeling badly about being here for a whole week without some stormin' to be lisnin' to. I'm working on my Southern drawl.

David went out to a dance last night. His second since we have been here. I can't even find my dance shoes! I am too happily busy, getting unpacked to want to go dancing just yet. He didn't just *go* to the Moose Lodge, *he joined*, and danced. He said the band was wonderful, but the dancers need some work. Uh oh, sounds like someone is looking for students! Should I remind him we are retired? Should I remind him *I* am retired!

While he was out I found the kitchen counters. I knew they were in there somewhere. I am really surprised, and pleased at all the counter space and storage we have. David installed pull out baskets in all the bottom kitchen cabinets that were large enough to hold them. After that, it's OK if he goes dancing! —*Love & hugs, Valerie.*

Leaving my siblings in the lurch with my Mom has taken some of the joy out of the move. They are certainly in my prayers. She is not doing well and the fact that she is harder to communicate with makes talking on the phone hard for me, but I promise to do better. —*Love you, Valerie*

Jane, from 1 Berrydale Lane, came down today to introduce herself, offer any assistance we might need and brought 3 nut cakes, one with cranberries, one banana, and one, to be a surprise. I'm hoping for lemon. She told us she was the one who picked up the movers and drove them down to #9 to see what they were in for. Her husband wanted to know what in the world she was doing picking up strange men in the street!

The trash man came today, and we did it right! Recycling is very important to me but apparently not to the trash man. This is another interesting new hitch in our Arkansas adventure. In CA you get the big bin and all the recycle stuff gets thrown in it and a big truck comes and picks it up. *Not so in Arkansas.* Things have to be sorted 10 ways to Sunday and taken to the recycle center. Plastic containers have to be sorted, #1's in one bin and #2's in another. They don't take anything over #2, so you need to be vigilant. Newspapers, magazines, cardboard, aluminum cans, must be separated. Bottles must be separated as to color (clear, brown, green). To add to all that, David wasn't overjoyed at the prospect of having all those bins *in his garage*. I managed to do it in four stacking bins and then I reminded him, It's my garage too... honey.

David and I had chicken for dinner tonight. My favorite, the one you buy already cooked and ready to eat. I was thinking about the time my sister Martha and I went up to see our cousins, the Trent's. We brought one of those chickens and after dinner Neil sat with the bones and picked them clean! I was sitting here in our kitchen, working on the bones, when David saw a wasp that had been visiting with me, in the kitchen, all afternoon. "Honey" he said, "How we are going to get it out of here?!" I was still very busy with my chicken bones, so I replied, "I think if we turn off all the lights in the kitchen and turn on the lights on the deck it will go out." The next thing I know I'm sucking on bones in the dark! David was out in the garage. The wasp took the cue and headed for the deck.

My son Larry called me today to tell me my granddaughter Kalyn had her first basketball game. They won 14 - 4 and Kalyn made 10 of the points! No wonder she isn't so hot to dance this year. That's fine with me as I don't get the 50% employee discount on dance lessons any more.

I am still using David's computer as he hasn't hooked mine up yet. I'm still looking for my office stuff so that I can get that room finished. I have been waiting to get my own computer up and running and connected to the internet. That will have to happen before you get this. I am keeping track of things on WordPerfect and will transfer it all then. I worked really hard on my side of the desk today, so I think there is actually enough room there now. I hope tomorrow will be the big day..

In answer to a query from my sister Cyndi; we both have our own computers because we had them before we were living together. *HOWEVER*, I would not want to share David's in any case. My computer is not installed as yet so I'm using David's. I wait until he leaves the house before I log on. I've got my own camera and drill for the same reasons. He is a darling and but more than just a little picky about his things. *The instructions seem to be required each and every time the item is used!*

Hey, y'all come by and see us when you are in the neighborhood. All we see when we look out our windows is green. The dogwood trees are turning red and we are told the rest won't be far behind. During the winter months, it's not quite as pretty but I still love looking at all those trees! —*Love, Valerie.*

Friday, we went to the Moose for dinner and dancing. Dancing started at 5 pm, $5.00 each to get in. Dinner started at 6, $3.00 each. Dinner was a grilled cheese sandwich, homemade potato soup, salad and homemade chocolate cake. We danced until the 7 o-clock break and went home. We Arkies are party animals!

We saw our first deer today. We were on our way home from Subway where we had lunch and it was just standing in the street. It looked at us and then showed us its little white tail and dashed in to the trees. We are still throwing deer corn out back and the chipmunks and squirrels seem to like it but so far, no deer. The neighbors assure us that once they find out dinner is being served they won't miss a day.

I put out our solar lights today. Arkansas is rocks! Two of our neighbors came over to get a load of the new kid on the block trying to put plastic posts in the rock beds out front. After much digging, sledging, and hammering I gave up trying to put them in the decorative rock and put them on the edges of the grass. Even then, the positions had to be moved about as there are rocks under the grass too. I didn't want the gardener to have to work around them, but he is on his own. Oops, I have been told, but I forgot. They aren't gardeners, they *are grass cutters*. Anything else you want to have done needs to be negotiated!

We needed the lights to find our way home after dark. There are no street lights on our cul-de-sac and after dark means really dark! David was having quite a time backing into the driveway at night, and we never leave the house without buying something that needs to be unloaded from the back of the car.

Still unpacking, I'm still looking for my office stuff so that I can get that room finished. *As I have mentioned before*, I have been waiting to get my own computer up and running and connected to the internet.

We are having a little rain today. It is mowing day across the street and that guy was out there on his riding mower anyway! There was a bit of hosing off after he was done but the yard looks good.

Hallelujah!! My computer is up and running. So here is the "News!" —*Love to all, Valerie.*

November. David got 4 eight-foot lights installed in the garage today along with 220 power. With all that power and light, I'll never get him to stop and come in at night! The electrician looked so cute in his overalls, and that Southern accent was a killer. It only took 4 trips to Lowes for things that needed to be replaced because something or other was missing in the package. David is now on a first name basis with the return guy. We'll be going out to dinner with him and his family in no time.

There are 2 neighbors out front wanting to know what we are up to now. The Mr. Katz has gone out to give them an update. Oh yes, and we are still unpacking. —*Love, Valerie*

Wow! What a day Saturday was. We were up and out by 8:00 am. We went to the bank sponsored rummage sale for the Animal Shelter. David had taken 5 or 6 boxes of our 'what in the world did we pack that for!' stuff to them during the week as a donation to the cause. We wanted to get a peek at what our donated goodies were going for, so we were there as soon as they opened and joined those who were buying little treasures. The top of the list of great finds was 4 wonderful pictures for our bathrooms. Then on to another rummage sale and 4 garage sales. We only left one without leaving some cash. We were feeling pretty lucky with our loot. We then went to an antique mall, where we found the perfect pot for one of my orchids and 3 very nice Delft pieces.

After a quick bite we were off to the tractor supply store for a 50-pound block of salt with which to lure the deer. We are not giving up until we see Bambi in our back yard! You should have seen David and me dragging that heavy hunk, or being drug *by* that heavy hunk, of salt down into the woods. We were trying very hard not to take flight!

Then on to a pawn shop where I got a GREAT golf bag for $6.99! We passed on the guns and rifles even though they were 50% of the inventory price. We stopped next at an art gallery and finished up at the hardware store. Quite the eclectic morning.

When we got home we found two little goodie bags on the front stoop, porch for you non-Arkies. One from #12 down the street with a cinnamon honey spread and two dip mixes, and the other from one of the local churches inviting us to join including a sermon on a disc, a pen with their name printed on it, and a decorative cross. I'm telling you, the people here are friendly!

The fun really started when we decided to go to Mustang Alley and do a little dancing. David loaded up the GPS unit, which will be referred to from now on as the TDM (That Darn Machine). We were on our way down highway 71 when TDM started using her favorite word, *recalculating*. I might add that she says this in a very condescending tone of voice. Then she seemed to lose her way and just kept repeating *THAT* word, mixing it up from time to time with, "follow the highlighted route" when there was no highlighted route to be seen!

We were now totally turned around and pretty darn sure all of us were lost, including the TDM. David stopped the car and called the Mustang place and got some none too clear instructions. Part of the problem is this question, which we seem to be hearing a lot. Are you on new 71, old 71 or business 71? Now how would two lost people from CA know that? I ask you!

In hopes of finding our way, David made a U-turn. The next thing we knew out of the darkness a sheriff's car appeared, lights and all, and pulled us over. As soon as the sheriff appeared at the window David said "Hi, were lost and the TDM was giving us all kinds of conflicting advice!" "Ah, Yes, *Sir*", the sheriff says, "I thought so, *Sir*". I think he had been watching us go around in circles for a while. "Those GPS things get confused out here and try to send everyone to the Mustang Road High School, *Sir*. The reason I stopped you, S*ir*, is you can't make a U-turn here, S*ir*".

Now I'm not kidding, it was so dark out there that when you did come across an intersection, and I use that term loosely, you couldn't really *see* it until you are half way through it *and then* only if you had someone with you to watch *for* it! Taking your eyes *off* the road is *not* a good idea. The sheriff was in the know as to where the Mustang Alley was, and was kind enough to give us excellent directions, and *no ticket*. I did get a little chuckle when the sheriff, who looked about 15, asked David if he was a *retired* police officer from CA. David did not tell him he only carries a police shirt in the window of his car to keep from getting tickets, but that he used to be in the uniform maintenance business and that was how the shirt got there. Uh Huh.

We started out again armed with some new instructions, when you know who, said you know what. We turned her off! The sheriff did say, "You turn left at the light, the only one between here and the state line, so you can't miss it. The Mustang Alley is *up the road a piece.* You go straight up Hwy 90 and you'll find it alright" That was the understatement of the day. *It was 9 miles, in pitch darkness, and not more that one of those miles was straight!* After we found it, yes, we finally did, we danced on a floor that was so slick we had to hang on to each other for dear life, so we wouldn't fall. But the people were wonderful. Going home as it turned out was *a much shorter drive.* David said, "This is a really nice road, isn't it?" I replied, "Yes". He continued, **"**I said that on the way out didn't I?". "Yes" I replied. He stated, with a chuckle, "Well it must be or I wouldn't have driven that extra 10 miles or so on it going out!" —*We love Arkansas, Valerie.*

Here's a little tidbit from our trip out here. The truck stops outside of CA are wonderful. About half way here we stopped at one that had a really big sign in the window. It said, Breakfast, Lunch, Dinner, Ice Cream & Shopping. They sell books on CD for $9.99 and $14.99. Yes, well known authors! I told David he could just leave me there because they had it all. He bought me some ice cream and a Michael Crichton book and told me to *get in the car*.

Now anyone trying to get me on my cell phone please note, it is no longer among the living. As soon as we can get to Verizon I will rectify that and let you know.

Yesterday we went shopping. Oh yes, we heard it was going to rain and the sky was dark and stormy looking. It poured! Except for getting soaked it *was* a good time to shop. No lines in the stores. At Sam's the cashier actually was so bored he unloaded our cart for us. The people here seem to have enough sense to come in out of the rain. We're learning.
—*Loving it in Arkansas, Valerie*

I now have a new job. I am the personal assistant to Bella Vista's new Master Cabinet Builder, one David Katz. I didn't even have to apply! I just had to answer the call. "Honey, can you come down here and help me for a minute". So, down the stairs I went. We are installing a row of cabinets in the craft room and they had to be moved around and have their bottoms trimmed about 3 inches, so the counter would be *just* right for my sewing area. Now, I haven't actually *sewn* anything in years, I'm more of a mender these days but now that I'm retired, who knows?!

My part of the job seemed to be getting things from upstairs in the garage that my Master Builder forgot to bring down with him. Unfortunately, he seemed to remember them one at a time, so there were many trips. At the same time, we were organizing the crawl space/storage area. The many cans of paint were no longer welcome there, so they needed to go up the stairs and into the garage. No, that did not save me any trips! The things going up and the things going down did not occur to the MB at the same time.

The sound of our next project gave me a little start! We were headed out to the garage to build a *cabinet carcass*. There was much lifting, measurements, gluing and nailing. I now know that the Original Titebond Wood Glue sets up in about 15 minutes, so you better get crackin' when you are told to push, pull, or square-up something. You would be surprised how fast the MB can repeat those instructions if you are not fast enough! Now this carcass is 8' high 3' wide and 2' deep. That sucker is heavy. We used the great glue, but to hold everything together while it was setting, a nail gun was required. It seemed to me that most of the time I was looking into the business end of that thing! "No honey, over there", was repeated many, many times as I tried to move to what I considered a much safer place. The really big level and the big square were used to make sure all the shelves would be level when we stood it up against the wall and screwed it in place. The next morning when the "*Oh no, oh no, oh no's*!" started to fly, the big square, the big level, the nail gun, and I were getting ready to make a break for it! However, all is well. All that was needed was a few well places wedges to level things up. I know what you're thinking, I'm not "a personal assistant", I'm just "the go-fer". But the MB fixes me a drink and gives me a kiss at the end of the day.
—*And yes, we are still unpacking, Valerie.*

Is there a breeze today? You don't even have to ask. You can hear it whispering through the trees out back. The trees that were green when we got here a month ago have turned and it looks like gold and bronze snow flurries when I look out the back windows. It is still warm enough to watch from the deck. I can wax poetic about the leaves because I won't have to rake them. They fall into the forest and stay there just as they should.

I wish they were falling on Bambi but no luck so far. Leaves in the front? Some, blowing about, but the only tree that would be making trouble in our yard is gone. When we decided to move here I asked David for a Magnolia tree. When he asked where I wanted to put it, I pointed to the tree that was already in place and said, "Right there". "You' want to take out a perfectly good tree and plant another one in the same spot?" "Yes" I said. "Why? "Because I want a Magnolia tree and that is the only place in the yard a tree would look good. That's why the builder put one there" I think my logic was lost on him. "I don't think so" he retorted.

Sooo, every time we were anywhere that was selling trees I was looking at Magnolias and I pointed them out each time we passed one on the street. I assured him that they were slow growing so trimming would never be a problem and we could plant it, take its picture and track it's growth each year. I mean, we won't be marking kid's growth on the doors!

With the flurry and excitement of actually moving here and all the other things we were doing, we have had so many other things to think about the Magnolia tree went out of my mind for a while. Not so my husband. He had some folks here putting in stairs down to the salt block, that steep trip was going to kill us! And did I mention it weighed 50 lbs.! They were also shoring up a retaining wall that led to the new steps. David came in to tell me what was going on and said, "Oh yes, please go out front and tell them where you want your tree". They had taken down the old one and planted my Magnolia a few feet away. *My Master Builder has a soft spot!* —*Valerie*

Our daily paper always has local news on the front page, a *human-interest story.* I take the time to sit and read the paper now. Here is one that caught my eye the day after the election. Arkansas passed a $300 million bond measure requiring annual legislation sessions, allowing the General Assembly to decide who will be election officials, *and* striking "insane" from the Constitution. Honest! It's right there, on the front page!

Also, news worthy, *and also on the front page, with a picture...* "Lt. Gov. Bill Halter greets supporters at Sticky Fingers Chicken

Shack on Tuesday night". "About 2/3 of the state's voters supported the lottery measure championed by Halter." I wish I could have been there getting my fingers sticky!

I can't wait to give TDM the instructions to David's woodcarvers meeting. I am still a little annoyed with her from the Mustang Alley incident. The fellow who hosts it sent these instructions via e-mail. "Take W 72 past the Hiwasse Post Office, left on Gordon Hollow, a gravel road, in 1 mile turn right on Fielding Road and go 1 & 1/2 miles to the 3rd driveway." That should give her something to think about. —*David better take his phone. Valerie*

For the first time in both of our lives, we had no trick or treaters. We didn't miss jumping up every 5 min. to answer the door, but now I have a big bag of candy hidden from the Master Builder. It's only a matter of time. He is really too busy to hunt for it and I do give him 3 pieces each night after dinner. It's a good thing Halloween was *after* I got my Magnolia!

He has been cracking the whip around the house and in the garage as well, as the rest of the house is starting to look beautiful. A tip for you girls... If your guy ever tells you to shape up or he is going to treat you like a *lag bolt*, run for the hills! We were out in the garage hanging a very large and very heavy cabinet carcass and all was not going well. He couldn't get the 3 1/2 in. lag bolt to take hold. "Bring me the hammer!" he said in a voice I know means *hurry*. He took it, and soon all was moving along much better. Apparently, when a lag bolt doesn't do what it is supposed to do you hit it on the head until it starts to screw right! Another lesson learned.

Also, I learn from the pearls of wisdom I receive from the MB. "Honey," he always delivers the pearls in a very sweet way, "Take some of those things to the garage now. You know, the job is never over until the clean-up is done". Uh huh.

We are still unpacking. The pace picked up this week as the MB still hadn't found the safe place he had picked to pack our

US Open tickets and my Savings Bonds. The *actual* safe was deemed *not safe*. It was not hard to find, and had already been installed. All is well, the lost is found, and we will be coming to town and enjoying the US Open with our friends. I still love Arkansas, but I do love my MB more! —*Valerie.*

November. My Mom turned 90 this week. I never, *ever,* thought I would miss this big event. I called her, and she said being in Arkansas was a pretty good excuse.

We have been told it is winter. Honestly, I think we had figured it out for ourselves. It gets down to the low 30's, sometimes the high 20's at night. The Ficus tree we brought with us is now in the dining room. We were just going to cover it but the prediction for a night in the 20's made us feel more compassionate. Someone told us that winter only really lasts about 5 weeks here. He was a used car salesman though, so we took that statement with a grain of salt. However, he was correct in telling David that the Chevy Cobalt can be towed behind a motor home, so my wonderful MB bought it for me. I think in-part, so we can *STOP* measuring the garage to see if it is indeed configured so that 2 cars can fit in it after all the cabinets David had shipped from CA were installed. I hope so because I would hate for the MB to have to leave his vehicle out in the cold. He promised me I could have mine *in* the garage.

The plan now is to drive the Cobalt to CA and pull it behind the motor home back to Arkansas. We are trying to make new plans about when to leave and what to take. It honestly seems like we just got here. Oh, maybe that is because we are *still* unpacking! —*Love, Valerie.*

David was a dance instructor in his former life, so he had a dance floor installed in the lower level of our house. He is anxious to "Let the Lessons Begin!" He had the installation done before we moved. Unfortunately, we did not have good information regarding cement floors and humidity. The lower floors are subject to lots of humidity. When we came to visit the floor had buckled. We have had it fixed but the jury is still out. There are places that crackle when we walk on it. The MB needs to walk a different route. He gets a very pained expression on his face and says, "oh darn" when he hears the noise. We have installed a dehumidifier. Every time I open the door and walk in the dance room the dehumidifier turns on, I think it likes me. :)

Also, my MB would like some clarification on his reluctance to replace the old tree with my Magnolia. He has asked me to tell you all that the tree that was removed had a trunk that was 3 feet across and it was 3 stories high. The new tree is about 8 feet high. I'm not sure just what his point is, but since I have my tree, I am learning to take orders... well, at least honor his requests. —*Love to all, Valerie*

My darling MB is learning. I was almost to the stairs yesterday when he called and asked me to bring something else down with me, therefore saving me a trip! When he unpacks a box, he puts the contents away. Now don't think for a moment that means it is where it belongs. Oh No! That just means it is up off the floor and out of his sight. We will be starting a whole new treasure hunt after all the boxes are gone. We are retired. What else do we have to do?

I would like to send a little thank you to those of you who have sent little notes back to me. It is good to know you are receiving and enjoying the "News".

I am making up with the GPS. We are, after all, driving to CA soon. I must admit however that we will probably need it less going to CA than to our airport which is only 1/2 hour away. The back way, through the beautiful countryside, is so full of twists and turns we couldn't find our way there without her. Oh, we could go the long way, but it is easier to start calling her the GPS again. (Giant Pain Somewhere ;-)

David went to the bank today, *His* first trip through the drive through. And, it was cookie day! When the girl handed him a cookie with his receipt, he asked if he could have another one for his wife. He gave it to me too! They also have popcorn day and you can get coffee, make copies and use the shredder every day, for free! You can find all that in a cozy room that looks like some golfer's study. I told David if I ever got mad enough at him to have to go somewhere to cool off, he could probably find me at the bank.

Our plan is to hit the road on Monday the 22nd. Your reporter will be out of touch for a while. —*Now packing! Valerie*

Dear friends and faithful readers, I hope you will forgive your reporter for not sending all the news to you, but some news needs to be further researched. We found out today that David has a cancerous tumor in his bladder. In the last two weeks we have been many times to the VA Hospital for tests, tests, and more tests. The diagnosis was confirmed today. We have a consultation with the urologist on Tuesday the 25th to see about a surgery date so our departure for CA may be delayed. We hope to be able to leave Tuesday evening for Los Angeles and be there for Thanksgiving dinner and the U S Open. —*Love, Valerie.*

For my lady readers I have 2 words. Shop Vac. A shop vac, is to the vacuum we use in the home, as an outhouse is to our bathroom. You don't have to be careful. You just go around picking up everything that's not nailed down and it keeps on working. Where was this when I was picking up after my kids? Remember the stuff they put down the toilet? If they had tried that in the outhouse they could go get it themselves or do without! Oh, you can clog them up, if you pick up enough leaves, twigs and small pieces of wood along with all the saw dust. Then you may have to ask the MB to clean it out for you, but since you have been hard at work in his shop, he won't mind.

I now have a smaller version for in the house. When asked by the MB why I needed yet another vacuum, at last count I think we have 5 items for vacuuming up stuff, I told him with mostly hardwood floors, and a Master Builder bringing in all sorts of things on his shoes, I had *new* vacuum issues. You can't be a good assistant without the proper tools. In defense of the MB, he did try to stop me a few times in my quest for a dust free garage to put my new car in. "Honey" he said, "Just leave it. I'm only going to mess it up again". I will have to ask his sister if he tried that one on his mother when she told him to clean his room. Oh, and once again, I know what you're thinking. Boy, does he have her snowed?! But ladies, he does the grocery shopping. Now that is a job I hate! —*Love to all, Valerie*

We have read the phrase "Tough Old Bird" in much of our in-coming mail lately, and I don't think it was in reference to the Thanksgiving turkey. I'm pretty sure the reference was to my very own Master Builder. We see the doctor tomorrow. Slow growing, noninvasive, very treatable, those are the phrases we expect to hear. We will be fine. —*Love, Valerie.*

So sorry all, David has to go back to the VA again tomorrow, so they can run a flashlight up his flag pole to get a better look-see. There is no way we can be in California by Thurs. Hopefully they will let us leave soon. I will keep in touch. —*Love, Valerie.*

Good News from Arkansas! It is Wed., and we have been cleared to go to CA. The Dr. said it was slow growing and it could wait to be removed until we get home the first of Jan. Thank you, my darling children, for postponing Thanksgiving. We will celebrate on Sunday!

Yesterday as we were leaving for the VA Hospital we saw 4 deer, 2 houses down from us. I was sure wishing I had my camera! About the VA; I know I have told you all how nice they are, but I would like to tell you why. They have a coffee cart that comes around each hour and they pass out free coffee to those of us who are waiting, David's nurse sat with him the whole time he was waiting for and recovering from his procedure, about 2 1/2 hours, and they have a store! They were having a sale, which they announced over the loud speaker! Since I have been slowly eating myself out of my clothes I took advantage and went shopping while David was in finding out what it was like to have your feet up in stirrups.

On the front page of the Benton County Daily Record today, in color, above the fold, a very large picture of a woman holding her cat. Patsy, the lady, was giving Mr. Lucky a kiss after being reunited. He had been missing for six weeks. Also, in a runoff for City Council, the *only* contested race in Bentonville, the challenger won with 197 votes. The looser got 128. When you win here, you really know how close it was or wasn't.

My children will hold Thanksgiving dinner Sunday afternoon instead of Thursday. Must go now, the MB is loading the car at warp speed and if I don't close down now I may not be in the car when it leaves. See you in CA!! —*Valerie.*

December. We had a wonderful Thanksgiving and Christmas with the family. Saw many of our friends and tried not to think about what will happen when we get home. We will hook up the car and make our Maiden Voyage in the motor home. Keep your fingers crossed. —*Love, Valerie.*

We got home yesterday and OMG we are unpacking again. On the way home David asked me what was the first thing I was going to do when we got there. After a few days on the road what I wanted was a real shower. The water tanks on motor homes are lamentably small.

On the 4th night out we stayed in a Motel. It is a good thing the place was almost empty as I stood under the shower for a *very* long time oohing and awwing. I was feeling so good after my shower that I actually hoped there would be some hot water left for David and any other guests the place might have.

I'm afraid the hot shower and the coffee the next morning were the highlights. When we called to say we did not have enough toilet paper, come on - 8 squares? Really? They asked *us* to come to the office and pick some up. The TV looked like it had been programmed for Christmas as the picture was all in various shades of red and green. David Caruso looks pretty good with green hair. The beds were so hard we were both up and down all night. Shera, our Rottweiler, was having the same problem with the floor, and kept coming and waking up David. Sooo, at 3am we put 2 of our pillows on the floor for her and we did not hear another peep out of her! I think she knew I was not going to be near as nice as David at being woke up in the night by a dog, so she kept away from my side of the bed. Oh yes, and the first thing I did upon reaching home was to sit down on the porch and brush that dog. After 5 days in the motor home it had come to my attention that the lovely soft black stuff on the dog was not there permanently. She *shared* it all over the place.

We have come to better terms with the GPS. We now find her antics cause for laughter. When getting off the highway to get some food we got her so upset all she could say was U-turn, U-turn!

I have spent quite some time today taking the motor home's refrigerator apart and cleaning it. It seems the coffee creamer was very curious as to what was on the shelves under it, so it tipped over on its side to have a look, and taking a cue from Shera, decided to share its contents with the rest of the folks on the bottom!

On the 5th day we stopped at McDonalds for breakfast. I ordered a sausage and egg biscuit. Thank goodness, we didn't use the drive through! First, I got a biscuit with a piece of chicken on it. Next, after taking it back, I got the biscuit and the sausage but no egg. On my third try the girl asked the cook to please add the egg and she looked at me like *I was the trouble maker*! I was being very nice and polite about the whole thing and was very tired from not sleeping the night before, so I didn't jump over the counter and kick her ass!!

But, I have saved the best for last. On day 2, we encounter snow, already on the ground, and the front heater decided not to work. David's feet were turning to ice, so he turned on the generator and I plugged in the little space heater we have. I was down trying to get the heater placed just right for his feet when a truck driver went by, looked at our positions, and gave David a big smile and thumbs up. I guess he thought David was getting some really dandy service!

We are safely home, and after a day of unpacking, cleaning, and laundry, we will very happily spend New Year's Eve right here on Bella Lane. We have been saving a bottle of Dom Perignon for a special occasion and we decided this was it. Happy New Year! —*Love, Valerie.*

CHAPTER 3

Arkansas News, 2009

January. My darlings, the time in CA went so fast. I'm sorry we couldn't spend more time together. The party on Christmas Eve was for sure *THE* highlight of the trip! We are still unpacking the motor home. I would be putting the clean stuff back in now, but David took off with the dog hours ago and he seems to have taken the keys with him. He was off to talk to the local Vet to get some meds for Shera's hips. When I told him I wanted to go home while he went *quickly* into the bank one day, he asked why. I told him he did nothing *quickly*. It takes him 10 minutes to drive out of our cul-de-sac for crying out loud. He has to stop and chat with everyone! He looked hurt so I told him that wasn't a bad thing; I just meant he was chatty. I now keep a book in the car.

On New Year's Day the only things I did were knit, watch TV and microwave some dinner. I needed a day off. Shera, our dog, is enjoying her freedom. Here in our new digs she can be out without a leash and she loves to explore the woods behind the house. When I whistle, she comes running, *usually*, and we give her a treat. I believe in bribery. It worked when I was potty training my children too.

VALERIE KATZ

We went to the Chevy dealer to pick up the paper work on the new car. You have to go to the Revenue Office to get your license plates. "No problem" we said, "Where is it". That's when the fun started. There were three men in the dealership and they all had an idea where the Office was. "You go down to 102", "No it's 85", "No it's 86", "Yeah but when you get to 85 or 86 you go to 102". So far so good, *David is taking notes*. The next set of instructions was just as informative: "It's across from the Sonic Drive-in", "Its kitty corner to the Hot Buffalo Wings place", "It's the building with the green roof". Luckily, the Revenue Office was in the phone book so we put the address in the GPS and found it the next day.

I wanted personalized plates and there were 21 different ones to choose from. I was quite taken with the ones with the butterflies. When I inquired about personalizing that one there seemed to be some confusion. It seems if you want to put your own message on your car you have to go with the regular plates. Bummer. I have sent for mine. You have to send in 3 different requests and in 4 to 6 *MONTHS* you will find out if you got one of them. If not, I will go back and revisit the butterflies. The answer to your question, there's always a question, is, because otherwise I can't figure which little white car in the parking lot is mine! I put some pretty pin-stripping on it too. I can just hear my friend Richard now. "Oh Valerie, you're such a girl!" Our new life is an adventure. —*Love to all, Valerie*

David had his procedure this morning. The doctor was pleased with the outcome and David will be able to come home tomorrow, the Good Lord willing and the creek don't rise. David has as yet, failed to feel overly pleased. It seems a certain part of him is more than just a little sore. He was complaining about how much it hurt and in the same breath he said they had him on *Morphine*. If that is the case, your prayers better be for me when he gets home. I have already been given the news as only my beloved MB can deliver it. "Honey!" Uh Oh! I always know something is up by the way he says that, "the doctor told me

I am not to do *one little thing* when I get home. Someone else should do everything for me". That Shera, I hope I can count on her! All kidding aside, I'm sure my biggest problem will be keeping him down long enough to heal. He is doing well, and I will go and pick him up tomorrow... honest.

Our friend Lee came to stay with me during the surgery. We visited with David until he went in to the operating room and then we were off to find something to eat. The cafeteria is under repairs, so they were dispensing goodies in a very small staff room. Lee treated me to coffee and a raspberry filled donut. I know, I know, but what better excuse for going off the diet than the surgery of a loved one.

A somewhat confused looking gentleman came in after we were seated, and Lee treated him to a cup of coffee also. The man then proceeded to tell Lee, in *great detail*, what he had been in the hospital for. Then up went his shirt for an impromptu look at his scar. I must say it was impressive! He left after that and we decided it was lucky for us he hadn't had his procedure the same spot as David! A look at that scar and I think Lee would have said more than, "Way too much information there buddy".

The MB loves to tell folks that if you want to know if your dog can count just put 3 cookies in your pocket and only take out 2. Well I'm here to tell you, if 2 people get a dog up at the gawd awful hour of 5a.m. and drag her out into the night, and only 1 brings her home many, many, hours later, the math does not add up. Shera goes between giving me the stink eye, meaning "Where is my daddy", and snuggling up to me just in case I really am all she has left.

One of my boys wrote to me last night and signed off with, "It's warm and windy in So. Cal". I wrote back. "Thanks for the warm and windy *crack*". We are supposed to get to zero tomorrow night. The MB told me he had been checking the weather each day for the past year and the temp between So. Cal. and NW Arkansas is always just a few degrees. When I get him home he will have to *define* a few degrees. Thank you all for your thoughts and prayers, —*Love, Valerie.*

Things did not go as planned today. David did not come home. The doctor decided to keep him one more day. Tomorrow they take out the catheter and as soon as he can urinate all by himself he will call me, and I will go to get him.

We had dinner together tonight. David had what everyone else had meatloaf, scalloped potatoes, carrots, biscuits w/ honey, coffee, orange juice, milk, an ice cream cup and a pear. They don't send around a menu at the VA, it's take it or leave it. I would have taken it. It smelled divine and David assured me it was. My dinner on the other hand was not so exciting. I had a fiber bar, a cup of coffee and David's milk. However, I did provide *the appetizer*. I brought us each an ice cream drumstick. We *had* to eat them first, they were melting! *Love, Valerie*

When we moved here David said it was *remotely* possible we could get ice and snow storms that would require stocking up weeks of provisions so retired folks like us would not have to go out in it. I explained to him, patiently, on many occasions, that the weather here was very temperate, he had informed me of that for the whole year we were waiting to move here! Snow! Ha!

I woke up today to a white world. It *DID* snow. And was retired little me able to stay home? **No!** There was a certain someone 40 miles away in the hospital who I needed to go see. Actually, the hardest part was getting out of our cul-de-sac. It was up hill and slippery. I had waited long enough for the salt to be delivered to the highways and for other drivers to melt the snow with their cars. *OK, OK*, so it took most of the day for me to get up the *courage* to venture out. But remember, I was in time to join him for dinner, and I brought ice cream. We'll try again tomorrow. —*Love to all, Valerie*

David called this morning. The doctor took out the catheter and "Houston we have splashdown". I am going to get him.

Things did not go as planned again today. The Master Builder is home, but the journey is not over. The cancer has metastasized so further surgery will be required. He will have to have his bladder and his prostate removed. We don't know when. He will go to Little Rock for this surgery and we have not heard from them as yet. The MB is taking it in stride and we still know that all will be well. It will just take a little longer than planned. *Valerie.*

Well folks, you can't keep a good MB down, or out of the garage. Before I was even up today he was out visiting with the neighbors. It seems our new neighbor's wife is an avid quilter, so David is going to set her up with our neighbor on the other side who is also a quilter. He is *in charge.* Someone besides his assistant to advise.

Yesterday he was out in his domain cutting and hammering away with just a few stops to see if I was making good use of *MY* time. He took the time to deliver his usual missive about the trash needing to be rounded up for pickup on Monday. My response was to gather it up and stick it in the bin outside. I must be getting soft; my usual response is to say OK and then get amnesia. It goes well with a cup of coffee. —*We are doing well, Valerie*

The MB woke me up today to tell me he could not get the dog to go out to do her business. Why? It has been snowing all night. Guess who is eternally grateful *NOT* to have to go out today? That would be me, but unfortunately, the dog does. So, I took her out and in a tone of voice she quite understood, my children remember the tone to this day, she went about doing her business. Just picture a dog, searching in vain for the scent required to deliver the goods. I do give her credit; she searched far and wide and out of site to do her thing. We were both relieved when she could come in out of the cold.

To the 3 of you who get the News and who live where it's really cold and snowy, forgive me my wonder at the weather here. However, the rest of my faithful readers live in climates where 2 days in the 40's is cause for grave concern about global warming.

The lights have been flickering. When I mentioned it to the MB he said he hoped the power wouldn't go off. Since food around here is definitely in the, it's the thought that counts department, it would not be good if the microwave was not operational.

I got a game disc from the CA kids and am now a fan of "Bejeweled" in a *BIG* way. I promised to get the disc back in a speedy fashion. However, we have snow again today, so the trip to the mail box is problematic.— *It's all new to us. Valerie.*

The sun is out today, and it is a warm 34 degrees outside. The ice cycles are starting to drip, and the forest out back looks like it has been strung with Christmas twinkle lights. It is our first ice storm and from our retired vantage point, we think it is beautiful. We are told this is an unusually harsh storm for this area. We are among the lucky ones who have not lost power. The internet and the phones were out for a few hours yesterday. It may have happened without me even noticing, but it was grave cause for concern for the Master Builder and when the MB is concerned, we *ALL* need to be concerned. It did make me remember my working days. When the phones would stop working we would be all smiles and hope the repair man was taking his own sweet time, so we could get some work done without all the interruptions. Those pesky private school parents have so many questions.

Maybe when the mail girl comes today she will be able to open the mail box without first hitting it over the head with a metal pole she carries to break up the ice. When I worked for the Post Office, a hundred years ago, things like that were frowned upon. I would have loved to have had one of those poles to impress some of the dogs I met along my route. "Neither rain, nor snow, nor dead of night..." has taken on a new meaning for me. Back then it was just a catchy phrase we recited when taking to the road with a hangover.

No new news on the MB's procedure. Still waiting to hear from the VA as to who will be doing it. The second opinion Dr. is scheduled for the 3rd. luckily the MB has enough projects in his garage to keep him busy. Cabin fever catches up to him quite quickly. Will keep you posted. —*Love, Valerie.*

Our ice village is melting. David wanted to get a snow shovel but cooler heads prevailed. We don't need a snow shovel, we don't have snow, *we have ice*. My Daughter Lili, an avid ice-skater, should be here. She could save a fortune on ice time at the rinks. Now you can be patient, (Not the MB's style) and let it melt or you can get a pick axe and take your chances. Not of getting the job done but of falling down and breaking something other than the ice. You don't need a shovel in the spring to plant your bulbs either, due to the rocks. *That's* when you need the axe.

When David was pulling his car out of the driveway yesterday, a chunk of ice he couldn't get to on the top of his car slid down and broke the windshield wiper off, the one on the driver's side, of course. We went to get a new one today and when the MB asked how to put it on, the guy said, "OH, I'll do it for you". And presto, out the door he went. The MB was still in the store putting his wallet back in his pants. With a smile, and 10 seconds the guy had the job done. Yes, 10 seconds and with a smile! Have I mentioned lately how wonderfully kind and friendly the people are here?

We went out last night, the first time since the ice storm started. David drove... I prayed... and we did not end up in a ditch. It was slippery out there!

The golf courses are beautiful. Bring your clubs; we have lots of tall tees. We'll bring a hammer and nail to make a hole for them. When the ball hits the fairway and encounters ice... well you can just imagine how far it will go! Not to worry about water hazards, they also have an ice cover, so your ball will just scoot across. Putting, on the other hand may be problematic. Not only will the putts fly at warp speed, the holes are filled with a flag that is sitting in a cube of ice, so we will have to make "House Rules", as to how close you have to come to actually score. Do we have any takers? Bring your hats and gloves. —*Love to all, Valerie*

February. It is Super Bowl Sunday and we are off to a good start. David went out to retrieve the paper and fell. We don't think it is anything serious, just a little sore on his left side. I guess he was unable to properly break his fall. He had the newspaper in one hand and knowing how slippery the ice on the driveway is, he had a cup of coffee in the other.

Remember when our kids were little, and we wanted to change our names, from "Mommy", to *anything* else? Well, someone who calls me "Honey" is using up good will that he needs to be storing up for more important times. "Honey, would you bring me the dip and the opened bag of chips? It really hurts to get up." Now, apparently my man, *who has no interest in sports what so ever*, has discovered that "Super Bowl Sunday", was *THE* day for snacks. It was to be observed, even celebrated. There was a big "TO DO" when we got home yesterday without the guacamole he was *sure* he had put in the cart. He went out for it this morning as it seems it is sacrilege to watch the Super Bowl without it. Then I made the required onion dip that he was requesting. I came back about 1/2 hr. later and it was *all gone*. "Did you eat all of that!?" I asked, politely. "Honey don't yell, my side hurts". *I repeated my question once more.* Then I said, "If you have a stomach ache later?" "I won't say a word" he replied. Alrighty then!

The smell of pizza was in the air, but the excitement was lacking. Since there was only the two of us, I figured a bet on the game would liven things up. When asked about a bet David said, "I don't even know who's playing". I tell him Pittsburgh and Arizona. "OK", says the man who had never watched a game all year, "You can have Pittsburgh and I will take Arizona and 7 points". He knew the spread for heaven's sake! In the end we decided to bet a $1.00 on each quarter, $1.00 for the total, and I would take the underdog *and* the spread. I lost $3 but it was a great game Next year I will probably take the underdog again. I just can't help myself. —*Love, Valerie.*

We have been to our second opinion Dr. and now have even more questions. He asked David to get the CD of his CT scan from the VA, so he could get a better understanding of the written report. He didn't feel the VA Dr's recommendation and the report matched. He did tell David that the option with the best possible chance of not having a reoccurrence of the cancer was to have the radical surgery. After viewing the CD, he will let David know what he thinks, hopefully tomorrow. David is leaning toward having the whole mess removed as he does not want to spend the rest of his life going in every 3 months to check and see if it is back. He told David that 75% of all men in his situation will have to go back to get the rest out and he may not want that hanging over his head. The whole mess means the bladder and prostate. Big decisions...

When we got to the VA yesterday the gates were closed, and yellow warning tape was strung everywhere. Luckily, we had discovered the back entrance on another visit, so we knew how to get in. The hospital was in one of the harder hit areas. They were working on generator power and had, had no phones for days. They were still using forklifts to pick up and stack the trees. The trees were no match for the weight of the ice. Our little area of Bella Vista got new, very, very, high power poles last year which we can thank for our power staying on.

Who would have ever, in a million years, thought I would live where there is snow. Not me, for sure! I guess it was very *little*

VALERIE KATZ

snow and *lots* of ice but right now the difference is lost on me. I hadn't even *heard* of an ice storm before.

Our friends and family still can't believe we live in Arkansas*!*
—*Love, Valerie*

We were out again today for a tour of the new Mercy Medical Center. The hospital is so beautiful I think it should be on a visitors list of things to see. It only has 130 beds, all private rooms, all with great views. We are watching the newspapers to see if their contract with Humana, our insurance carrier, pans out. However, I did have to tell David he *may not* stay here. A private room! No one to talk to! He would be calling home every 5 minutes!

God bless David, I would be a hermit if not for him. I have all the social graces of a water buffalo and have a devil of a time talking to strangers. It helps that almost everyone here is from somewhere else, so they want to find out how you got here. My "Eric Estrada invited us!" always gets a smile. They all want to meet you and let you know that you are going to *love* it here. The big question this week has been, "Now that you have been through an ice storm do you want to return to CA?" "*NO WAY*" I *do* love it here!— *Love, Valerie.*

Our 2nd opinion Dr., Dr. Brekelbaum suggests restaging (going in again) after 4 or 5 weeks for a new biopsy. If the results are negative to then start radiation and check every 3 months for a year and then every 6 months for 2 years. Then David may not need to have the organs removed. So now we are waiting for a response from the VA. My darling MB is being very patient and is keeping his chin up. —*Valerie*

Apparently, here in AR, the TV guide is taken quite seriously. On Sunday, that's what I always look for! The TV guide here is a *BIG* disappointment. Now, I am not the only one who thinks so. I have taken to reading the Letters to the Editor portion of our paper and for the past month or so the big topic has been the TV guide. It must have been changed recently and the majority of the readers are outraged. There are 2 to 3 letters *a day* on this subject! There have been 2 that have caught my eye this week. One man said that with the economy, global warming, and the war he thinks someone needs a reality check if all they have to complain about is the TV guide. And another said to get over it already; she uses hers as a coaster. I'm staying out of this one, my grandson Alex had a magazine drive at school and I ordered the TV Guide Unlike the AARP Magazine and the Readers Digest, it never gathers dust or goes unread. —*Love, Valerie.*

The news from Arkansas today is about my Mother, in Oxnard. Her dog has been sick. She was pulling an all-nighter with the dog and told the care giver to go lay down, she would call her if she needed anything. Well, she needed to go to the bathroom, didn't call, and fell and broke her ankle in 3 places... *the good leg!* So, she is in the hospital and the girls have the care givers coming anyway to make sure the dog gets his meds every 4 hours. $15.00 an hour to feed the dog! If Mom doesn't come home today, board the dog out! It's a good thing I still had a bottle or two of wine left. ...—*Valerie*

The VA Dr. was not happy about the 2nd opinion Dr's opinion. David has an appointment to see them, but could not get in until March 3rd, so we are still on hold.

We got news from CA. They're getting lots of rain! The weather man here must have gotten jealous when he heard about it. It rained buckets here last night with a little bit of hail. The wind was gusting so strong that the fan on the deck looked like the electricity was on. Maybe it got wet too and some of the dust washed off. I am not looking forward to cleaning it in the spring. It is a bamboo thing with lots of grooves. But... the MB DOES look good on a ladder :-)

David is trying to break some kind of record for joining the most things in the first few months of living here. He goes one Sat. a month to the Wood Turners meetings. The search for the proper lath has taken on the proportions of the early search for gold. He has been hither and yon, talked endlessly with other turners, and checks the ads in the News Paper daily. (I check the Paper daily too, but just to satisfy my curiosity as to how long the folks around here will continue to write in about the TV Guide.)

He also goes to a meeting of the Wood Workers (not to be confused with the Turners) one Sat. a month. The Welcome Club Golf 'n' Burgers group will meet two Saturdays a month. I sure hope they aren't the same Saturdays as the Wood folk as that is the one I want to join. Of course, I can always join as a single. It is time to dust off the golf clubs

He has been reading in the Paper about the Property Owners Association (POA} closing a 9-hole golf course. He is getting their E-mails too, and how he got on the e-mail lists I *do not know*. The POA's Recreation Committee had pushed this through without going through proper channels. Apparently, they just took it off the golf list and put it on the Parks and Rec. list without so much as a by your leave. He is going to the POA meeting!

When he left I wanted to tell him to play nice, but I let him venture out unchecked. He said he kept his mouth shut (hard to believe) but there were lots of things he wanted to say. The next meeting should be fun. I may go with him and sit in the back. —*Love, Valerie.*

Today he went to his first meeting of the Scale Model Electric Train Club. He said it was perfect for him. They meet every Wed. for lunch and shoot the breeze. When he's right, he's right!

I have been getting some inquiries from my MB as to how I am spending my time. The MB is full of plans and thinks I am not using mine wisely. Well, *I* am still reveling in the fact that I don't have to do anything! I stay up late and sleep in, in the morning, and that suits me just fine. *Love, Valerie.*

After another talk with the VA Doctor, David has decided to have the surgery. Dr. B, the second opinion guy, has agreed to do it, so it will be done here locally. That is what David really wanted. He was not fond of the idea of me in a motel in Little Rock for 10 days while he was in the hospital. I would have pushed really hard to take the motor home and the dog I would not have felt at all safe alone in a motel. So, there you have it, I'm a bit of a coward. I want my Rottweiler! We don't have a date yet, but I will keep you informed.

A little tidbit about one of our meetings with the surgeon; After the decision was made to do the surgery David wanted to know, "After the surgery when can Valerie and I have sex again?" The doctor's reply? "Oh, your sex life is over." I was sitting behind David. He turned to me with a stunned look on his face and asked, "Did you know this?" Yes, I did. I honestly didn't think a man got to be 67 years old not knowing the sex was over when the prostate vacated the premises!

On the way home he wanted to know if I really did know, and if so, why hadn't I told him? My answer was that I wanted his decision to be made, on his health issues not our sex life. I can do without sex, I *need* my MB. —*Love, Valerie.*

We have joined the Welcome to Bella Vista group and went to their monthly breakfast last Friday and to a concert on Sunday. The entertainment at the breakfast was provided by the Sophisticated Ladies of Bella Vista. You should have seen them dance. Now that is a group I may decide to try! The MB thinks it would be great fun if he could join too. Hmmm... David and the Sophisticated Ladies? It does have a nice ring to it. If I was in, I think I would be one of the younger girls.

The concert entertainment was a very nice jazz group who, when not traveling, perform at Disneyland. We have decided to get season tickets to the upcoming events. This week we will be joining the Welcome group for bowling and dinner, not on the same day. With the MB spearheading these events, my days of *not doing anything*, may be numbered.

I am trying to become the Arkansas champ at Bejeweled (the computer game). Of course, I must be ever ready to answer the call, "Honey, can you come here and help me a minute?"
—*Valerie*

This is the Bible Belt. There are more churches than banks, and there are plenty of banks. We have been invited to join our neighbors on Sunday mornings but so far have not done so. My friend Becky invited me to join her for a Bible study series her church was sponsoring, on Tuesday mornings. Twelve weeks, at 9:00 a.m.? My alarm will need to be set! *Yes, Yes, I do remember how.* She said if she was in my shoes, new to the area and dealing with David's issues, she would want someone to invite her to such a group. I must admit, I was dubious. She gave me a *study book*, with *questions* in the back, for each week's lesson. Then she asked if I had a Bible. My first reaction was, *Oh no! Study? Homework? Take tests?!* She said to underline passages and make notes in the book, which I did *not* do. I did my reading, made notes in a separate book (I didn't want to look like I hadn't done *any* of my homework) and went to the meeting.

I am so happy I did. Not only did I meet another group of wonderful and welcoming women, towards the end of the meeting I actually spoke up and contributed. Two of the questions were, 1 - How would you describe talking to God and 2 - How do you think God feels when you do. I said talking to God was like talking to my Mom. No matter what I do she will always love me and when needed forgive me. Another lady said she thought God probably felt like we do when our children come to us for guidance or just to chat. And yes, I decided to write in my book, and I am going back.

Last night we went to the monthly Welcome Club dinner. It was at a Chinese restaurant. It was a buffet. I don't usually like Chinese buffets, but this one was huge, and every item was better than the last. I ate until I thought I would explode. And the people, OK let's all say it together, *were so nice!*

One of the ladies at our table works at the animal rescue shelter, a place that is on top of the "Favorite places to raise money for" list here in the Village. She also works at the local TV station on Wednesdays. The talk was lively and when she found out David teaches dance she asked him if he would be interested in doing a TV dance series. *"Interested?!"* It is a very small station and only operates 4 hours a day, but David is jazzed. He is dying to get back into teaching. He is also talking with the man who runs the restaurant at the Country Club about teaching there one day a week. His idea is to teach in the afternoon, so the lesson would end at happy hour when the music starts so maybe the folks will stay to eat and dance. He is determined to keep the place open. It is so charming, close to home, and the food is wonderful. We almost have the place to ourselves when we're there, but David is bent on changing that. The doctor better hurry and schedule David's surgery or he won't have time for it. —*Love, Valerie.*

Good morning, it's official. I have Bejeweled arm. I have played so much; my right arm is too sore to use, and I have to play with my left hand. My left hand is not very proficient, and I find it hard to get the Jewels to go where I want them too. I feel like I'm in physical therapy after an arm injury The fact that I have been playing this much is a little tidbit that I am quite sure my daughter Denise won't want me sharing with my grandson Alex. I won't be sharing this with the MB either.

I got an e-mail from Denise yesterday. They are coming to visit June 27-30 on their way to a Morefield reunion in Illinois. Our first company!

St. Jude's Hospital has invited me to a 2-day event in April. It is an appreciation dinner and tour of the hospital for those of us who are regular contributors. I sure hope David's surgery schedule allows us to go. No date set for that yet. We are *still* waiting for the paper work to get to Dr. B.'s office. —*Valerie*

We have a date! David will have his surgery on March 10th. We will meet with Dr. B next week and get all the particulars. I will of course, keep you posted.

We started a new activity. Bowling with FUSS, Fifty until Sixty-Six. They bowl at 5pm each Friday and those who can make it bowl, in what can only be described as, a very loose league. The fee is $10.00, but only when you show up, $8.00 for bowling and $2.00 for the end of the season party. It is not sanctioned so members just come when they can. There is a system of keeping track of wins and losses, but that part was *way* beyond my understanding.

The bowling alley is brand new and has 10 fully automated lanes. Sets the pins, keeps the score, and returns your ball :-) There is one red pin on each lane and if it comes up in the #1 spot and you get a strike you get a free game or a free drink of your choice. David and I each won. David had a beer and since they don't have wine, a serious flaw I have graciously decided to overlook, I had green tea. I got off to a great start by falling down during practice. No damage. I'm fine! —*Love, Valerie.*

March. David woke me up at 5 a.m. today. Yes, he is still alive, I didn't kill him. He was taking his 1/2 of the bed on my side. He usually takes it in the middle. I was hanging on to the sliver that was left when he nudged me to ask if I was awake. Now, those of you who know me well know that that was *highly* unlikely at 5 a.m... He wanted to tell me that our neighbor Freda had called the night before to remind me that today was the day for our eagle watching trip. Neither one of us could go back to sleep so at 5:45 we got up to face the day.

He waited until later to tell me the "e" had fallen off the word lathe on my last e-mail. He said he had no idea what a lath was but that all of you would get the message. He should know that folks who complain about typos no longer *get* mail.

At 7:00 a.m., when we were letting Shera out for her morning walk, we discovered a white world. We got a little dusting of snow so there will be no eagle watching for me today. Not my idea, the outing was cancelled.

David has wood turning this morning and then lunch with the train bunch. He had asked me to make meatballs for the wood turners meeting, which I had done. Lucky for him, he asked *before* the early wake-up call. Me?? I may be up to having my nails done and taking a nap. (Yawn)

As he was taking snow off the car, I reminded David he was not in CA anymore; I did say it with a very sweet smile. — *Valerie*

David is scheduled at noon on Tues. for his surgery. He went for all the prelims today, so he is ready to rock and roll. All good wishes and prayers are much appreciated.

The people who were going to rent David's house never moved in. The house they had sold fell out of escrow and they filed bankruptcy. However, there is some *really* good news. The house in Agoura Hills is in escrow! David lowered the price and in 2 days there were 6 offers. One of them has asked to be the backup in case the first one falls out. This is great! David won't have that hanging over his head while he is recuperating.

The strain is finally starting to show on David. He was up Thursday night throwing up and his stomach has been off ever since. He also spends a lot of time in the bathroom and has lost 5 pounds in 3 days. He thought he had food poisoning, but we had exactly the same thing for dinner. We had a drink and the early bird special, something small and easy to digest. That was followed by another drink and an order of onion rings for dessert. Tomorrow is the big day and we are ready. — *Valerie*

The surgery was long, 1:30 p.m. - 7:30 p.m., but the outcome was good. The doctor said David did great and should expect no complications. Hooray! —*More later, Valerie*

Coming home from the hospital today I noticed all the changes around me. The first trees are in bloom, the new bulbs are coming up, and little yellow flowers are blooming everywhere. The golf courses that were covered with ice and snow just weeks ago now have greens and fairways a beautiful emerald color. Spring must be on its way!

At the hospital I talked to the doctor who said David caused him lots of trouble in the operating room. What with needing 3 units of blood, extra bags for his new potty pouch, and having such a small or crooked throat that a specialist had to be called to put the tube down it, therefore making the surgery last longer.

What did David have to say? "When I get home we really have to get our taxes finished". And "Where is the plunger for my morphine"! *Not* necessarily in that order. He and I thank you all for your thoughts and good wishes. —*Love, Valerie.*

David is out of ICU and in a regular room. He is still on a full liquid diet which they have gotten wrong, 4 out of the 5 times they have brought him his meals. He thought he had graduated to a *regular* diet, along with the *regular* room he was moved to yesterday morning, so he ate the bacon and eggs he was served. I don't know for sure if that was the cause of his discomfort later in the day, but he was in a world of hurt. They got him up and walked him around just before I got there. He asked for pain meds and they gave him some morphine in his IV. He was miserable the rest of the evening and asked for another walk so maybe he could get rid of the gas that was causing him his miseries.

The Hospital *staff* doctor was in this AM and had all 4 of the people in charge of David's care in for a *stern* talking too.

Besides the food fiasco, he is supposed to be up at least 4 times each day for a walk. Then, *believe it or not*, he asked David if he wanted to go home today. That would be a big *NO!!* David's *regular* Dr. should be back tomorrow.

When they brought him his dinner I pointed out the error of their ways (nicely) and they brought him his liquid dinner. They told me I could have the other one if I wanted. Do you think they were trying to make nice? Of course, I had already eaten the roll and butter.

David is in good spirits in spite of all of this and due to his new living quarters, I can spend more time with him so I am in good spirits too. So... we are doing fine. —*Love, Valerie.*

It has been a looooong, looooong day, but our MB is home and sleeping in his own bed. The first few days home from the hospital have been interesting, so many new things to learn. On the day he came home we were scheduled for a lesson in ostomy bags, changing them and learning about taking care of the immediate area. It was scheduled for 11 a.m. I set my alarm... I told David the timing would work out well as then I could leave a little earlier and to go the market. I had been staying with him until 9:00 pm or so each night, then another 45-minute drive to get home, so groceries needed to be purchased.

David called me to tell me the Dr. had been in and he was coming back to send him home so could I come as soon as possible. Normally, going for these six-hour visits, I pack my book, some food, and a couple bottles of water and green tea. I figured I wouldn't need these items, we would be coming right home! It has been my experience that hospitals want you out before noon so off I went, armed with nothing more than a smile and my purse. I mean, how heavy is that little paper back? It fits right in my purse!

I would like to tell you now that many times, in the last few days, David has told me how much he loves me and how he just doesn't know what people do who don't have a *me* at home. When he introduced me to his many nurses and aides they almost all said, "Boy, he talks about you all the time. He really loves you". It's a good thing too as he really needs to be on my good side now, while I *still* have a good side!

Well, Cyndy, the ostomy nurse, didn't show up until a little after noon and the Dr. didn't show up until after 3 p.m. A prescription for Percocet was needed! (60 tablets) and had to be filled. *That* required a visit to the VA, not in the homeward direction.

When we got to the VA David asked me to find a vending machine, so I could bring him something to drink to take the Percocet with. They had also received a script for all of the items David will need for his care at home, so they were trying to find all of that stuff. It was taking a little *longer* than normal and we didn't really need anything but the pain pills. The hospital nurse had sent me home with *mucho* supplies. So, while I was going to the basement to find the vending machines, and waiting for David's name to come up on the "your prescription is ready" board, David called me *twice* to find out what the holdup was!

On a normal day that little habit of continual calling does not bode well with me. Today, I knew he was in pain, so I was trying to be understanding. It was 5:30 pm and I was tired, hungry, and getting a *little cranky*. I went back to the car, gave him his drink and a pain pill and headed for home. My good side was fading fast and his phone was on my hit list.

I asked him if he could hold out for a few more minutes while I ran in to Allen's, a little grocery store that is small, easy to get in and out of, and where they take your purchases out to your car for you. (Just try and do it yourself!) David really wanted to go right home, but he had had his Percocet and his good side was properly medicated, but said to please hurry. I did. We were out of bread, milk, and eggs and the Dr. wanted him to have Ensure as he isn't really eating much of anything and he needs to get his strength back.

I got him home, got a banana, a pop cycle, and an Ensure down him, fluffed, arranged, and rearranged pillows, and it was lights out for him. Me? I needed a glass of wine and some TV.

Two hours later he called me. When I had arranged his night drain the last time, something we were not so sure how to do, I had closed it instead of opening it. We had a real mess. We are scheduled for home help. *Soon* I hope. *Love, Valerie*

Getting David out of bed is no easy feat. Now he is worried about the sheets, the bed, etc. etc. and all I want is for him to *get out of bed,* so I can assess any damages. I'm afraid I used "that" tone of voice as he all of a sudden turned his attention to doing just that! Sheets were changed, and I got David back into bed. I crawled into bed too, and he said, "Honey, I hate to bother you again, but could you please get me a sleeping pill, and a flex straw to help me take it with?" "Sure Honey, no problem" I said. No tone of voice either. I'm so proud of myself. Now back in bed, just after 1 am, he reached over to touch my shoulder and said "Honey, are you going to be OK with all of this?" I took his hand and assured him we were going to be just fine.

And we will be, just fine. —*Love to all, Valerie*

Friday was a better day. The visiting nurse was coming to change all of David's dressings and we were really looking forward to that. Since she was coming any way, no reason to keep the dressings dry, I decided a shower for David was just the thing. He said he didn't think he was feeling strong enough, but I wasn't having any of that. I told him he would feel like a new man. I did not use that tone of voice, but I was ready to if necessary.

I was correct, he did feel like a new man, or maybe just felt more like my MB. He actually wanted food today and when it was delivered he didn't just pick at it, he *ate* it. We are both feeling very good about things today and know that every day will be better. He will be back in the garage before I know it.

Someone turned us in to the Animal Control folks. They came to the door today to ask if Shera (the big black dog) lived here. Luckily, she was resting in the house when he got there. He explained to me that the regulations state that she must be on a leash when not on our property. He actually said he could "*Read*" the rules from the manual to me if I wanted him too. He was really being very nice about having to deliver this news.

Unfortunately, Shera *doesn't* understand about the rules. She likes to go visit with the neighbors on each side and they like it too. I took her with me to get the mail and our neighbor was out in his yard. Shera gave me the stink eye when I took her in and didn't let her out to play. She lay in front of the door for quite a while hoping I would change my mind. After dark I can let her out. No one will see her then. Oh dear, breaking the law after dark. I guess we will be getting the invisible fence for her. —*Love, Valerie*

What a difference a day makes. It is Saturday, and when I got up this A.M. David was already up, OK, OK, he is *always* up before me, and had made himself some breakfast. He asked for lunch, ate it all and wanted dessert. Now, his menu was not exactly what I would have desired, bologna and toast for breakfast and bologna, cheese, and tomato open face on a bagel for lunch. My MB loves his bologna. Dessert was a different matter. I opened up some shortbread cookies I had purchased when we were in CA for Christmas. I have been on a diet, so I was *afraid* to open them. They are my favorites! I don't really *know* how many calories are in them, so I can't *actually* put them on my calorie list, sooo, they must be free! No! Don't bother writing to me about the little box on the back of the package that contains information I neither want or need.

My MB went in to the garage this morning to look around and see what he can relocate. He loves to move that stuff around. I was sure any minute he was going to pick up his tape and measure something. He has been watching "This Old House", one of his favorite TV shows, all morning. He is starting to really believe that the light at the end of the tunnel is a good thing and not a train fixn' to run him down. —*Life is GOOD, Valerie.*

I am sitting here listening to a bird calling to my dog. I wondered why she no longer came running when I whistled for her. Then I was out doing just that, and I heard my whistle coming right back at me. My first thought was, "I never noticed that echo before". Then I realized it was a bird mimicking me... well, mocking me, since we have Mocking Birds. It has gotten my whistle absolutely perfect too.

Overnight the little buds on the Dogwood tree, that were little spots of ice last month, have turned into little buds of green. We know from our visits here last year that once the Dogwood makes its appearance the rest can't be far from turning our world green.

I went out to get the paper and the wind was blowing so hard it had actually blown our rolled-up newspaper 4 feet into the street. I made it back into the house just in time to beat the rain. It came down so hard and for such a short period of time that it was as if God had dumped a huge bucket of water down on us.

For those of you who have asked, yes, I am saving my e-mails. I suspect that the time will come when the wonder of the area will begin to fade. I will then be able to pull up my notes and remember just how *wonderful* we know it is here. Oh yes, David *is* doing well. ;) *Love to all, Valerie*

Yikes! We have had our 2 steps backward. The last 2 days have left us in tears. The darn apparatuses have not been the least bit user friendly. After going through 3 of them on Tuesday, without success, I was in tears. This was *very* upsetting to my MB, poor thing. I handed him both his cell phone and the house phone and told him "If it rings and it's for me, I'm not here to anyone but my Kids". Then I took my cell phone and put in a call to my Mommy. I asked her caregiver if Mom was having a good day. When she said yes, I asked to talk with her. I told my Mom that she may have been having a good day, but I had called to *fix that* and we both had a little laugh. Here I am, 67 years old, and still calling my Mom when I am frustrated and reduced to tears.

We called in the pro, home nurse, and she came and helped. Then on Wednesday, I woke up with a very yucky looking right eye. Now for those of you who may not know this, on Sept 1st of 2005 I got that ungrateful eye a new cornea, a lens implant and a cataract removal. I made an apt. with a local Dr. and left for my apt. at noon. They had an emergency and were running late so I didn't get out of there until 3 p.m. Then off to Wal-Mart to pick up a prescription for the eye infection and do some grocery shopping. While I was away David's appliance sprang a leak and when I got home, he took one look at me and broke into tears. I hugged him and asked him if he wanted to call my Mommy. Then I put on a new apparatus and *it leaked...* We watched the "How To" video again, and gave it another shot. So far today we are a success. David got dressed and we went to the bank and then out for lunch. Oh, happy day. —*Love, Valerie.*

Things are looking brighter today. I woke to find my MB sitting in his chair in the living room, thoroughly enjoying himself, dividing his time between watching the spring snow come down through the big window and watching 101 Dalmatians on TV. He said he had a small leak, but was not very much perturbed by that piece of news. Equilibriums are being restored. Smiles all around!!

The newspaper arrived with a full color picture of local tulips, and was wrapped in a plastic bag with samples of Fiber One toaster snacks and oat & raisin cereal. Good reading and a yummy breakfast for me. What's David eating? Nothing in the kitchen is safe. His appetite is definitely back. —*Love, Valerie*

April. This is the first "News" I have attempted since I had the "Brain Storm" about changing from aol.com to Cox.net. I announced the change to all before finding out what a royal pain in the keester it was going to be to transfer my e-dresses. Yikes, what a job! I quit at 3am this morning and am back at it today. I have a few that still need to be transferred but AOL and COX have decided not to "Play well with others" this morning. Some of you have received some strange e-mails from me, I know, as I was trying to figure out the easiest way to get the job done. There isn't one.

The reason for the change from AOL, which I happen to think is the BEST and most user-friendly system there is, is AOL keeps getting kicked off as it has to go *through* Cox Cable, and the only way I can get on to it now is as a guest and then I don't have all the goodies I need. My daughter and her husband have Cox and seem to like it and it comes with our cable package so I decided to give it a try. That's when the trouble started. I called Cox, set up an e-dress and discovered I had a version of Microsoft that would not let me use Cox with the tool bars. No File. No Edit. Get real! When I asked David for help, I was ranting by then, he discovered his Cox e-dress was not working now either and wanted to know *"WHAT I HAD DONE!"* I had already talked to the HELP line, both *here* and in *India*, and had been told they could help me for the bargain price of $59.95. Sooo, it was David's turn. He started with the *HELP* person and was soon asking for the *supervisor*. He always does. :-) After 2 glasses of wine and an ice cream sandwich (for me) and 2 hours with the supervisor and going from one computer to the other (for him), we were ready to get started. You will know how successful we were if you get this and future "News".

About my MB... the apparatuses are still a challenge that keeps us up on our toes, and at times, down in the dumps.

The lining of the stomach which is usually about 1 inch was for David 3 inches, so his stoma does not come out to boldly meet the world, but shyly, just barely, peeks its head out. After a frustrating day for us, we had yet *another* professional out yesterday. She wasn't even out of the driveway before the leaks started. After 2 more tries we managed to get the apparatus on and so far, today it is still holding. We meet with a new specialist tomorrow at the VA.

We had to make another visit to Dr. B this week. He said on Monday he didn't want to see us for 6 months but David had a fever of 102 so he changed his mind and said to "Come on Down". Tylenol and an antibiotic seem to have cleared up that little problem. As a precaution, he is scheduled for a CT scan.

After a frustrating day earlier in the week we decided to put things in perspective and watched "Patton" and "Midway" on TV. Now those were some "#@%*@# times"! It is now 6:45 and I am going to try to send this thing, *again*. Valerie.

Monday was a big day. We went to see David's primary Dr. and the VA Ostomy specialist. She took one look at David's stoma and said she could certainly see why we were having so much trouble. However, she said, she had a new type of apparatus that she thought *might* just do the trick. She spent quite some time on skin prep and then attached the gizmo. When it was in place she had a look on her face that we recognized immediately. It was the, "This is never going to work" face. But she said we should try these new models, check the Internet, describe our problem, and ask for some samples.

I was having a very bad "Back day" and was not my cheerful self. When we got home the Dr. had called to say the antibiotic David was on was resistant to the now grown cultures so somebody had to go back to Wal-Mart for new meds. After finishing a treatment on my back and taking 4 Advil, I went. I called David from the Wal-Mart line to request that he call and order some pasta and garlic bread for dinner and I would pick it up on my way home. He asked how he was supposed to do that as he didn't have the phone number to the pizza place. I gave him some *very direct advice* on how that could be accomplished. He did just fine.

Today is day 3 with the new model apparatus and it is holding. We are so happy! David has been in a much better mood and has been out in front walking about and visiting with the neighbors. Tomorrow we have to change it so I thought I would write while we are still smiling. "OK" everyone, "Cross your fingers!" —*Thanks, Valerie.*

Yesterday was my birthday. When my MB asked what I wanted, my answer was "A really good steak". It just so happens there is a Ruth's Chris Steakhouse just 20 minutes from here. David made reservations, I took a nap. Thank goodness, we were eating at 7 and not at 5 as we had talked about. We were getting ready to walk out the door when I heard, "On no! Oh no! Oh no!" David had sprung a leak.... the decision was made to make the change and hope for the best. We got a new seal on him in warp speed and we were out the door.

Steak, lobster, and yummy drinks were enjoyed by both of us. Nothing would do but that the restaurant would furnish a birthday dessert. After finally convincing our waiter that there was absolutely no more room in my stomach, he went through the dessert menu again pointing out which ones were best when taken home. I chose the caramelized banana pie. What was I thinking? Everyone knows what happens to bananas when they are sliced. My only excuse is my brain was numbed by the amount of food I had eaten. The drinks may have played a part in that also. I tried it today, but it looked bad and didn't taste so hot either, so most of it was fed to the garbage disposer. It, like the dog, will eat anything. It was a great way to spend my birthday.

Today the couple who run the Starlight Dances, two Wed's a month, called David. They have been doing it for 13 years and wanted to know if David would like to take it over in Sept. It looks like we may be back in the dance business.

This Easter was the first one … *EVER*… that I have not been with my kids. So they put a call through on Skype and I could see them, and talk to them, almost like I was there. This move would be so hard were it not for Skype and E-mail. Wonderful ways to keep connected to you all. *Love to all, Valerie.*

> *This is a note David sent out via e-mail.*
>
> *To Val's Mom, children, siblings & relatives,*
>
> *Thank you for having such a wonderful person as Valerie in your lives. I don't know what I would have done these past weeks without her and I will never be able to repay her for her kindness, love and devotion.*
>
> *I am sorry that it is I who has kept her from being with you this Easter, but I hope you understand. I love you all, David.*

I did not know he had sent the note until I got an e-mail from my daughter Denise. Isn't my MB the best. —*Tearfully, Valerie.*

UNCLE! I am back on AOL! We got our AOL straightened out and I moved back. I am soooo spoiled by how user friendly and quick it is. Last night while trying to send out an E-Mail on Cox.net and moving my e-mails to the already read folder, which was taking an eternity, I played many levels of one of my computer games. I could keep track of the little Cox gear in the corner spinning around from the game screen. Then I would go back to Cox and give it another task. I am so sorry to have to ask you to change my e-dress again but here it is! —*Thanks, Valerie.*

Today has been a good day. "The Gear" went on smoothly, no hysterical crying and calling of Mom's today. Then it was off to the community in-door garage sale. It is the first one Bella Vista had tried and all the tables were sold out immediately. It was so crowded we could hardly drag my bag with the wheels through the throng. Yes, this time we actually remembered to take it with us. A good thing too, just inside the door I stopped and bought 6 candles in glass jars and would not have wanted to carry those heavy things around.

On our way out, I spotted a wonderful mantle clock. The lady had purchased it in Germany and her husband had been complaining about it ever since. It chimes on the hour and on the quarter hour. David was not impressed, and we left shortly thereafter. We took in a garage sale on the way home and as we were leaving it I told David I really wanted to go back for the clock. Lucky for me, it was still there! When we got home, David looked it up on the Internet and, *yea howdy*, it's worth much more than I paid for it! So now it is on David's "Good find Girl" list. David just hollered in to tell me how nice it sounded but did I think it would chime *ALL* night. He will get used to it. When we have our neighborhood garage sale on May 1st & 2nd it will *not* be out there because *my* husband was complaining. *And the best thing?* David drove to the sale, his first time behind the wheel since his "procedure". He is already enlisting my help to vacuum the garage. He is on the mend. —*Love to all, Valerie*

David got cut off from one too many calls on his cell phone. He called Verizon only to be told that we were in a poor service area. He tried several rooms for the best possible place for service. (*There wasn't one*) Another call to Verizon got him in touch with someone who was "*IN THE KNOW*". After about 45 min. with a distraught MB she told him that since Verizon could not give full service in this area, they could not hold us to our contract. New service was now a top priority

He interviewed the neighbors to find out *what* service they used, and *were* they happy. Then he borrowed one of their phones for a trial call here at home. Alltel was the winner. He got them on the phone. The land line of course. After much ado, the gentleman told David to go to the Alltel store, pick out a phone and then come home and call him again as he could waive start-up fees and beat any deal the store could offer. We were in the car and headed to town in short order.

While David was getting the low down on phones that might fit his needs, *I had picked mine out in about 5 minutes,* he sprang a leak. He was very calm about it. He went to the car for a towel to stem the tide, and, in a slightly more hurried fashion, made his decision. We went home to take care of more pressing matters.

The next day he called the Alltel guy. *I kid you not*, it was 2 hours on the phone before all the details were agreed upon and the Discover card was put to work. The Alltel guy said he would overnight the phones. They got here 3 days later. We unpacked our new toys and went to work. Since we were changing carriers our info could not be flashed over to the new phones. Now *my* biggest problem was getting the back off the phone to put the battery in. Not so my *MB*! He had opted for a touch screen phone with GPS, e-mail, and more things I can't remember. He went through the instructions many times and then called Alltel. 45 min. later, the girl was practically begging him to go to the store for more help. She had done all she could, and no, she did not have any one who "*Knew more*" than she did that he could talk to. Believe me, by then I was on her side. I was also asking him "Please honey, hang up and go to the store"! He did. In no time he was sending me an e-mail from his phone. Peace and happiness was restored. A good thing too, his next stop was the new chiropractor and she would have had her hands full if he was still wound up about that phone.

When I went to cox.net for my email my friend Charlotte said if I changed my e-mail address again she was cutting me out

of her Will. Then not only did I change it again, but I got a new cell number. I told her not to worry, her grandson could probably show her how to change it for her and if not, she only lives a few blocks from my granddaughter Jennifer, and she could do it for sure. I'm still out of her Will. It's too late to make a long story short, so just change our phone numbers.
—*Love, Valerie.*

May. Most of the folks who live here are among the gainfully retired. Good stuff doesn't have to wait until the weekend. Dances, dinners, lunches? Good stuff any day of the week. Therefore, garage sales are held Thursday, Friday and Saturday. We had ours last weekend. The only thing missing... Garth Brooks should have been singing "And the Thunder Rolls". Garage sales here are held *in* the garage. We got 4 inches of rain! However, the garage sale was a success. There were 6 or 7 homes involved and my little promoter had done lots of advertising around our Village. I guess the golfers were looking for somewhere to go so business was brisk. David was in his element. Lots of folks to visit with! We had one little visitor both days. A hummingbird!

Sunday is the exception. That day is for going to church. We are ready. We are now in the process of joining our many friends and neighbors who have invited us to join them on Sunday and give their church a try. We went last Sunday to the church we have been invited to by our next-door neighbor, one of David's wood turner friends, and a really friendly gentleman from the garage sale who loaned me his umbrella while he shopped so I could go out to the mail box. David had been at the church at the end of last year to help with a project they work on all year, making toys for needy children at Christmas. After a very nice and eclectic service, the minister came over to introduce himself during the cookie and coffee portion of the morning. David was introduced to him as "The dance instructor". "Oh, I need a couple of beers to try dancing" he replied. Hmmmm... Good vibes here. *Love to all, Valerie*

We have had a good week. David has mastered "The Gear". He can do it solo with no leaks in sight. I am out of a job, no longer needed. In front of David I am being very brave, stiff upper lip and all that. Behind his back, I am dancing a little jig. —*Love, Valerie*

We have been very busy around here this week getting flowers planted, cleaning up the deck, washing windows. We could not find replacement blades for our fan on the deck, so we took down those dirty and moldy items, cleaned them up, and painted them. It was good to see the MB up on the ladder, taking charge.

He was also up on the ladder balancing the ceiling fan in the living room and replacing the light fixture in the laundry room. That light was today's last project. The MB and his assistant were getting tired. The end piece, on the light fixture, was not going on easily. Then, in a tone of voice I haven't heard in some time, my MB said, "Hand me the hammer". That little piece of plastic understood that it was time to get cracking and go where it was supposed to go, *or else*. And what has kicked this frenzy of activity into high gear? The kids are coming! At first it was just my daughter Denise and her family. Then Donald and his family decided to join in and it looks like some of the rest might come too. We don't have a clue where everyone will be sleeping, but we will figure it out. We have until the end of June!

For you who have asked, no, the local newspaper has not gone out of business due to the flagging economy. I have just been so wrapped up in my "David" duties that I have not had time to read it. It seems our citizens have given up on the TV guide. No amount of pleading and complaining managed to change it back to its former glory. However, we do have a new cause. It seems insult has been added to injury in the form of a new crossword puzzled format. It has taken on a "We will get a little harder every day" attitude. Most of the mail is from folks who have been doing it for years and now find Wednesday to be the limit of what used to be a full week of puzzle enjoyment. The puzzle now seems to be coming from Los Angeles and is full of clues that are designed for "Valley Girls" and "Hollywood Types" and mean absolutely nothing to the locals. I didn't know the locals even knew about Valley Girls! I, personally, am of the "Crossword puzzles are a group endeavor" state of mind. I can't do them by myself but love to join in with someone who can. I am a veritable font of trivial, and on the whole, useless knowledge.

One more thing about the paper... If you are one of the masses who are thinking you would love to vote out the bone heads in Washington DC who don't seem to understand just what we want, but have no clue how your representatives actually vote, look no further than our little paper. The "Here is how Arkansas' U.S. senators and representatives voted on major roll call votes during the week that ended Friday" was followed by a list of the items up for a vote and exactly how each and every one of our legislators voted on them. I may have to start making notes for future reference.

We have had 11 inches of rain since the beginning of April. We find the evenings punctuated by thunder and lightning to be truly wonderful. —*We still love Arkansas. Valerie.*

I took out the electric mixer, the big mixer bowls, flour, corn meal, and the P-nut butter... Dusting off an old cookie recipe for the soon to arrive grandkids? No... *We* have a bird feeder. I am making pudding for the birds. I have waited a week to tell you this as I wanted to make sure the birds would be more receptive to our attempts at friendship than the deer have been. There are still no deer in our little section of the woods. For the first few days I was feeling very disappointed. I took corn meal off of the grocery list. The birds are shy, and don't just rush to the new snack shop. They check it out very carefully first.

Just as I was giving up hope I noticed that 1/2 of the pudding was gone. We spent some time hiding in the house, watching for the little guys. Sure enough, they had accepted our offer of friendship and were enjoying the fruits of our labor. The Welcome Club had left us a list, complete with pictures, of the birds in the area. I can't find it! I think our biggest fan is a red-headed wood pecker, but can't be sure.

Now that the deck is clean and ready for use, I have spent many hours out there drinking coffee or lemonade and reading. I position my book, so I can see the pages and the bird feeder without moving my head. That way I can see the birds without scaring them away. I will try to get pictures.

This AM, while enjoying the birds, my coffee and the newspaper, it started to sprinkle. I had listened for several minutes, trying to figure out just what that lovely sound was, when the drops finally made it through the trees. A gentle rain goes even better with coffee than amnesia. *Love, Valerie.*

June. I'm up early this A.M. I was out on the deck, listening to the birds and enjoying today's first cup of coffee. I was away for 2 days and when I returned home David told me I had received a couple of complaints during my absence. I asked him if he had informed the complainer that my complaint box had a permanent closed sign on it! It turned out the complaints were from my new feathered friends. They had run out of pudding while I was away and wanted the situation rectified. I didn't get right on it and one little guy, not so shy any more, sat on the top of the feeder voicing his distress. Now all is well in the aviary cafeteria, even with its limited menu.

My absence from home was due to a small stay in the hospital. It was, after all, my turn. I went in with no fan fair, not bothering to tell friends or family, many of whom are now knocking on the "Closed" sign of my complaint box for this break in etiquette. This trip was small and insignificant when compared to that of my MB, but it was in the same general area.

For several years I have been bothered by something that ails many "Ladies of a certain age". As my mother would say, I have been having difficulty holding my water. I told the MB that nothing could be done about it. Anyone ever try to tell David that? During one of his follow up visits with Dr. B he announced "Valerie has a problem too! Tell him Honey". Need I describe his tone of voice? The next thing I knew, I was scheduled. "Outpatient", that's what I was. Start at 11:00 a.m. and home the next day at 10:00 a.m. Not so fast… My "I don't do well with anesthesia" talk fell, as usual, on deaf ears. Their "Anesthesia has evolved" talk fell on my dubious ears. Two days of throwing up made my point but impeded my progress. I couldn't stay upright long enough to do what was required for my release. I couldn't tinkle. The catheter was reinstalled, and I was sent home.

David and I were quite the sight, walking around the house for 2 days with our respective gear. I will never hear the phrase "Fill'er up" again and not think of yesterday when they filled me up, with water, *through* the catheter. There was a, not so veiled threat, of sending me home with "Do it yourself mini cath's" if the deed was not completed. Cath out, water out, done. Let's go home! — *Valerie*.

My Matron of Honor and best friend for 30 years, Charlotte, has told me for at least the last 20 of them that *she* is in charge of my life. She's the one who has held my hand during stressful times and held the paper sack for me while I was hiding out in the store room of the school hyperventilating during really rough times. She sent me an e-mail letting me know how she felt about me going in for surgery without so much as a note to her. I sent her a very quick response.

"Hi Char, Sorry, I don't know *what* I was thinking. I didn't tell anyone I was going in to the hospital. I should have known that was OK for my family but not for *you*!!" ;) David knows how Donald is though and as soon as they would allow him in my room he asked me if he should call Donald. The rest apparently had to wait for an e-mail. I know, I know. These things happen when I forget just *who* is in charge of my life!

I was in the hospital to have some bladder and bowel repair. The doctor is pretty sure I won't be peeing in my dainties any more. If David doesn't stop moaning and groaning every time he moves and giving me updates on his bodily functions, I will have to shoot him. Now he wants to ask *me* every hour or two if I have pooped! What is he expecting? I didn't eat for 2 days as I was throwing up due to the anesthesia! My patience is running thin my friends. Pray! —*Valerie*

We had decided that our decks were in need of some color and water seal, so we purchased a deck sealer with the color mixed right in it. We have brushes, sponges, wipes and are ready to rock and roll.

However, the weather man has warned of impending rain storms, so yesterday we took heed, and put the task off. We then enjoyed the most beautiful, sunny, spring day. Today, we are set to go.

I quietly listened to, and patiently observed, the MB's instructions on how the job was to be done. Then the tools were passed to me. My MB apparently thought I had not been paying attention. He kept returning from his garage with *continued* instructions until he received my request to "Go to your garage and leave me alone or I am going to quit!" Done! I started in the middle of the deck as we had shoved the items that normally sit on the deck to the sides. A good thing too, it is pouring now. The thunder and the rain, which I do so enjoy under most circumstances has shown up with a vengeance. The deck is covered, mostly, but the wind has joined the party. But, heck, I HAD received my instructions. The part closest to the door was dry so I finished. 10 min by 10 min sections. The stuff has to be rubbed after 10 min., so I set the timer and just kept going. I guess we will have to wait until tomorrow to see how the job turns out.

When I was a kid, my Mom used to mop the floor that way. She started closest to the carpet and mopped her way out the back door. We knew better that to walk on the wet floor, so Mom had a few child free moments to enjoy. Apparently, I forgot that critical part. My MB was on *my* side of the door. It worked out OK though. After being banished to the garage, he was busy practicing his wood turning and doing a beautiful job. Ahhh... team work. —*Valerie.*

The top deck is done... and so am I. When I sent David to his garage he went, and did not return. He was kind enough to come out and paint the top of the 2 posts that were too high for me to reach and was very good about bringing me my tools and cleaning the brushes. After the staining was done, railings, deck and all, came the finish work... I washed down all the stuff that had been piled high and moved about during the job. Table, chairs, storage bin, Bar-B-Q, bar, and anything else that couldn't get out of my way. There is a big black wasp that took great interest in what I was doing. We made a deal, I would ignore him, and he wouldn't bother me. I kept to my part of the bargain and he kept his... *Thank goodness*!

This morning I enjoyed the fruits of my labor. I sat out on the deck with my coffee and the Sunday paper and felt quite at peace and happy to be alive. Uhhh... about the lower deck you may ask. Well, I think it will be one of those things that you need to take a break from and forget just how hard and what a pain in the ass it was. —*Love, Valerie.*

July. The kids have come and gone, and it is quiet here this morning. One week ago, we picked up my son Donald and his family, wife Debbie and daughter Sara. The next afternoon my daughter Denise and her family, husband Kevin and children, Samantha and Alex arrived. We greeted them with B-B-Q steaks and sweet corn. Beds were assigned, the cork screw was set to warp speed, and the scale was banished under the bed. Let the fun begin!

Denise and family were only here 3 days. We took the nature hike through Tanyard Creek the first day, went river rafting and canoeing the second day, and took in Eureka Springs the following day. David and I have been too busy to see the area around us so we all explored together.

Since Dutch pancakes were on the menu the Eureka Springs day, we got off to a late start. We were slowed down for a few minutes by two young ladies whose stomachs were a bit queasy from the crooked road. That gave Kevin, Donald, and me a chance to climb the observation tower. I must admit to not making it all the way to the top. Three quarters of the way up, the wind that had been tickling the tops of the trees whipped it's self into a frenzy. We were way above the trees, so there was nothing to slow it down. I got a little case of vertigo at that point, so I stopped there and the guys went to the top. I may have to stop there again on another trip. I hated not being able to finish!

When we got to Eureka Springs we discovered a charming little town that needed, not one afternoon, but possibly two days to see properly. We did make it to the train ride. It turned out to be a longer walk to the station than we had anticipated, and I was very worried about David. He was moving pretty slow and his face was quite red by the time we got to the station.

The conductor was a hoot and had quite a nice supply of interesting stories about the railroad, and a wonderful way of delivering them. When the locomotive was detached and was turning around for our return trip, he asked any of us who were interested, to come out and place a coin on the tracks. There is a precise way of doing it that includes, spitting on, not just licking, the coin and placing it, just *so*, on the tracks. It was great fun.

Sara and I played many games of cards in our time before and after her cousins joined us. She kept a running total of wins and losses that did not show my gaming skills in a very good light. She had 15 wins and I had 7. On the Friday they left she and I went down to our little 10 lane bowling alley and she kept to her winning ways. 2 1/2 games for her, 1 1/2 games for me. Well, I may have spotted her some pins.

Now I have to explain to my stomach just why it will be getting no more cookies, cakes, and most of everything else it has been treated to this past week. The scale is still under the bed. David and I decided to leave it there for at least a week.

On the way home from the airport David was treating me to a list of things he wants to get done. My answer was always the same. "Maybe tomorrow Honey". He was so engrossed in his list; he failed to see the Patrol Car following us for several miles, with its lights on. The siren worked quite a bit better. It seems the MB was going 17 miles over the posted speed limit. After *MANY* questions about how long we had lived here, and just when our home in CA and been sold, she kindly gave the new guy just a warning about the speed limits and a very real warning, that the grace period for registering a car in AR is one month. We were dangerously close to a rather large fine if we didn't get David's car taken care of! I kept myself busy looking through the pictures on my camera and did not correct the MB when he said our CA escrow had closed just 2 weeks previously. ;) It was a good week.

I hear the thunder. It is time to grab some coffee and the paper and go out on the deck to enjoy the rain. —*Love to all, Valerie.*

I started my day in my favorite way, on the deck reading the paper. I have been quite distressed lately that this was to be a thing of the past. If you could have seen my shoulders and legs, you would have thought I had the measles. It sure felt like it. I was thanking my lucky stars for hydrocortisone cream. I must say that my MB was very quick to answer the call. "Honey, call the exterminator."

The exterminator called back and suggested fleas. Since I was scratching, and my furry friend was not, I said I didn't think so, and furthermore, fleas never seemed to bite me in CA. He came out and sure enough, not fleas. He gave us the super service and as he was leaving I asked him about the tiny little orange spider looking things I see on the deck. "Oh" he said, "Those are chiggers!"

We had been warned about "The dreaded chiggers", but no one told us you could barely see them with the naked eye. If I hadn't been doing a jigsaw puzzle out on the deck, with my glasses on, I never would have seen them. It seems they like to do the puzzles too, so they gave themselves away.

The exterminator gave us a tip that he said we would never see in the exterminator's manual. Apparently, his wife walks every morning and was having trouble with the chiggers. A neighbor told her to put drier sheets in her shoes and that would solve her problem. So, armed with a drier sheet, I rubbed it on my arms and legs just to be sure, I went out to read my paper. I was joined out there by an unexpected ally. I felt something crawling up my arm. It was a quite large praying mantis. Luckily, I had not hit it too hard. Now I know these guys are wonderful to have around, they eat all those annoying little critters that bite you and eat your plants and all. However, He had to be reminded two more times *not* to crawl around on me. —*Valerie*

It has been three days now and I have no new bites. My little praying friend is still out there doing his job, and I can enjoy my coffee and my paper. Sometimes David comes out to join me. We have no problem sharing the paper. He likes to read about politics and the business section. I prefer the more important items... a picture of 4 deer watching traffic go by on the highway, the letters to the editor, and of course... Dear Abby.

Taco Tuesday... we had heard about it but had not yet attended. It seems to be a small "Rite of Passage" for folks new to the area. Their biggest night they served over 2200 tacos, in 4 hours. So, on Tuesday, after running errands all day, we found ourselves at 3:30 p.m., starving. The bowls of cereal we had had for breakfast had long ago run out of steam. It was just the right time to try Taco Tuesday. It goes from 4 p.m. until 8 p.m. We were a half hour away and I was driving. I really didn't think I could drive that far without something to eat. So, we stopped for a quick and healthy snack. I had an Almond Joy, David a Three Musketeers.

We received our instructions. Pick out the room you want to sit in, there were 4 to choose from or you could go out on the patio, pick a table, check the table number, come back and order. Our food would be delivered. *We were ready.* We scouted around for a room with a good view of the golf course and ordered… four tacos, two each, chips, salsa and of course, a pitcher of Margaritas. That was followed by two more tacos, one each. Well, they were only $.75. How could we possible stop at two! We couldn't have chosen a better night for our maiden voyage to "Taco Tuesday". While we were eating, a Barbershop Quartet started to sing in the next room. I went in to investigate. Four men were standing in front of a table singing a beautiful version of "Let Me Call You Sweetheart". As they sang, they motioned for a young lady who was sitting on the other side of the table to stand up. Then, at the appropriate point in the song, one of the singers took a box out of his pocket, opened it, and produced an engagement ring. The girl nodded yes, and he slipped it on her finger. On our way out, we stopped to tell them how happy we were that we had been there for such a special night. The guy had organized and carried out a great event and had never missed a note. The girl assured us it had been a complete, and very welcome, surprise. "Taco Tuesday" was deemed a success in every respect. —*Love, Valerie.*

Today is our second anniversary. It has been four months since David's surgery. When you have your prostate removed they tell you sex is a thing of the past. Not So. Oh, it's different, that's for sure, but after we had gone out for dinner, we had a most wonderful, intimate, and satisfying time in bed. I think we are really on the mend. —*Happily, Valerie.*

August. I have gone to CA for a month to visit my Mom, my kids and grandkids. David stayed home to be with his 10-year-old grandson Ryan. On their first night alone together, Shera, who had been enjoying her late-night excursion out in the woods, came home covered in poop. She had found some and had rolled around in it until there was barely a spot left clean. Boy was I happy I was half way across the nation! So, around 9:30 or so, David and Ryan were out front giving her a bath. It was necessary to give her two, to actually get her clean and smelling good again. After drying her and confining her to the laundry room for an hour, she was released and told to "Go to bed!" She did not have to be asked twice.

Around 2:00 a.m. David awoke to the sound of crying. It seems sleeping down stairs alone had gotten the best of Ryan. He was scared. So, David proved to be the good Grandfather. He explained to Ryan that Valerie was in CA and her side of the bed was vacant and wouldn't Ryan like to sleep there. He did not have to be asked twice either. —*Love, Valerie.*

David called this a.m. He said he had a severe kidney infection. He had gone with Ryan to the VA hospital and they had put him right into ICU. Our wonderful neighbor Don had gone over there to pick up Ryan and would keep him until David could go home, maybe Wed. or Thurs. I told him I was coming home. I have had kidney infections and there is no hospital stay involved. You get a prescription and are shown the door! He started to weep and said "Please don't come home. You deserve this vacation."

At the beginning of the summer my 16-year-old grandgirl, Jennifer, had been diagnosed with a cancerous growth on her ovary and the growth and the ovary had to come out. She was feeling better and trying to rescue what was left of her summer by working 2 days a week at the Long Beach Aquarium as a Volunteer. She wants to be a Marine Biologist. I was supposed to be watching her for the next 3 days. We picked up Kalyn, another one of my grandgirls and went to Jennifer's to play cards (Crazy 8's, Go Fish and War) and to spend the night. When I got tired of those two girls kicking my butt at War, I retired to get in my PJ's and listen to my girls giggle.

We were up early and off to the Aquarium. After much coaxing, Kalyn put her hands in the stingray / shark pool for a petting session. After that it was, "Look Grandma, this one likes me, he keeps coming back for me to pet him" We had a great day... I'm going home. Jennifer will stay with her Uncle Don's family; Uncle Don will take me to the airport. The wonderful woman at the airport wanted to know why I was there. I told her that my husband, who had had cancer surgery a few months ago, was back in the hospital and I had to go home, *now*. She worked with us for about 45 min. She managed to get me on a flight just after midnight with no additional charges. Well, there was that little charge of $15.00 for my suitcase. ;)

I'm home. David is still in the hospital and the news has not been good. I'm so glad I didn't let him talk me into staying in CA. They found 2 modules in his liver and 1 in his lung. They will biopsy tomorrow. David says the nurses and the Dr. have been looking pretty sad when they come to talk to him.
—*Pray please, Valerie.*

The news today is not happy news. David is still in the hospital and has been diagnosed with liver cancer. We are waiting on a biopsy tomorrow, so we will know how to proceed. When I went to see him today the nurse was telling him some important things to remember; A good attitude, a good diet, and not to lie around and let me spoil him. He didn't look too worried about that happening! We decided to take a walk down the hall. There was music playing! "Hey", he said "Want to two-step?" My answer was, of course, "Yes". So off we went, two stepping down the corridor, David and I grinning like fools and the people going by giving us the thumbs up. You can't keep a good guy down.

David is still being held captive at the VA Hospital. No ransom demands have been made but I am keeping a record in pictures of his treatment. After this ill treatment, he was caught trying to bribe his grandson, Ryan, to help him escape. No news on the biopsy yet but I will keep you informed. *Valerie*

The biopsy has been done, the bone scan has been done and the results are in. There is no good news today. The cancer is in the liver, both lungs, and the bones. The prognosis is daunting to say the least. We have listened to the experts and my MB will start his chemo tomorrow. But we are putting on the gloves and are ready to fight. WE HAVE OTHER PLANS! Thanks to all who have written encouraging notes and said much needed prayers.— *Love, Valerie.*

David had his first treatment and *we* are home. The chemo nurse told him again he had to do things for himself. She said he should have a hot sudsy water treatment 3 times a day. When the MB asked what that would do, she said, "It will get the dishes clean. You should do them" Will let you know how the next few days go.

We will be gradually moving his days of treatment, so they are on Mondays, not on Thursdays, so he will be at his best for the weekend. You know, dinner & dancing ;-) — *Valerie*

A Good morning, David is up and feeling pretty darn good. He is weak due to the fact that he has been in the hospital for 2 weeks, but his spirits are good. We had breakfast together on the deck. We had a welcome home thunder storm last night and it is a beautiful morning. Then I turned the shaggy dog I brought home from the hospital into my MB. He got a haircut and got his mustache trimmed. Then it was off to the shower. How do the used car companies describe it? He has been overhauled and is ready to go. He is feeling so good he thinks he will have the dance next Wed. as planned. The dancing is the next best thing (I am the first) that he loves. As long as it works for him, I'm in. —*Love to all, Valerie*

I'm afraid my MB is a little backward. Chemo is supposed to make you sick. He had his chemo on Thurs and felt really good on Thursday & Friday and then was back in the hospital on Saturday. We called the paramedics to come and get him. He was having severe chest pains and his fever had spiked to 104. He is now at Northwest Medical Center in Bentonville which is so much closer to the house. He has new doctors looking into his case. A pretty drastic way to get a second opinion don't you think? His white blood count is off the chart, so they may have to postpone his treatment this Wed. On Friday while he was home we picked up our new motor home. It's a 2000 Winnebago that we had purchased before I left for CA. The fact that it was still at the dealer was weighing heavily on David's mind. It is now parked temporarily in our driveway. On Sat. morning, when David was starting to feel puny, he went out and just sat in it for a while. I followed him out to keep an eye on him and got a few boxes unpacked. Please keep praying and we will keep on fighting. —*Valerie.*

There is no news on David's health. He remains the same. The news is on his care. The new hospital is taking wonderful care of my MB. The staff is plentiful, and is, if not at his beck and call, very attentive to him. Since his pain is in his chest they have a heart monitor on him at all times. His heart is not in question; the chest pain is believed to be caused by pneumonia, although they still are not sure, therefore, no chemo for him this week. He is closer to home now, so I can spend more time with him. Since he is in a weakened condition, I can boss him around. Today I made sure he was using his breathing thing (probably not the technical term) at least once an hour. I also took him for a walk around the floor twice. After the second tour three different ladies came in to see him as they had detected an elevation in his heart rhythm. I told them not to worry. His heart skipped a beat when he saw one of the ladies pouring candy bars into a dish. *His brakes work darn good*, as he came to an immediate stop and asked if he could have one.

His blood sugar was off the chart later so no more candy bars. However, the food is really good, so he isn't as willing to share. I would complain, but I am still enjoying some homemade lasagna a friend brought over for us. Thanks for the prayers, we are still fighting. —*Love, Valerie.*

September. It is Thursday morning and we are again *home*. I would like to say it all went smoothly... but I cannot. Oh, all was well on David's end. It was his taxi driver that had the mishaps. I was so excited about going to get my MB that I was almost to the highway, about 3 miles, when I realized I had forgotten to bring some clothes for him to come home in. So, I was making a quick U-turn and my coffee cup tipped over. How could that happen when it was sitting in its secure little holder you might ask? Well, it seems there were 2 pennies and a toothpick in that little holder and they disrupted the coffee cup's equilibrium just enough for it to tumble out. That cup has also tumbled out of the "My favorite cup" category.

Whatever is wrong with my MB, there is nothing wrong with his eyes. "Honey, what is that all over your shirt?" was his second greeting, right after "There's my honey now". When I explained about the coffee, he said he hoped it wouldn't stain as it one of his favorite. It wouldn't dare! —*Love, Valerie*

Our clue to a change in the weather is, once again, the Dogwood tree. Just as its white flowers were the first sign of spring, now their leaves turning red is the forecast that fall is on the way.

There was a very unusual breeze today. It was one big puff, and then it was gone. My MB and I know how it originated. It was our collective sigh of relief as we left the Oncologist's office.

For the first time in weeks we got something besides gloom and doom from a medical professional. Our lab results were good, the next chemo will be tomorrow, and the doctor gave us some much welcome hope. David had many questions. To make sure he didn't forget any of them, he had a *LIST*. The last of the questions was "What about alcohol? May I have a Scotch from time to time?" "Have two!" said our new best friend. There we were, armed with this good news and ready to celebrate. And we know how! We are from Southern California after all. We were off in a flash to Lowe's and bought a new vacuum cleaner for the motor home! Thanks for your prayers, don't stop. We will continue to fight. —*Love, Valerie.*

(A note to David's Daughter)

Dear Marcy,

This is a note I can send you now. I would have sent it regardless of the outcome yesterday, but I am so relieved that yesterday was good news.

I was terrified. Your Dad seemed to be getting weaker by the day. His remarks about what I was going to do when he was gone were getting more frequent. He was telling people that he wasn't going to be doing the dances anymore because he wanted to spend what time he had left doing other things.

I spent the weekend working in the motor home, getting it ready to hit the road and wondering, secretly, just who I was getting it ready for. Were we really ever going to be able to use it?

I was so afraid we would get to the Dr's. office and they would tell us his white blood count was too high and he was too septic to receive treatment. As I write this to you there are tears running down my face, tears of happiness and relief.

> The rest of the day your Dad's comments were, "Honey, I can't believe how good I feel. Those pains in my back and sides are so much better, almost gone." I kept telling him, "Yes, good news and hope are great medicine."
>
> I know, we still have a huge hill to climb and I make jokes in the "News", but believe me when I tell you, I am scared every day. Ready to fight, and pray, and be there for him, but scared just the same.
>
> Please know, you will always get the facts from me. Good or bad. I won't be hiding anything from his children. I just want to be sure what the facts are before I send them along.
>
> We are in this together. Love, Valerie.

When we left the Oncology clinic on Tues. we were told, "Come back tomorrow. You will be out of here in about two hours." We arrived at 10:00 a.m. The Chemo room is quite large. I didn't count the recliners, but I'm sure there were at least 20 of them. David was given his choice of several and took one that looked long enough to house all 6' 3" of him. The staff was plentiful, and all were armed with a full dose of Arkansas kindness. "Have you had chemo before?" and, "Did you have any negative reactions?" Were asked, and answered with "Yes" and "No" respectively. While they got David hooked up, I settled in next to him with my 2004 AARP magazines. I had been saving them until I had time to read them.

The first 1/2 hour was uneventful as the only thing going into my MB was anti-nausea medication. When they started the chemo, David, true to form, asked me if I would go get him something to eat. A 6-inch sub from Subway was the something of choice. The staff said that would be OK, gave me directions, and off I went to get our subs, with cookies!

When I returned, I looked over at my MB and he was surrounded by staff and had a wash cloth on his head. When I got to him he said, "You missed all the fun". I looked in his eyes and answered, "I don't think I missed it all". My man looked terrified. He told me later that he was sure it was "All over" for him when the reaction started.

After I had gone, he had had a very bad reaction to the chemo. His blood pressure had dropped significantly, he was flushed and sweating, and his abdomen was cramping. The chemo was temporarily turned off and he seemed to be stabilizing. Then the shaking started, head to toe. I called out to the staff, they came right over and started calling for more med's. David said he felt like he was in one of those TV shows where someone calls out "We need some help in here!" and a bunch of people come rushing to surround them. The staff got things under control, assured us that that was a common reaction to chemo, they would slow things down, and all would be well. David was pooped and took a nap. I kept one hand and one eye on my AARP magazine and the other hand and eye on my MB.

At 4:30 p.m. we were on our way home, armed with prescriptions to take next week before we go in, to minimize any adverse reactions. At this rate, I will soon have an empty space in the cabinet where those AARP magazines have been stored for so long they should be growing mold. We are up for the fight. Keep praying. —*Love to all, Valerie*

Today was chemo day. There was quite the scene again today, but my MB was not the star. He took his chemo without all the hullabaloo of last week and felt good enough afterward to ask to go to Sam's Club for a hot dog.

The scene today was caused by the professionals. It seems one of the guests was having a birthday. He was treated too much singing, giggling, and tons of Silly String. For those of you who don't know, it is a string like, sticky something or other, that is dispensed from an aerosol can at an alarming velocity. Someone thought pay back was in order, so the Birthday Boy was given a can and gave as good and he got. Then we all enjoyed his chocolate chip cookie which was the size of a large pizza.

I, for one, enjoyed today's entertainment much more than last week's. I'm sure David did too as he got out his phone and started taking pictures.

I'm not sure if it is the chemo, but everything the MB has eaten, and have I mentioned there is nothing wrong with his appetite, for the past 4 days or so has had an attack of shyness and has refused to come out. My poor guy has been in such pain tonight. We have tried many, not to be described; things and we have had success. It looks like we will need a plumber tomorrow. "Yes David, it can wait until tomorrow! It is 10:30 P.M. We have 2 more bathrooms!" I'm heading for the wine. —*Valerie.*

We love our little airport, just a handful of gates to come and go from. We tell people coming in "We'll meet you at the bottom of the escalator. Don't worry, there's only one". Luggage is then retrieved, and we are on our way. From the gate to the car takes about 15 min. Come visit. You will love it too. The drive to the airport is also wonderful. The road winds lazily through the ever so green country side. It is a lovely introduction to the beauty of our home here.

David's son Howard is here. He got here at 10:00 P.M. on Wed. It was raining so we left a little early so we wouldn't have to worry about being late. As it turns out, being late was the least of my worries. The trip only took 20 min, even in the rain! However, after dark is no time to be thinking about anything but where in the heck the road has gone. It was, "I can't see my hands in front of my eyes", dark. Our annoying little friend, the GPS, was doing her job, but when she said to turn at some street or other, the problem was finding it. There are no lights out there to mark the street corners. There is one turn in particular where she is always mistaken. (She lies) We know that now, so when we get there we just go straight.

When my MB asked why we were approaching the intersections so slowly, I reminded him that not only was it pitch black out there, but we were approaching intersections where visual indicators were now nonexistent. Other comments, "Be careful, oh Honey look at that, and do you have your bright lights on?" were mostly ignored as I was too busy staying on the road to acknowledge them. I do know, now, that those ugly little school bus yellow signs with big black arrows are there for a purpose, and not just ugly irritations on my lovely drive to the airport. I make no apologies. I needed them, and I used them.

Howard leaves on Tues., in the "AM" I am happy to announce. We will be sorry to see him go. He has been a real God send. He has been helping David do so many things that he just is not up to right now. I have been quite shameless. I have taken full advantage of his visit. He is spending his time with my MB so I have been resting. They go out to run errands and I take naps.

Howard has the iPhone, and now so does David. The two of them have spent many hours getting it set up and ready to work. Someone on the iPhone help desk doesn't have a clue how lucky he is that David has some in house assistance. No, "I want to talk to a supervisor!" calls to date.

David has been having some back pain, but on the whole, is doing very well.

"This is God. Today I will be handling all of your problems for you. I do not need your help. So, have a nice day. I love you" ... "Put your worries in a basket and leave them for God." This was sent to me today from a reader of the "News" I'm getting ready to fill up that basket. —*Love, Valerie.*

We went to a concert last Sunday. It was called "Nearly Neal". The guy did all of Neil Diamond's music and it was wonderful. David went but was in so much pain he couldn't enjoy it. During intermission there was a parade of our new friends coming over to ask how he was feeling and to wish him well. It was really heartwarming and meant a lot to my MB. —*Valerie*

Last Tues. when David got his chemo we saw the Dr. and after hearing about the pain he was in, ordered a steroid shot. It was one-part, fast acting, and another part long acting. David felt like a new man! He wasn't able to leap tall buildings in a single bound, but he was feeling much friskier than I have seen him in a long, long, while.

Every week David has his blood drawn and then an IV for the treatment. They are really having a devil of a time getting his veins to cooperate. This time our nurse tried both arms and then called in the pro. During his treatment, the nurse was talking to David about permanent-port implants. They are put under the skin so no problem with showers or any other activities. The nurse said she could set it up with the surgeon for him. David was quite adamant about not scheduling it until she had talked to the Dr. She explained to him that the Dr. didn't usually weigh in on the implants, but David was insistent.

She came back later, said she had talked to the Dr., and he thought it would be a really good thing for my MB. So, he made plans to have it done. After she was gone, my MB gave me a big smile and said, "What good news honey. The Dr. must think I'm going to be around for a while or he wouldn't say I was a good candidate for the port". What a wonderful Dr. we have. He dispenses his medical advice sprinkled with good doses of hope and encouragement.

Friday night we went to the Country Club to meet friends for dinner and dancing. We danced several nice dances including 3 slow East Coast Swings. However, this is Bella Vista. The music starts at 6:30 and by 8:30 we were on our way home. All those prayers are really helping. —*Thanks, Valerie*

October. We are home again. This time however, there was *NO* hospital involved. We have just concluded the shakedown cruise of our new, well new to us, motor home.

We left on Thurs. and went to the Down Stream Casino in Oklahoma. It turned out to be closer than we thought, only 46 miles. It was a pretty uneventful trip, no narrow country roads or anything like that. Good thing too, I did all the driving. My MB said I did a wonderful job. ;-) We were lured to that particular location by the promise of free RV parking and full hook ups. There was also a shuttle that David put on speed dial. It came in minutes to pick us up from, or deliver us to, the casino.

We had a small glitch getting started. We stopped to get gas and after 15 min. and the help of a stranger walking past we were no closer to pumping gas than when we pulled up to the station. My MB had a plan… he called the previous owner of our new home away from home for help. He told us to unlock the cap. Well, there *was* this little silver thing covering the key hole.

On Friday night we treated ourselves to a wonderful steak and lobster meal. The special of the day was a 22-oz. bone in porterhouse steak with a crab stuffed lobster tail. I'm pretty sure it would have fed a family of 4, so we opted for something a little smaller. We had Shera with us on our little trip, so the manager gave us a one of those really big steak bones for her. She is a great traveler, but she won't get her treat until Tuesday. She will be home alone all day, so we will leave her out on the deck with it. That's the day we go for chemo in the morning, and then straight to the VA for a CT-scan in the afternoon, to see just how the treatments are working. We won't get the results for another week. We are on pins and needles knowing how very important this will be. An extra prayer for our nerves and sanity wouldn't hurt.

VALERIE KATZ

We didn't have much luck gambling, terrible luck actually, so we decided to play the penny slots. Yes, pennies. The end results were the same, but the cash lasted much longer.

There was one smaller problem that we never did get solved. We could not get the hot water heater to work. I could heat enough water in the microwave to wash my face, and, as my mother used to say, treat the hot spots, but we would have had to be away for more than 2 days to get this girl in a *cold* shower. We will be getting that fixed before we venture out again.

Our favorite part of the trip... David found he could sleep on his side, the new apparatus has made that difficult, so for the first time since March we were able to sleep all cuddled up like spoons. We had a great time. We hope to be planning more outings very soon. —*Love to all, Valerie*

Yesterday the MB's chest was numbed, and the new port went in. When it thawed out, *OH BOY!* My man was in a world of hurt. Those pain pills are a wonderful thing. I woke up that morning with a sore throat and a general "Where is the pesky VW that ran me over" feeling. As the day wore on the VW turned into a truck and my sciatica decided to join the party. I went to the chiropractor and started making plans for today.

I was worried that maybe I was getting the flu and would share it with my MB. *THAT* would not be good. I had to go with him for his chemo and then on to the VA for the CT scan. My plan was to stay in the car. There is a sign in the chemo room that says, if you have a sore throat, a runny nose, etc. etc. you *must* wear a mask while you are there. Since I was feeling most of the above, staying in the car and just being the chauffeur seemed like the best idea.

I made my plans. I packed an apple, some nuts, a large coffee and a container of lemonade. I washed my face, and without a backward glance at the drawer that holds my eyebrows and blush, off I went. Oh yes, I was going to stay *in* the car. I guess

I should mention that I had on my slippers and some sweats that looked very much like PJ's. That pesky bra was left at home too. I did remember my pillow, a book, an afghan, and 4 days of crossword puzzles. As I said, my plans were made, and I was going to be comfy.

David went in for his treatment. Of course, he did ask me if I had my cell phone before he went in. I told him "Yes, I put it in my fanny pack last night just to make sure". Not long after, I realized the error in my plans. I had to visit the ladies room. Oh well, there are people getting treatments dressed in all kinds of outfits. I figured I would blend right in. And as long as I was there… they have really good coffee, so I got some more.

I was just getting settled when there was a knock on my window. David's nurse was there. It seems they were having a bit of trouble with the new port and David had been trying to call me, to no avail. Oh, I *had* put my phone in the fanny pack, but I had so many other things to take with me I had left it at home. My MB was far too busy with the reluctant new port to come out and deliver his usual little talk about not leaving home without my cell! Out he came after his treatment. I was thinking that a drive through for something to eat and a trip to the VA and we would be on our way home. That was *my* plan…. the MB had *other* plans.

Harbor Freight is very close to the VA and not so very close to Bella Lane. Sooo, a stop there was necessary. I was up for that. I know where the rest room is and I was pretty sure I wouldn't see anyone who knew me in there. Hobby Lobby is in the same area as Harbor Freight and since we were looking for some things for the house, we stopped there too.

Find a drive through, no way. We had to go in to a KFC. They have a buffet, and as I may have mentioned before, my MB has *not* lost his appetite.

The VA was next. By then, I had almost stopped wondering what people were thinking. Is that woman running around in her

PJ's? I went in and used the rest room. Two stops later, we found the items we were looking for. We were on our way home.

We won't get the results of the MB's scan for a week. Will keep you posted. Shera would like me to tell you that she got her bone and it was every bit a delicious as promised.

Keep in touch. —*Love, Valerie*

This is going to be a looooong week, waiting for test results. Today is the day after chemo so David is ready to leap tall buildings again. He wants to be busy, so he is off to the bank and the Subway and has the heater in the garage going so that he can tackle some projects out there. I want to be as big a help as possible, so I've got lots of laundry for him to fold. :)

David has wanted me to go with him to his wood turning session. The one held once a month in a converted garage out in the boonies. He was only going to visit for an hour, so I agreed to drive him. I am so glad I did. Words could not describe the beauty of the area. It is situated next to a river and the grounds are lush. I had no trouble identifying it as the boonies however. These words on a very small diner described it perfectly for me. "Stop here for Killer Chili and Bail Bonds."

Sending out the "News" is good for me. I am able to keep in touch with all of you, and yes, I am saving them, for my children. My plan has been to live my life so that when I'm in my dotage my children will not think of me as an "Old Lady", but as a "Character". I know sometimes, when they were younger; they were wishing I would tone it down a bit. One of my best perks?? People begin to write back and share their stories with me. —*Love to all, Valerie*

If it's Tuesday, it must be chemo. We have been very apprehensive, and somewhat sleep deprived, knowing today was the day for the first results on how the chemo is working. The first thing the nurse asked was for David to sign a paper, so the VA could send the test results. My eyebrows shot up into my hair line as I asked, "You mean we don't have results today!?" As she beat a hasty retreat she assured us that she would fax the paper immediately and the VA would reply just as promptly.

It was good news, bad news. The chemo has kept the cancer from growing, but it had not caused any shrinkage. So... today we got a new recipe. A much stronger version, that takes 4 1/2 hours to deliver. We got there at 10 a.m. and left a little after 5 p.m. David was cautioned about the effects. Stronger meds may mean more of a reaction. The word nausea was delivered to deaf ears. During the treatment he wanted me to go get him some chili from Wendy's. When it got to, "Are you still here. I'm hungry!" I told him I had been waiting to see if he had a bad reaction. If there was a replay of, "Oh my, what in the heck is happening to Mr. Katz?!" like when he first started his chemo, I wanted to be there. I missed the first showing and did not want to miss the re-run.

There is no Wendy's near the oncology clinic, so we settled for Taco Bell. The man has a cast iron stomach and the appetite to go with it. When we were on our way home he wanted to go to Sam's Club for a hot dog. When I told him I was not hungry, he asked if I wouldn't I like to take him for one anyway. No Way! I had the bit in my teeth and was headed for the barn.

Time will tell. So far, he feels fine. Yesterday he was feeling pretty punky and tired. I told him not to worry. He would get a dose of his vitamins (chemo) today. The nurse said the new meds would probably ramp him up pretty good tonight. She said not to fight it with sleep aids. Just go with the flow, read a book, watch a movie, and enjoy.

Oh yes, there is something I forgot to tell my CA friends about his new chest port. The doctor wanted to know if he was right or left handed and what arm he fired his rifle with. The kick back could damage the port. Now, *there's* a question you don't get in CA. I will keep you posted. Thanks again for all the prayers. —*Valerie*

No one is feeling like leaping over tall buildings here today. My MB knows he has had chemo. He has been feeling really tired and somewhat achy all day. However, everything in his stomach is staying just where it belongs. We are grateful for small things.

There is a woman who visits the Oncology Clinic with her dog. He is some kind of a Setter, but he is marked just like our Shera. She brings him in to visit the folks having treatments. He is enormously sweet and has a scarf that says, "If you can read this, start petting". We did! —*Love to all, Valerie*

We had big plans for this weekend. On this weekend each year, Northwest Arkansas gets crafty. There are 11 different sites for these craft fairs. The one near us is huge, and nothing is sold that has not been handmade. We loved it last year and could not wait to go again. Also, there was one in Pea Ridge, just a few miles down the road, where David's woodturning friends were going to be exhibiting, and selling, their wares.

Then this afternoon, the church (barring bad weather) was throwing an afternoon pontoon party at one of our lakes for folks new to the church this year. The weather man cooperated enough to not send rain, but at toasty 45 degrees, I think plan two may go in to effect and it will be held at the church. We were really looking forward to that.

But it is still true… life is what happens while you are making other plans. My wakeup call on Sat. was the sound of David falling down in the bathroom. We managed to get him up, but he was a little disoriented and seemed to just kind of melt right down to the floor again. I wanted to call the paramedics, but David said "No, this was just a ploy to get me up to fix him some eggs". The way to this man's heart is still, definitely, through his stomach.

I went and got his office chair; it has wheels, and got him up and on to it. Then we glided to the living room and his new electronic chair. I brought him his morning Ensure, a nutritional drink for folks who need a little extra help with vitamins and energy, and then I fixed him his eggs.

This morning, I heard a noise and looked up to see David just outside our bedroom door rocking in place and looking like he was about to go down again. I grabbed a chair and got it behind him, just in time. He was again disoriented. I brought him some Ensure and helped him to his electric chair. When talking to him later he didn't seem to remember the incident.

Now we have questions. This new chemo cocktail has kicked some serious booty around here. The doctor has some splanin' to do. I keep reminding my MB that he can't expect to feel great when he goes in every Tuesday to be poisoned. This too shall pass, and then... well, we have plans. —*Love, Valerie.*

There was no Chemo Cocktail this week. My MB's blood count was too low for the treatment. We had the exact same thoughts on hearing the news. "Oh no, will this delay our trip to CA", and "Oh boy, maybe he will feel better without the treatment and we will be able to use our tickets for River Dance on Sunday".

I had a talk with the doctor about a walker and some home care help. David is very unsteady on his feet right now. I try to escort him when he feels the need to move about the house, but he is a foot taller than I am and has me by about 90 pounds. The only thing I really could do if he fell, would be to throw myself under him to break his fall. When we do get the in-house help, I am going to ask that one of the days be Wed. Mahjong is calling. We both feel better when I have had some R&R.

Just to make things a little more interesting around here, David changed the ring tone for his iPhone. It sounded like the doorbell. After several quick trips to the front door, I figured it out. Now, if we got as many visitors as David gets phone calls, we would definitely need a swinging door. However, when one of our wonderful friends and neighbors decides to pay us a visit, we don't want to leave them cooling their heels on the front porch while I wait for the MB to answer the phone. I'm not sure what his ring tone is now, but he has agreed to change it.

When I woke up this a.m., at 7:15, I could hear the MB talking on the phone. My first thought was, "Oh my gosh, who could he be talking too at this hour. It's 5:15 in CA!". As it turned out, he was visiting with someone from the iPhone help line. My man loves company, and when push comes to shove he can always find someone to visit with on his iPhone. My wake-up calls are certainly varied. —*Valerie.*

I love daylight savings time. An hour more of daylight pleases me immensely. However, after explaining the "Fall Back" concept to 13 of our clocks, the bloom is off the rose. There is one clock in the kitchen that I can't reach and another one in the living room that I can't figure out how to get the back off of. I'm sure my MB will be delighted to tackle those in the a.m.

My MB did get his chemo on Tuesday. His blood platelets were still very low, but they gave him a shot of something that was supposed to encourage them to "Get crackin'" and then gave him the chemo. Next week he just has labs, no chemo is scheduled. A week off is always good. The fact that the MB is feeling pretty rotten today is not so good. I had him call the Doctor's service and they ordered him some antibiotics pronto. I think they said something scary to David. Pneumonia! He has had a very sore throat, and a cough that is a side effect of the treatments, but it has gotten worse and now seems to have gotten, productive, but no fever, so that is encouraging. I on the other hand have had a pretty good week. I managed to make it to Mahjong two weeks in a row, and I won. This week I won a whopping $1.60. "No, no, don't call." I am a firm believer in the "Never a Borrower nor a Lender Be" way of thinking.

Last night I went to a dinner and play at the church. Met some new people and thoroughly enjoyed myself.

Last Tuesday, while David was getting his treatment I went and got my Arkansas driver's license. I took all the things my new friends here warned me I would need. My new marriage license, my old divorce papers, my passport, and my CA driver's license. When I plopped down my stack of papers, the very nice gentleman decided I must not have anything to hide and settled for the CA license and the passport. I gave him my new address and then confirmed that all the rest of the information was the same. Eye and hair color, height and weight, yes to donating body parts. He must not have guessed that I was being a little less that truthful, I did fudge a little on the weight, as he then asked me if I would like to register to vote. I choose to think of it not so much as a lie, but as a bit of wishful thinking. Thanks again for all the prayers. Keep em' coming. —*Love to all, Valerie*

November. After 2 weeks without chemo, the MB was feeling pretty frisky. When we got to the chemo lab on Tuesday he had his vitals taken and then we had a visit with the doctor. We had been to the VA last Friday and that doctor was concerned about his heart rate. It was running from 99 to 117 which seem to be too high. We now have a blood pressure cuff to monitor that stuff.

The chemo Dr. said the high heart rate was due to the treatments. He then told us that it was a day for the 4 1/2-hour treatment. That's the one he had when he was falling down and woozy for 2 days. Oh dear! I needed something to sooth me. I went and had my nails done.

Today my MB is feeling pretty darn good. He had someone over while I was playing Mahjong to look at his speakers and all the other DJ stuff he has. He sold it all, a pretty big step for him.

Now here is the best news. We have met an Angel. Her name is Carol. She will be coming to help us for 2 hrs. 3 days a week. She cleans, does laundry, cooks, and changes the sheets. She will do whatever we need. She has a great sense of humor and we both love her already. She asked David if he was going to try and get up out of bed without calling her. When he didn't answer right away she said, "Don't make me jump up there and throw my leg over you!" She told us all her other people were very old and either deaf, blind, or both. Her husband drives a big rig and is gone most of the time. She is really looking forward to having someone to talk with. Also, she doesn't hover. She wants David to let her know just what he needs and wants. Let's see... Talk, give orders? Sounds like my MB alright. Next week she can help us load the motor home. We are still planning to come to CA and I told her that when we get back, if they try to give us someone else, I am going to raise hell and put a block under it!

The News is *good!* David had his CT-scan on Monday and the chemo is working. When we went for his treatment on Tuesday his red cells were extremely low. No wonder he could barely get out of bed. He will need one of the big chemo treatments around the 8th of December, but we will try to get it at the VA in LA.

We are loading up the RV and plan to hit the road on Sat. There is excitement in the air! When we get there, we will make plans to be at 1 or 2 of the dance venues and hope to see most of you during that time. California here we come!

After 3 hours of help from our Angel, Carol, and 2 hours of the same from our neighbor Don, we are off to CA. It is 1:15 p.m. and we are already worn out but we are excited to be on our way. After 250 miles we lost the light and the will to drive one more mile. We pulled in to a rest stop to spend the night. David is still very tired from his dose of the Super Chemo so a quick chicken pie and he was off to bed. He is always cold, a side effect of the treatment. We left the heater on all night. He was under the spread and 2 Afghans.

I know that Texas has certain standards. They do things in a big way. They are in to Big Hats, cowboy boots and Western music. I'm pretty sure it is against the rules here, maybe even the law, but I threw caution to the wind today and drove through Texas listening to the movie sound track of Camelot. Well, not *all* caution. I kept my eye out for the sheriff and when I saw one I stopped singing along. Well you never know, they *may* be able to read lips.

As the sun was setting we stopped at a McRestaurant, thinking there was a rest stop 35 miles down the road. I got back on I-40 and discovered it is every bit as dark as the little road to the airport in Bella Vista. Yikes! I was nervous about keeping up with the trucks who seemed to know their way. Then there came an 8 mile stretch of road that was being worked on, so it was down to one lane each way with only the cement divider separating the lanes. The oncoming traffic was like driving into the sun. Lucky for me, there was a truck that was as hesitant as I was, so I was able to cozy up to his bumper for guidance. I was following so close I was afraid I was going to be DQ'd for drafting... it's a racing bike reference... phone a friend. The 8 miles was finally over and I saw the sign that made my heart so happy, rest area 2 miles. Halleluiah! Then the next sign... rest area next right. Yippee! And right under that a big orange one that read, "Rest area closed". About that time my co-pilot got up from his nap to inquire just why I was *still* driving.

We are parked along I-40 in a gas station. We will spend the night here along with some truckers who I assume are likewise displaced. I am catching up on "The News" and am well into my second glass of wine. I am praying tonight for "Traveling Mercies"

1:06 A.M.? **Me**... "David, Honey, what are you doing? It's 1:00 in the morning." **Him**... "No, It is 6:00" **Me**... "Nooo, I just

checked my cell phone and its 1:00". That is how today got started. I had been unexpectedly awakened by the sound of the coach starting and moving. We were not overly thrilled with our accommodations last night so the MB decided to move us. I had been asleep for 2 whole hours. David said he hadn't gotten much more than that but he was nervous about where we were and could not go back to sleep. So, we were off. It took about 1 ½ hours to find the next Loves Truck Stop. We were both lulled to sleep by the sound of dozens of humming generators. The sign said no overnight parking, but, technically, we didn't get there until morning. So, no harm no foul.
—Love to all, Valerie

December. We have been in CA for a week now. Things have been very busy!

Thanksgiving was wonderful! We were at my son Larry's, the house I lived in for many years, and we had a great meal. I was told the evening before, by his wife Luz, that she didn't like anyone in her kitchen, so not to come in and try to help. She said it with a big grin on her face so I got the message. "You have enough on your plate, relax tomorrow." I promised to stay out in the motor home and arrive with the first guests. I know a good deal when I hear one! I will instigate a vote to meet here for Thanksgiving dinner next year!

We were joined after dinner by my sister Martha and her kids and grandkids. They had had dinner with my Sister Cyndi's group and then came to see us. Michele was here from Canada so it was a great treat to see her. I must admit that my eyes puddled up a bit. The house was full of family and little kids were running around having a boisterous time. It reminded me of all the Christmas Eve's I had spent in this house with my family as they grew up and had children of their own. Great memories!

Friday, it was off to the US Open Dance Championships. David has been looking forward to that! He did quite well.

There was a *lot* of walking and stair climbing. We rested when we could. The events lasted each night until midnight, that's 2:00 a.m. Arkansas time! *Love to all, Valerie*

David had been very tired and had been complaining about a sore spot on the inside of his thigh up near his groin. We had an appointment at the VA to meet with an oncologist on Monday so I suggested we go early and have it checked out. Well, here's how that went! **Him,** "I don't have a doctor here" **Me,** "You can go to the ER. They have that here don't' they?" **Him** "I don't want to do that." **Me** "Well, OK. But if you don't go and have it looked at, you have to stop complaining about it. I don't want to hear it anymore!" I know, I know. I really do have a remarkable bedside manner.

We got to the VA at 10:00 am. We got in to see a doctor around noon. She said David had a lovely abscess and called in a surgeon. Due to his other problem, they drew some blood, and discovered his red blood cell count was down to 7. We asked what it should be. "14" was acceptable. A blood transfusion was called for.

The surgeon came and said he would have to lance the abscess and clean it. It would have to be packed. Could I repack it every day for him? "Well", I said "Let me watch you so I will know how." *WOW!* That sucker was deep! The doctor said it would be a big help if I could help keep the area open so he could see better and use both hands. Did I mention it was in his groin area? Well, let's just say the doctor passed me the ball and I kept it out of play.

Then it was off to a quick consult with the oncologist. He said he would be happy to give David his chemo here on the 8th. Great news!

Back to the ER for the blood... At 10:00 pm we were only half way through the first unit, with one more to go. At least six more hours were needed. I asked David if he would mind if

I went out to the car to sleep for a while. Well, he was sleeping! At that point he got all riled up and wanted to know why they couldn't just keep him all night so I could go home and get some rest. Believe me, they got the message! I was on my way!

Those of you who know me well, will not be the least bit surprised when I tell you the next turn of events. Leaving the hospital, I got lost. I drove around for a bit and then remembered my good friend, the GPS! Well, she did help me find the freeway but I was pretty darned sure she was taking me the wrong way. I wasn't that lost! I had lived in this area for 60 years. I turned her off and on 3 times before I realized, "Home" was Arkansas! I wanted to go to my old home in Canoga Park. I think she was starting to get hoarse from having to repeat, "Recalculating". —*Love, Valerie.*

When I went to pick David up in the morning, he had asked the nurse to pull out the packing and repack it so I would be relieved of having to do at least once. The Dr. had really packed that sucker. They had to give my MB Oxycodone *and* Morphine and the written orders said to do it twice a day instead of the once a day the doctor had initially told me. The nurse kept patting me on the shoulder and giving me sympathetic looks. When I asked for a few rubber gloves, she handed me a whole box of them and some waterproof pads for the bed.

We decided to take the motor home up to Oxnard and keep it there for a few days so I could see my Mom. When we went out to the coach for the first "changing of the packing", David told my Mom that if I hurt him he was going to kill me. I told my Mom to just take me out of her Will and bid me goodbye. I was "Going to hurt him." Does anyone out there write music? I think I have the lyrics for a Country Song here! *Love, Valerie.*

Rookies, that's us. Motor homing is great. We get to move around, see the family and have all of our stuff with us. No packing, unpacking, strange beds... we love it. However, some things that are not the usual fare for us need to be watched. We've got the need for gasoline covered. The guy riding shotgun reminds me to watch that gage *every time* I pull the coach, or my car, out into the street. We are learning about new things though. Black, grey, and fresh water tanks, as well as the propane tank, all have to be closely monitored. I must admit, the MB is the one who has his eye on these little, potentially serious, dials.

So, there we were, all cozy, electrical hooked up to son Larry's house, slides out, levelers deployed. Not a care in the world. Then the question came from my MB, "Honey, have you checked the tanks lately?" I jumped up to do so. My report to the MB went as follows..."Black tank full." Uh oh, that's not good! When we flush we really do need things to go down. "Grey tank full." That's not good either! Propane? "Well that one says empty", also, not good. David went to the Yellow Pages to find a place to dump the tanks. It was time to get my nails done.

When I got home (My nails looking lovely) it was, slides in, levelers up, electric unplugged, and we were off. The station David found did indeed have all the things we were in need of. I drove our 35-foot home on wheels in to what turned out to be an entirely too small area. Once we were safely off the street David went to inquire as to the location of the dump station. It was in a rather narrow area on the side of the station and I was headed in the wrong direction. Turning around an SUV in that area would have been a little tricky not to mention a 35-foot motor home! At that point, 2 men from the station came out to assist the "little lady", more than likely hoping to avoid what was starting to look like an incident that would require a call to their insurance company.

I was happy for their help on many levels. One, if I ran into anything it was less likely to be "All my fault!" Also, when I am moving the coach around the MB gets nervous and upset and the flailing arms and hollering lead less and less to any kind of usable help. So, I kept my eyes on the other sources for what I was hoping was going to be useful information. The major problem for me was that I thought I was turning around to pull back on to the street, go around the block, and try it from another angle. They were positioning me to back up to a dump site I *had not yet located*. After many "Don't worry, I won't let you hit anything" from the new helpers, and even more "Honey! Watch outs!" from you know who, I was in the correct position for dumping. These instructions were repeated twice more when moving to the propane pump and then to the gas pump.

Apparently, it follows as day to night that when the black and grey tanks are full, the fresh water supply is similarly diminished We were just about out. Due to my MB's condition, these dumping and filling duties are mostly left to me. Let us now just call a spade a spade. It was already dark, and I was tired and cranky!! Filling the fresh water tank was not going to happen until the next day. After relaying my decision to hop in the shower and wash my hair the MB expressed his doubt about there being sufficient water for the job. I informed him that my disposition would, in all likely-hood, not be improved in that eventuality. Luckily, there was just enough.
—*We are learning, Valerie*

The next morning, I was up, hair clean and looking good for a trip to Pinecrest School to see my Granddaughter Kalyn, get a Student of the Month award. Looking good was sort of important as I had worked at the school for 34 years prior to the Arkansas move. I wanted them to see I hadn't turned into a hick.

As I was stepping out of the coach my MB said, "Aren't you going to get me some fresh water before you leave?" There was nothing to say except "Yes". I went out, got the hose out of its locked compartment, hooked it up, shoved the business end of it into the tank and turned the water on, hard! Maybe... possibly... a little *too* hard. As I was walking up to the coach, the force of the water shot the hose out of its hole, and water was going everywhere. It was making absolutely no effort at all to miss me! David said now maybe a hat was in order, better yet a paper sack with the eyes cut out. Yes, Yes. His sense of humor is a killer. It is true, no good deed goes unpunished. I gave myself a quick swipe with a towel and off I went.

My ex-boss was happy to see me and called me up to the front of the auditorium when Kalyn's award was given. She asked me to tell the folks about my move and how I liked Arkansas. Her final instructions... Keep it short, not like your e-mails. Sorry about this one Betty. —*Love, Valerie*

Tuesday was chemo. Platelets were quite low again but after much hemming and hawing the Dr. OK'd the treatment. No more until we get back to Arkansas. *Y—eah! Valerie*

Today started with a bang! We had an equipment malfunction. David was looking for water wings. There was some leakage, OK, *lots* of leakage. I was awakened by the cry for help. "Quick Honey, Get some towels!" A bag change and a repacking of the abscess, no time for pain med's, followed in warp speed. I'm getting good at this! When we are getting ready to re-pack the dreaded abscess I tell David to "Call me when you're naked". I must admit this phrase has taken on quite a different meaning lately. —*Love, Valerie*

We were **this** close to a perfect weekend. Oh, we had a small warning. When we were getting ready to drive down to Orange County to spend 2 days with my daughter Denise and her family, I noticed some nickel size, red spots all around the sides of David's feet. I was worried about them as bleeding can sometimes be a problem with chemo. I wanted to stop at the VA Hospital but David was adamant about keeping to our plan to visit the kids. We did not take our home on wheels as we were worried about the slope of their street and we were, after all, only spending one night. We arrived like gypsies, our "stuff" shoved in to 4 plastic bags.

VALERIE KATZ

My daughter and her husband, taking into account the medical necessities involved, gave up their bed and bath so we could take care of matters in a more private setting. The guest room shares a bath with the children and we saw no need to chance an accidental encounter with them while I was torturing my Honey.

We had a nice BBQ, and watched a movie on Saturday. On Sunday Denise and I went out to lunch and shopping. David's feet had looked worse that morning so we called the "On call nurse" in Arkansas to tell her just what we were seeing. She said it was probably nothing to worry about but maybe we should have his blood drawn and checked.

After a spirited game of Pictionary, we left Orange County around 5:30 p.m. We stopped at the VA Hospital about 7:00. After 14 hours, 2 units of platelets, and 1 unit of blood, we were again on our way home. David's blood count was low and his platelets were down to 11. 100 is a minimum that they look for. The doctor said that if we hadn't stopped he would have started bleeding on the way home.

I spent the night in the car, trying to get comfortable, stay warm, and get some sleep. David spoke to one of the ER staff who said it was too bad David couldn't call me, his fancy iPhone won't work in the ER, I could have come in and slept in the lobby. I must say I did look around the lobby. There was quite the eclectic group sleeping there. Since I had spilled catsup, cinnamon butter, and coffee on my shirt, I guess I shouldn't have been so uppity.

We had plans for Monday morning. I was going to have lunch with a friend, take the motor home to dump the tanks and move out to Simi Valley to stay with my son Don until Christmas Day. I called my friend and canceled lunch, called Don to say we would be a little later than planned and we went to bed. We slept like bags of sand until 3pm. Our journey is certainly not dull. —*Love, Valerie.*

Christmas Eve was off to a swell start. David asked me to look at a sore in his mouth. He thought he had a canker sore. I got out my little flashlight and there were so many dark purple areas in his mouth that if he had been a dog I would have sworn he was part Chow. I handed him the phone and said, "Call Arkansas and talk to the chemo nurse." She then talked to the Dr. and he said we were not to start our trip home without having David's blood checked. We decided we had spent enough time at the VA so we found an Urgent Care place in Simi that could do the job and we were on our way. After having a brief chat with David, the Dr. ordered blood labs... stat! Twice! He didn't think we should be traveling with David's numbers so low but the Dr. in Arkansas said we were good to go. All of this only took about 1 hour. Now there was a number we liked!

One of the things I wanted to get done while in CA was have my car detailed. We love Arkansas but in our little corner of the state there are no full-service car washes and that little car was a disgrace! We were running out of time! So, establishing yet another Christmas Eve first, I had it washed inside and out and then had it waxed. My family thought it was a little pricey but I reminded them I had been saving that car wash money all year!

The rest of Christmas Eve was wonderful. Don and Debbie have taken over the event and their second annual party was a huge success. Everyone from the oldest, my Mom who is 91 to the youngest, Sara who is 10 were in attendance. We all ate, drank, joked, drank, sang, drank, and had a most wonderful time. —*Love, Valerie*

Merry Christmas!! The day started with Debbie making pancakes. Then with some help from Don we got the car hooked up to the coach, that means Don did the lion's share of the work while we watched, and we were on our way to Christmas dinner with David's sister Sharon and her very entertaining husband Arnie, in Palm Springs. I have been telling folks that I have been eating so much I was going to have to have my mouth sewn shut when I got home to Arkansas. With a lovely dinner that included turkey, ham, and prime rib, with all the trimmings, I guess I better be calling to make that appointment.

Arnie said he made the best scrambled eggs ever, so of course we had to check them out this morning. Yum! The bagels, cream cheese, etc. were darn good too. Somebody bring me that phone! One of our neighbors in Arkansas sent David a picture of our neighborhood. Bella Vista had a white Christmas! It is time though. We have our trail all mapped out, we have the bit in our teeth, and we are headed for Home. Arkansas, here we come!

P.S. There is one more, very small, almost insignificant, item that will make David very unhappy if it doesn't make it to "The News". On Christmas Day, while driving the main drag of Palm Springs, our side view mirror reached out and struck the side view mirror of another motor coach parked on the street. Now I was more than happy for David to do the macho thing and go to investigate the damages. He, on the other hand, thought that since I was driving, I should go along and face the music. There was no one in or around the other coach, but miracle of miracles, there was no damage to it. Honest! Our mirror, on the other hand, was hanging by a series of wires. I was dispatched to "Fetch the duct tape". After using some of my best golf language on it, the tape convinced me that it was now, and would forever be, stuck to the shelf.

While the tape and I were conversing, David managed to put the mirror back together like a shiny jigsaw puzzle. The mirror however, has as yet, not come up with a satisfactory explanation for the bad behavior that caused this entire hullabaloo in the first place. —*Love to all, Valerie*

We woke up this AM in Amarillo Texas. We were in a nice RV park. When we checked in last night the guy said "Good luck tomorrow. It's supposed to snow again". David got out his iPhone and confirmed that snow was due in Amarillo today and in Bella Vista tomorrow. We hit the road pronto! Except for gas we did not stop. The 11 hours of driving was well worth it. I really don't do snow. —*Love, Valerie.*

HOME! The hot water heater is perking; the heater is on, the fire place is blazing, we are happy to be home. If you were here you might wonder why I am so busy putting the plants left in the kitchen for easier watering, back where they belong. We have a big ass cork screw on the counter in the kitchen. We put all the plants in the kitchen so our neighbor could easily water them. They were in front of the wine opener! After driving 11 hours, all me by the way, I needed a drink!! —*Love, Valerie*

CHAPTER 4

Arkansas 2010

January. Happy New Year y'all! We have watched the Rose Parade and David is expressing some interest in the Rose Bowl game. We have made no New Year's resolutions. It is almost 4:00 pm. I must be getting rested, I'm starting to care. Care about what? That the coach really should be emptied out? There is a bunch of dirty laundry out there. I did go out this morning to get the eggs and bread. 3 1/2 days of dishes were sitting on the sink. Oh yes, the food was still on some of them. The car is still attached to the coach and still sticking just a little bit out into the street. Neither David nor I have gotten out of our PJ's since we got home. And that the plants that were NOT in front of the corkscrew are still in the kitchen.

I cleaned the kitchen and am thinking about, well, maybe thinking about, a resolution or two. We don't need the car until it is time to go to church on Sunday, so it can stay hooked up to the coach. The paper was delivered this morning. The sun is out, and the deck and the crossword puzzle are calling but it's way too cold to go out there. Wait a minute! I've got a resolution. I resolve to not think about the rest until tomorrow. *Have a wonderful 2010!* —Love, Valerie.

Yesterday was not good. David has been very demanding. It all came to a head in the evening and I shouted and told him he was taking advantage, he was not an invalid, and he needed to do things for himself when he could. Of course, this morning, I felt terrible. I told him I was so sorry. He hugged me and agreed he had been pressing his luck a little but promised to do better. We're working on it together.

You know the expression, "I think I died and went to heaven"? Well, I think I died and ended up in South Dakota. When I stirred my stumps this morning the first surprise was that David was still in bed. Then he delivered the amazing news. **Him**, its 7 degrees! **Me**, Where? **Him**, Here! **Me**, did you get up and check our thermometer to make sure?! **Him**, hell no, I just turned up my electric blanket. And, in almost the same breath, he wanted to know if we were having banana smoothies this morning.

When I got up to check the temp for myself, I was sure he was kidding, David said, "If you want to know if it's cold out just ask Shera. She will take one look out the door, see the snow, feel the cold, and come right back in the house. Then she will want a cookie." Now that furry black acorn didn't fall too far from the daddy tree, did she?

Before anyone got anything to eat, I got dressed, put on my jacket and boots, and went out to get the paper. My crossword puzzle needs to be addressed when I am having my coffee in the morning. I asked myself, "Who is this person walking in the snow in this cold place to get a newspaper." In CA I never even read the paper and anyone who has ever known me knows, "I don't do snow!" But, I don't have to leave the house and the fireplace works just fine. I just checked, twice! It is now 4 degrees. I think it's time for me to snuggle under that nice warm blanket. *Yes, we still love Arkansas! Love, Valerie.*

My friends, this is Arkansas. I was looking through the paper yesterday and found a craft workshop being held at the library. Its name? "Ductigami". This is a class dedicated to making things out of duct tape. There was a photo showing just how to make a lovely red rose. I didn't even know duct tape came in red and green!

Sorry to say, I will not be passing on these "Duct Gems". The class is for 13 to 18-year olds. I'm quite sure it is a prerequisite to auto shop, where they will really need a good working relationship with the gray tape.

My man had a CT-scan and a checkup at the VA on Thursday. The dreaded abscess is almost healed. NO MORE PACKING! We will get the results of the scan on Tuesday. I will, of course, keep you posted. —*Valerie*

The "News" today is fantastic. We went to see the oncologist and he said all of David's tumors have shrunk, significantly. We are thrilled. *Thanks again for all your prayers. Love, Valerie.*

February. When I got up this morning, I had a big decision to make, should I go get the paper for my crossword puzzle or not. The problem was the snow. It has been snowing now for 24 hrs. And it is beautiful! However, no paper and no mail. We don't have to go out, just sit in front of the fireplace and take pictures of the birds. There sources for food are also covered with snow.

Shera is once again wondering where all the good smells have gone that tell her just where to go when she gets the order to "Go do your business". I took a picture of her after she had buried her face in the snow looking for a good spot. The snow is up to her knees. Some deer were spotted this afternoon also but were too far away to get a picture.

David has been showing the effects of the "Big" chemo treatment he got on Tuesday so he doesn't want to go anywhere, anyway. I guess he has run out of shows on the DVR as I can hear Dragnet coming on and One Adam Twelve just finished.

It's time to get out the Soprano's DVD's we got for Christmas, pop some popcorn and settle in. We love this place!! —*Valerie*

I couldn't sleep this morning, so I am watching our Village wake up. The snow is still on the ground. As beautiful as it is, it does come with some drawbacks. It snowed on Thursday and we have not seen the mailman since. The newspaper only missed one day! I have always held to the "No news is good news" theory, but I haven't seen a Newport News catalogue for weeks and I promised two ladies at the Moose Hall that as soon as I got one I would call them and give them the order code for the jeans I was wearing. It is also my granddaughter Jennifer's birthday and I'm sure her birthday card is in a frozen state out there in the mailbox.

Yesterday I ventured out and, you better sit down for this, shoveled snow. I would be more than happy to just hole up here with the MB and wait until it all melts, BUT my sister is coming today. We are going to need the car! She is flying in at almost 9 PM. I am thinking that this will be a good time to find out how to get to the airport the long way. No dark winding roads for this girl tonight. —*Valerie*

What a day this turned out to be. It was just going to be a quick trip to the Oncology clinic and back home. David has been very weak and did not get out of bed all day on Monday. The Super Bowl party he went to with a friend on Sunday was taking the blame for this but I'm so glad he went. He had a day out of the house and had some guy fun.

Today, getting him out of bed, dressed, onto his walker, and out the door was a real challenge. Since it was not a chemo day it was OK to be a little tardy. Unfortunately, it wasn't a Carol the Caregiver day either. David actually let me go get a wheel chair to get him in the clinic. They took his blood and when the nurse came out with the results she told us, in what can only be described as the epitome of sound medical terminology, "Mr. Katz, your blood panel looks like shit."

The Dr. was advised, and we were sent off to the hospital for more bloodletting. That was necessary, so they could get right down to business tomorrow. We have to be back by 8:30 am so he can get a transfusion. Eight units of platelets! The poor man. No wonder he can't get out of bed. The low normal for platelets is 100. David's were at 13. Tomorrow, new blood and a new man. I will not forget to bring my book tomorrow!

Now another word for my friends, Ensure. For those of you who are unfamiliar, it is a vitamin enriched drink for folks who are not eating very well due to Old Age, Medical Problems, etc., etc. We qualify in several areas.

When we were on our little trip to CA I had completely misjudged the amount of coffee creamer I would need for the trip. I had however, put in an ample supply of Ensure for my man. I don't like my coffee without cream, so when I ran out, I decided, any port in a storm, I would try the Ensure. It worked out so well that I continued to use it. I figured one bottle a day would surely be good for me too. So, I put it in my coffee and on my oatmeal. *AND*, if there is any left at the end of the day... it mixes really well with Amaretto. The elder folks answer to the White Russian ;) —*Love to all, Valerie*

It must have been having good friends and family that did the trick in CA. either that, or the folks in CA just have better blood for the transfusions. Our Guy is having a really hard time rebounding from his last chemo. I thought having the platelet infusion would bring him bouncing right back but this has not been the case. He spends the lion's share of each day in bed and never ventures away from it without his walker with either me or Carol bringing up the rear.

When my children were young, and I came home from shopping announcing I had brought them a present, the news was not met with the smiles you might expect. The reason? Well, the "Gift" was more than likely a new broom or rake. Yes, I know, it is a miracle they love me. My son Don laughed about the gift that I got our caregiver Carol, resplendent with a red bow. Well, she had been asking for a new mop! —*Enjoy, Valerie*

David is a Veteran. What good news for us right now. They have been so helpful in getting us the help we have needed in all the journeys we have taken this past year. There is a reoccurring theme in the journey of David's life. In his teenage years he learned to dance. It wasn't high on his list, but his sisters dance group needed guys and he was tall and available. The bonus? A way to meet girls. He joined the Navy, served his country, and the bonus? Girls love a man in uniform.

He started dancing again in his 30's and once again, girls love a man who can dance. He told me that at one point in his life he had wanted to be a Rabbi. I think his change of plans has something to do with "The Bonuses" but he denies this.

When we were in CA in December, David's friend Cliff combined one of his dances with a birthday party for David. Yes, we know, his birthday isn't until May, but we may not be in CA in May and there was cake, so what the heck, we celebrated! After the cake ceremony David and I were going to dance a few steps and then have the rest of the crowd join us. Cliff had a surprise planned for us. He asked me to tell the folks about a reoccurring comment I got when I was working the door at David's dances. Women were always coming up to me and saying, "I used to date David you know." At that point, Cliff announced that it was the last chance for all the ladies to do the right thing. They should come forward, right then and there, and return any of David's keys they might still possess. The crowd erupted and no fewer than 12 ladies (and one man) rushed up to hand me keys. Cliff, I'm *almost* sure, had given all those ladies the keys. It was hilarious! Me? I am his final bonus and happy to be so. —*Love, Valerie.*

David and I have had a very scary two weeks. The treatments for his blood levels did not have any effect on how he was feeling. He just kept getting weaker and weaker. He slept most of the day and needed his walker to get around. We went to see the Dr. and David's blood panel was almost normal, but he just kept getting worse. We were already pretty scared, and the Dr. was very concerned and quite puzzled. With his blood tests so close to normal he was also wondering why David was failing to rebound. He had lost his appetite and didn't have much to say. This was serious!

He sent us for an immediate CT-scan. David had his Barium Cocktail in the car. The scan was taken, and we were sent home to wait. We had to wait until 5:15 p.m. the next day, but it was worth the wait. As it turned out, pneumonia was the *good* news. So, antibiotics have been ordered and my Man is starting to feel much better.

The man from the bank called this morning. Could he come over with some papers for David to sign? "Sure", says David. "Is 30 min. OK?" says the bank guy. Another "Sure" from David.

"Will you be able to open the door for him?" This question was directed at me. Why?? We were still in bed! My comment, "Couldn't you have asked for at least an hour?" fell, again, on deaf ears. Don't worry, He has had a rough two weeks, I didn't hurt him. —*Valerie*

March. It was another hard two weeks for David. Apparently, the Chemo heard that he has been tolerating it with ease and decided to "Kick his Butt". My man is feeling somewhat better though. I know... His appetite is back. He is still feeling pretty weak and therefore not up to spending time in his garage or handling any "Honey Do" lists, but progress is progress and we take what we can get. —*Love, Valerie*

I have a new word, "Respite". It means "Take 6 hours and do whatever you want. No questions asked". The VA has granted me 30 of these days and yesterday I took one. David seemed to have plans for *MY* free day! There were lots of "Honey, on your respite day you should" being thrown in my direction.

I managed to stop the tide by telling him, in no uncertain terms, to enjoy his day with Carol. I could, and would, do just as I pleased. He took the advice remarkably well.

I left at 12:30 and went to the movies at the mall. I saw Crazy Heart, loved it, but then I think Jeff Bridges is eye candy. Then I went to the food court, had coffee and a smoothie, did my crossword puzzle, read a little in my book and then went back to the theater and saw Valentine's Day. Sheer… uninterrupted… bliss.

I had been toying with the idea of stopping on my way home. I had a half hour left, and picking up some of those wonderful biscuits that The Red Lobster makes and eating them in the car on the way home sounded yummy. I love those things. But, as I left the movie I discovered that the person who holds my hand and walks me to my car was missing. I made a B-line for Bella Lane.

David had had a pretty good time too. Carol had been his "Beck and Call" girl all day. The highlight of which was a lovely soaking of his feet in Epsom Salts that was kept at just the right degree of warmth by the regular adding of hot water to the tub. He said he told Carol that we should have more of these respite days. He liked not having to wait "Just a Sec" when he called for service. It looks like his sense of humor is returning. He gave me one of his smiles and said he would like another foot treatment today. I smiled back and said, "OK honey, Carol will be here soon for her regular visit". See, my sense of humor is back too. Our first Respite Day was a total success. —*Love, Valerie*

David went to see the doctor last Friday. He was still not rebounding as much as we had hoped. The doctor said he thought the treatment just might be killing him so no more chemo until we see him again the second week in April. He also encouraged us to go to Branson the end of March to meet our friends from CA. We are really looking forward to that.

David got up and dressed today and spent most of the morning working on the piles of paperwork that his desk is using as a disguise. Can't fool us!

The weather here has been wonderful. I got started on the flower beds, taking out the remains of last year's goodies and some weeds that were not at all welcome. Now that the weeds are gone I see new sprouts coming up. Spring and daylight savings time will be most welcome. As is most always the case, I got caught up in the idea of spring and just didn't know when to quit. My biggest project is the round flower bed in the front yard. It would have to be the front yard, because we don't have a backyard, just the forest. A really nice exchange, and far less work.

My CA friends, this is what has become of me. Not only am I trying to make the flower bed round again, but I am digging up all the decorative rock that has been overtaken by dirt. To paraphrase Randy Travis, "I'm just sittin' at home digging up rocks". I was thinking that when I was done, I should pull out the hose and rinse off those filthy rocks. I was getting a little tired when I remembered, I live in Arkansas now! It rains here all year long. Rain can't be very far away, and it will do the job for me. Another reason to love it here!

I was sitting next to a nice lady in church on Sunday, and after the service she invited me to play golf with the ladies on Wed. I'm thrilled! Carol will look in on David, so I am dusting off my clubs and hoping it won't rain. Those dirty old rocks are on their own! —*Love to all, thanks for the prayers, Valerie*

April. David is still not feeling up to par. We have taken the motor home in for service in anticipation of our trip to Branson, but I continue to be worried about how much he will be able to enjoy the trip. Just the move from his bed to his chair in the next room tires him out. Keep your collective fingers crossed. We are taking things one day at a time.

Well, we had a wonderful time in Branson. My friends, Ira and Donna, were great. Ira pushed David around during the day in a wheelchair. In the evening we would retire to the coach for cards. When he had had enough, David would excuse himself and go to bed. The rest of us would have a glass of wine and continue playing cards. They have been good and supportive friends for a very long time.

The weather seems to think that if change and uncertainty are the norm for us, it will try to go with the flow. Yesterday I was out digging up more rocks in a warm 69 degrees. Today? We are watching the snow fall. —*Love, Valerie*

We went out last night! We were invited to a home cooked meal and an evening of cards by some of our new friends. David said he wanted to go and I was instantly in for the occasion by the lure of home cooking and cards. The plan was to dine upstairs and play cards downstairs. I was telling our hostess that I wasn't sure David could do the stairs when I was informed that he was already on the lower level. It seems our host has a "Shop" down there and that was a must see for David. The shop was impressive, and my MB was in his element. I could tell going back upstairs was a trial for him, so I threw caution to the wind and followed him up with my hand on his hind quarters for support. I'm quite sure the fear of falling, on me, was instrumental in his successful ascent. I do what I can. ;) —*Valerie*

Old Man Winter did not go quietly into hibernation. He had a few tricks to up his sleeve for Miss Spring. She was getting all the rave reviews and he wanted to give her a parting shot she would remember. The last day of winter had a dramatic drop in temperature and in the afternoon, it started to snow. A record breaking snow fell all night, followed by the sound of ice hitting the windows in the morning and rain the rest of the day. Can everyone say, "So there!"

When we were in CA our neighbor put our porch tree in the garage for us. No mean feat as it is in a huge pot that I filled with rocks and sand so the tree, that was quite short, could be seen. Last week we decided the worst of winter was over and he put it back for me. Winter's last fling gave it a lovely new snow coat. We will have to wait and see if it survives.

The rain was a blessing. It undermined the snow, Spring sent the sun, and the snow is gone. I guess Spring had the last word after all. Our bulbs are coming up and at 10:30 this morning it was already toasty 53 degrees. Did this CA girl just say 53 degrees and toasty in the same breath?! —*Happy Spring to you all, Valerie*

April. Our guy has had some very scary days. On Wed. we went for his bone scan. After the scan they took 20+ X-rays of his hip area and then returned him for more bone scans. Today we got the results. The cancer has spread to all his bones from his shoulders to his hips. Chemo does not work on bone cancer so next week he will start radiation. He will get it every day for two weeks and then he will be tested again to see if it is having any effect. He is taking this devastating news pretty well. I'm so proud of him. To those of you, who continue to call him and keep in touch, **Thank You**! It means so much to him. I will keep you posted. —*Remember to pray. Love, Valerie*

David has been duly marked for his upcoming treatments. He has 5 red lines on his chest and has been fitted for a cast like contraption. Don't you just love Medical jargon? So, he is ready! We are waiting to hear from the Dr. as to when his treatments will start. We are hopeful that it will be this coming week. My MB has been relying heavily on the pain meds and the radiation is supposed to alleviate this.

Last Wed. was my birthday. We went out with friends to the Red Lobster where, I'm sure you will be surprised to learn, I almost ate myself into a coma. Steak, lobster, those fabulous biscuits, and a couple of Margarita's. Mmmm!! My children put "60 Sizzles" on my cake when that age arrived. I have been trying to live up to their expectations, and since this is the last year of the 60's for me, I tried to start it with a bang! I have been telling them for years that I intended to live my life so that when I was in my dotage they would think of me as a character and not an old lady. They have a whole year to think up something delicious for my 70's.

Then we went home to play some Crazy Canasta. The gentlemen completely forgot whose birthday it was and absolutely creamed us girls. David's birthday is next month and I hope to treat him to a similar fate. I'll continue to keep you posted.
—*Love, Valerie*

We met with the radiologist today. What a great meeting!! He needed to meet with us, as he had looked at David's scans with a fine-tooth comb and David was going to have to tell him just where the pain was because he couldn't see anything significant enough to be causing it. Oh, he saw lots of little trouble makers, but big ones? No. He said that sometimes as these little critters grow and get just big enough to press on a nerve and then the pain radiates around. He will start with radiation on the spot-on David's lower spine and after that there is a new therapy that consists of a homeopathic something or other... that medical jargon again ;), that they make radioactive and administer through an IV. The little guys look and act like calcium and go directly to where the bones are trying to kick out the cancer. The radiation kills the cancer cells so the bones can get crackin' on that healing thing. What wonderful news.

David told the Dr. that what he wanted was to be pain free and stick around as long as possible and that the VA had given him a very discouraging diagnosis when all this started. The Dr. said there were some parameters involved with this whole thing and some people go down that predicted road. "However," he said, "You don't seem to be going down that road". No sir, my MB will make his own path and we are betting on a long one.

We are taking a clue from Spring. She is pushing all sorts of beautiful flowers up from the ground and giving the trees new coats of lovely green leaves. Everything looks renewed and hopeful.

We stopped on the way home at Staples. David needed a ream of paper. Me? Well I needed some Dark Chocolate covered Almonds. We all celebrate in our own way and it is way too early in the day to open the wine. —*Thanks for all the prayers, Valerie*

May. The ease with which our guy managed the Chemo is but a fond memory. The Radiation is a whole new ball game. It is kicking him quite firmly in the keester. In response to this, the pain meds have also been kicked up a few notches. However, his spirits are still good and he is coping quite well.

David's son Howard, his wife Alisa, and their children Nathaniel and Marin were here for a week. We brought the motor home to the house for them to use as their own little home away from home. My heart was quite warmed by the site of Marin, who is 2 ½, carrying around the blanket with her name on it I made for her when she was born. It's a little tattered, but it is never very far from her.

While they were here Nathaniel turned 6. He was very much in charge of my computer while they were here so if you have been e-mailing me, that is my excuse for any tardy responses ;-) He was having a little trouble getting a game to load properly and came to ask me for help. As I was working on the problem he started to complain about my progress in a very unsatisfactory tone of voice. I gave him both "The look" and "Tone of voice" and reminded him it was my computer and if he wasn't careful he might lose the privilege! "OK!" he said as he pointed to the other room. "I'll go there and be back in 8 minutes." It was all I could do not to laugh. At the same time my good friend and "Matron of Honor" Charlotte, was here for three days. We had a great time. We explored the sites around here the first day and then went to Little Rock for two days. We went to see the Clinton Library. It is wonderfully done. The Arkansas Art Center was having a Pharaoh Exhibit, so we were able to see that also. We stayed at the Peabody Hotel and were quite enchanted by the march of the ducks. They have 5 Mallard ducks that live in the fountain in the lobby of the hotel. At 11:00 AM each morning they are brought down, in the elevator, from their "Suite" on the roof and they march on a Red Carpet to the fountain. At 5:00 PM they roll out the red carpet for them again and they march back to the elevator and ascend to the roof for a night of rest.

Except for the fact that you can't get a cocktail with a friend if you happen to get there early, we live in a dry county, we have a most convenient little airport. While we waited for her plane, Charlotte and I had time for a hand of Spite and Malice, a friendly little card game I taught her to distract her from the "No Cocktail" issue.

My daughter Denise will be here for three days for Mother's Day. Yeah!! The direct flights from Los Angeles on Allegiant Air are on Monday's and Friday's only. On the Monday after Mother's Day I will take her back to the airport where I will pick up my brother Dennis who is coming in on the very same plane thus saving me a trip. I mean, it is a whole 30 minutes! We are having company. I guess all my talk about what a wonderful place this is, is finally luring folks here to see for themselves. —*Keep praying, love Valerie*

Denise arrived for her visit and it was wonderful to see her. While she and I were our having lunch David sent Carol out to get us both flowers for Mother's Day. He told Carol to make sure they were both beautiful but to be sure my arrangement was a just a little bit bigger. My Man is such a treasure.

Denise went home, and my brother Dennis arrived and spent his first whole day here in Arkansas at home with the dog. David went for a CT scan on Tuesday and while there his heart rate went to 190 and his blood pressure went south. I went out to get the car when the technicians called for an ambulance. They were in the ambulance with David for about 20 minutes.

THE NEWS FROM ARKANSAS

I finally went up to the door and they told me they were ready and would proceed shortly. I found out much later that they had lost him for a few minutes. He was in the hospital overnight and we don't really know why this happened. There is a big chunk of Tuesday that he can't remember.

I was with David Wednesday when the Dr. came to visit. He has had a Cardiac Event' and there are significant problems with his liver, along with the rest of the stuff our guy was already dealing with. The Dr. wanted to make sure there was a document on file as to our wishes on heroic measures. Then he asked me if I was prepared for him to be home. I said yes, of course. He was scheduled for two units of blood and we were hopeful this would fix his blood enough to go home. We were trying hard to process this scary information. I got home about 9 PM. Dennis was ready with a hug and a glass of wine. I am sooo glad he is here. I really needed that hug.

The transfusion worked its magic and our guy is home. I am so happy to have him here. He asked me how I was doing, and I said, "Fine Honey". "Well" he said, "You do look a little the worse for wear". I will swear till the end of time that he got that black eye in the hospital.

Will keep you informed, keep praying. —*Love Valerie*

My Dear Family and Friends, the News today is distressing. My MB and I went to see the Oncologist. He said that David had a couple of options. There were some new protocols that were being tried on his type of cancer but that had not as yet been OK' d. He said he could get some for David, but our insurance may deny the claim. The other option was just to keep him comfortable and not in pain. David chose the protocols.

He has been in constant pain, even with the Morphine he has been taking for the last week. So, the plan was to give him enough Morphine, so he wasn't in pain and then prescribe the Morphine accordingly. He was still in a lot of pain and they were giving him some more morphine when he said he was cold and he started to shake. His heart rate went to 180 and his blood pressure tanked, again. The ambulance was called. He is back in the hospital. I hope to be able to bring him home tomorrow. I'm headed for the wine and some mind-numbing TV. —*Keep praying, Valerie*

Hospital food, now there is a phrase to strike terror in your heart. It is usually a choice of, "What sounds the least yucky", or "Take it or leave it", if you are in the VA Hospital. Here he has quite a nice menu to choose from. I ordered him a nice breakfast for tomorrow. It is his Birthday and after breakfast he gets to come home.

We got the news today that there will be no new protocols for David. He will be home with Hospice care. A hospital bed has been ordered. His pain is so severe that keeping him comfortable is now our only option. It has been a more than difficult decision, but we will do the best we can. —*Love, Valerie.*

May 28. It's David's birthday and he did get to come home. The Hospice Nurse and Doctor came to give David an evaluation. Then they asked me to come into the kitchen where we could talk. They said they were pretty good at predicting how much time a patient had left. They gave David about four days. I called his kids. —*Love to all, Valerie*

David's son Howard has come to be with his father. He told me he and his father were never close when he was a child. Things got better after our wedding and his trips here to see him. They really bonded over those iPhones.

He and his sister Marcy were raised in Toronto, Canada, by their mother. David liked to tell people he lost his wife in the earthquake. We had a terrible one in California in 1971 and he said she got scared, went home to Toronto to be with her mother, and never came back. I don't know if he ever shared that version of the events with his ex-wife. Marcy is distressed by the fact that David wants to be cremated so has chosen not to come. The thing David was hoping to live long enough for was Marcy's son Ryan's Bar Mitzvah. He and Ryan had a special bond. David went to Toronto every year to celebrate Ryan's birthday and the Bar Mitzvah was something not to be missed.

We had a party on Memorial Day. My answer to "What are you doing on Monday" was "Nothing" The force of nature known as "Carol the Caregiver/Nag" said "Oh yes you are". She brought the food; she brought her husband and son. She shoved me out of the kitchen to play cards with them. Howard got the shrimp and BBQ'd it along with the steaks Carol had brought. She also made a huge meatloaf. I had mentioned to her that I didn't really care for cold or reheated meat except for meatloaf which I would eat every day until it was gone. There were 5 of us in all and we could have easily fed 10. A truly wonderful and welcome diversion was had by all. —*Thanks Carol! Love, Valerie.*

The most asked question of my CA friends is, "When David passes are you coming home?" I tell them, "I am home. Bella Vista is home now." The most asked question from Bella Vista friends and my family is, "What are you going to do?" My answer is this. "I am going to take my phone, David's iPhone, and my Rottweiler, get in the motor home and head for CA for at least a month. The response to that has been unanimous. "No! You know that is not a good idea." They are entitled to their opinions, but that is my plan.

June. Howard has gone to the store, armed with my list, and my admonition that if he didn't want to starve to death while he was here he should buy something he liked. He did a great job and has been a true treasure while he has been here. He has not complained even once that the air conditioner has taken a vacation. There are some things a son should never have to see. Howard has seen many of them in the days he

VALERIE KATZ

has been here, and he has truly risen to the task. I don't know what I would have done without him. And when told to "Start pouring" he makes a mean drink. The Hospice folk are here daily and doing their thing. We are settling in. —*Love, Valerie.*

The doctor and nurse were here together from Hospice this a.m. The doctor said David probably had less than a week and was wondering why he is still here. I have made arrangements for Carol to be here 6 hours every day to help me. My Donald and our CA roommate and David's Best Man, Richard, will both be arriving on the same flight tomorrow night. I am well taken care of. —*Love, Valerie.*

June 10. I guess God was ready for his dance lesson. He took our favorite teacher up to be with him today. —*Thank you all for your friendship and your prayers. Valerie*

Howard and my son Donald are here for the funeral. The ladies from the church have been arriving all morning with food to be served at a small gathering here afterward.

The service was warm and wonderful. As we greeted all the attendees on their way to the coffee and cookie portion of the morning I introduced my boys. Not less than 90 percent of them said to Donald, "You're not going to let her drive to CA by herself, are you?" He has assured one and all that he will be with me. Our conversation had gone something like this. "Mom, I had a one-way ticket here. I will be going to CA with you. If you want to talk to me fine. If you don't that's fine too. I'll just be there for you if you need me." I did.

Donald and I are enjoying Margaritas, meat loaf, potato casserole, and apple pie. This is our first day on the road and we are doing well. The day started at 4:30 A.M. Howard had to be at the airport for an early flight. He woke me to say goodbye and Don took him to the airport. The early wakeup call had limited effect on me or my boy. I went back to sleep and Don went back to bed.

THE NEWS FROM ARKANSAS

My bank, Delta Trust, had sent a beautiful floral arrangement to the church. Since going to the bank was one of the errands I needed to attend to, we took the flowers for them to enjoy. I did my business with the teller and introduced her to Don. She said, "You aren't going to let her drive to CA all by herself, are you?" He assured her he would be with me and on the way out the door he said, "Mom, even at the bank!?" "Yes", I said, "Now you won't be worrying about me being here all alone. You see, everyone is looking out for me." After a few more errands, hooking up the RV and getting gas, we were off....at the crack of 11:30. What Else?

Today we are having our Margaritas in Texas. We found a lovely little RV park. I misunderstood the directions to the spot where we were to be parked. I ended up on this tiny road and we had to go several miles in the wrong direction. I made a U-turn across a median (it looked pretty packed down to me) and got on another 1 1/2 lane road. As I was making this somewhat dubious move Don looked up and hollered "Don't look David!" It sounds like quite a storm outside. We are going to pull the slides in and hit the hay. We are looking forward to tomorrow.

What with the right rear-view mirror falling off and a few more "Don't Look David's" we fared pretty well. For those of you who remember my little accident in Palm Springs last year when I bumped the mirror pretty hard, it did finally bite the dust. When we stopped at the next truck stop we bought a 7 1/2 in. convex mirror and Donald strapped it on with the motor home owner's best friend, Duct tape. This turned out to be number three in the "Don't Look David" list. Number two was the stretch of road, most of it uphill, going into Barstow that we entered with just over 1/4 tank of gas. I don't know about a wing, but there was definitely a prayer or two requesting that we not run out before we could fill'er up. David was up there reminding me that I should never, ever, let the coach get to less than 1/2 tank. I could hear him! And

I was certainly seeing the virtue in his advice by the time we got to a gas station. Somehow, I don't think "All's well that ends well" was what my MB would have been thinking.

We have made it safely to Simi Valley CA. I will spend the next few days with my Mom. This is a good time for me to be with her as we are moving her from her home to a private residential home for seniors very soon. Not a good time for any of us. —*Love, Valerie.*

I spent today resting and swimming with my 10-year-old Grandgirl Sara. Now it's off to bed. The time is flying by. I will be heading home soon and still have so many folks to see. Be patient, I'm trying!!

Yesterday I met with my great friend Richard for a game of golf. The folks here have been puzzled by the weather. It had been cool and overcast, prompting this comment from me. "Correct me if I'm wrong, but this is July? This is southern CA? Right?" Well, the weather straightened it's self out for my day of golf and I have the golf tan/burn to prove it, red ring around the neck, brown ankles, white feet, etc. For someone who has not had the opportunity to play much golf, six, 9-hole rounds in 2 years, I was playing pretty well and having a great time. Then came a large sand trap on the back nine. It wasn't too deep, so I had Richard drop me off. Armed only with my trusty 7 iron, in I went. Proving, once again, that if you take your eye off the ball the chances of hitting it correctly are pretty darn slim, I swung and was still in the trap. My next shot was successful and rake and club in hand I headed out. On the lip of the trap I lost my balance, fell, and rolled to a stop, on my back, feet in the air. To their credit, no one laughed… until I did. I could see a Marshall overlooking the scene. If he was going to tell us to pick up the pace, he changed his mind, probably figuring that those 3 men already had their hands full. This is golf folks. As in life, you dust yourself off, find your smile, and finish the game. —*Love to all, Valerie*

July. I have been busy...... It has been an emotional time but with the amazing help of family and friends, I am doing remarkably well.

David's friend Cliff arranged a Memorial Dance in David's honor. With approximately 200 in attendance, it was a party David would have loved! There was dancing, eating, drinking, and reminiscing, with tears and laughter.

Halfway through the festivities Cliff stopped the music and gave those who wished to, a chance to share some memories of David. Richard Schissel brought the house down with his telling of the "Ham and Meatball Debacle", at one of our US Open parties.

Here is the story... Every year David had a big party at his home for all this dance students. On Thanksgiving weekend there was always a big US Open Dance Competition. It goes on for three days and David always got the videos. Then one week in February he'd have this party and show all the videos while people either sat and watched or went upstairs to the dance room and danced. It was my first time to be with him and help host the party. We ran out of name tags at 200 so it was a big deal.

We were getting ready! The big table and every location that could be used for food in the garage was covered with tablecloths and dotted with balloons. It was a potluck and all the food would be out there. It was festive! David was in the retail laundry business so real cloth napkins and silverware were used. No paper and plastic for this party!

My Rottweiler, Hoover, had completely stolen David's heart when we moved in with him and nothing would do but that she would be included in big event. After I had reminded him of Hoover's delicate stomach and propensity to upchuck anything but her own food, David made signs complete with her picture. "Hi, my name is Hoover. I have a delicate stomach. PLEASE DON'T FEED ME!"

David always provided a Honey Baked Ham for the event and I was to make a big batch of my meatballs. David wasn't really a seasoned dog owner. He took the ham out to the garage and placed it on the table. Not in the middle where it would be safe, but on the edge. We looked around and Hoover had pulled the ham down and was chewing on it! David's "Oh my gosh what are we going to do now", was followed swiftly by orders from me. "Take it into the kitchen, wash it off and put it back on the table! In the middle! And put *that* dog out!"

We then went to get the crockpot full of meatballs. We picked it up by its handles, started for the garage and one of the handles fell off. Meatballs went crashing to the floor! I hollered to David "Quick lock the door!" Guest arrival was imminent! Spatulas and big spoons were fetched, and the meatballs were returned to the pot, taken to the garage and plugged in. After David's, "Are you sure we can do that?!" I reminded him that the whole place had been scrubbed to a fairthy well, so everything should be just fine. Mums the word! There were lots of amazed looks and "OMG, I was at that party!" My daughter wanted to know, "Mom was that true?" "Yes, I'm afraid it was." I ended that portion of the evening by telling the story of how David and I met. It is a funny story that David loved, so no tears were shed.

Next on my agenda was my Mom. It has become necessary for her to leave her home of 50 years. My Sister Cyndi found a marvelous private home for her. The caregivers couldn't be nicer. When we were putting the room together for Mom the husband of another resident stopped by to reassure us by telling of the wonderful care his wife was getting. There were some tears, and the inevitable question "Why", which has had to be answered daily, but all in all she has done pretty well. Her good spirits seem to have rebounded and she has described the food as "Delicious!" On my visit on the 4th, my bother Dennis, my cousin Penny, my Mom, the other 4 residents and I enjoyed a great performance and sing-a-long by a fellow who resembled Burl Ives and sang in the same folksy way, inviting request and bringing smiles to all faces. —*Love to all, Valerie*

I now have 2 more weeks here and I am planning on seeing as many family and friends as I possibly can. Then, accompanied by my sister Cyndi, I will head back to Arkansas where our other sister, Martha, is trying to make herself at home at 9 Berry Lane. She left before us in order to be there when her furniture arrived only to be told that it has, as yet, not left CA. I am afraid that her settling in has been further disrupted by the remote control to the cable box. I gave it strict instructions on how to behave, but from the phone calls I have gotten from Martha, my admonitions have gone unheeded. —*Love to all, Valerie*

Oh, that double edged sword known as "The joy of being a homeowner" does apply to six-wheel homes and will follow you across state lines. As this is my first voyage without David and I am still learning just how that amp gage works, mistakes were bound to happen.

First, my son Don stopped me with "Mom stop! Not that cord! Remember, we had a 30-amp receptacle installed because on your last visit your coach kept kicking off the electricity in the house." When I went to my Mom's I tripped the breaker there too. But thanks to my big brother Dennis, order was restored, and I was dispatched to my sister Cyndi's. Luckily, she has a dedicated line for my type of visiting as she has another relative who visits often with a large coach.

Later I arrived at the home I had lived in for 33 years, the place where I had raised my family. I'm quite sure I don't have to point out the obvious, but I will, this house is no Spring Chicken. I plugged in to the same receptacle as we did last December, set the amp meter at 20 and was all set, or so I thought. Last Dec. it was quite a bit cooler than it is now, about 30 degrees! I needed the air conditioner running and the fun began. The air went off, I checked the coach breaker panel, I was pretty darn proud that I knew where it was! Not the problem... then I opened the door and listened for the water fountain on front porch of house that is on the same fuse as the coach. It was silent. Uh oh. With many years of experience at this address, I knew where the house panel was too. A switch was flipped, and all was well, temporarily. The temperature went over a 100% and the air was working, but it was struggling. That's when I had my brain storm. The air was kicking off over and over, having a struggle getting started again, so... I figured if I started it with the generator and then flipped it over to the amp power it would have a running start. When I pulled that little stunt the amp meter shot up to 45, the coach went silent, and so did the fountain on the porch. Flipping the switch again had some effect. A fan that was on the same circuit in the house started again, but not the fountain on the porch or the air in the coach. On further investigation, there were several other areas in the house that were not working. A very forgiving and understanding son and daughter in law, Larry and Luz, actually plugged the coach in to a receptacle in the house that was still working so I could have air in the coach. I found that if I turned the refrigerator over to propane and didn't use more than one light at a time, just to be safe, the air stayed on.

An electrician was called and a new panel, with a dedicated line for my future visits, will be installed. He thinks it will be on Monday. My Arkansas departure date will be postponed by at least one day.

I sure hope my MB was busy giving dance lessons because this was a *BIG* "Don't look David!" —*Love to all, Valerie.*

It's time to get the coach ready for the trip home, but I can't get started. All I can do is bawl. I can't seem to get myself under control. I called my daughter Lili, only to get a busy signal. If the phone is busy, she must be home. I got in the car and headed over to her house. When I had visited with them earlier in the week I had knocked on the door and her husband, Scott, had said "Mom, you don't have to knock when you're here." So, when I got there, the garage was open, and I went right into the kitchen, crying so hard the whole family came running and exclaiming, "Get some tissues, it's, Mom!"

Lili and I had gone through the sickness and death of my son David, so she was the one I needed to talk to. We spent the whole day talking about both of our David's. We cried, we laughed, and we sorted out what this morning's tears were really about. It wasn't about getting the coach ready for the road by myself, it was the knowledge that when I get home my beloved MB won't be there. —*Love, Valerie*

Today is the day I set out for Arkansas with the rookie, my sister Cyndi. She has already let me know, in no uncertain terms, that the thought of driving the coach scares her silly and she won't be able to help me in that area of the trip. I said goodbye to my Mom, picked up Cyndi and Shera and we got ourselves settled in the coach. We cracked open a bottle of champagne and played a few games of cards, none of them won by me! We were ready for our adventure. You can't start an adventure like that on an empty stomach, so we were off to McDonald's for pancakes.

Next stop was to fill the propane tank, and the first of the Don't look David's! I pulled up to the tank and was told by a somewhat agitated young man that I was on the wrong side and would have to pull in from the other direction. The propane tank is situated in a gas station, on a corner, and the road is divided and busy. Sooo, I pulled to the front of the station, yes, where the pumps are, and proceeded to make a 3-point turn. As I was dispatching Cyndi out to make sure I didn't run into anything, or anyone, a rather concerned looking gentleman hurried to the door of the station and started making frantic gestures designed to help me. So, I told Cyndi to sit back down. The gentleman was also working the cash register, so his help stopped before my job was done. Hence, the now broken tail light.

We were now on the road and stopped for gas and a bite to eat. I wanted to park near a tree so I could let Shera out on her leash to stroll around in the shade. Totally misjudge how close I was to the tree until the scraping started. Don't Look David!

We stopped around 6:30 P.M. for a potty break and Cyndi said, "Is the road going to continue to be this straight?" When I answered, "Yes, this straight, all the way to Arkansas." She replied, "Maybe I could help with the driving." So, there she was, first day, behind the wheel. She had me call a whole list of folks who needed to know we were cruising down the road and I was in the passenger seat. Her decision to drive may have had something to do with the following. She went for a potty break while I was driving. The road got a little rough, I had to tap the breaks, and apparently, she landed in the shower. Then she found out that if you are not the driver, you are the go-fer. There were several requests from me for items in the back of the coach, including water, *with ice*, that resulted in her being tossed about a little bit and prompting the following. "And I didn't want to drive" and "Damn it to hell!"

We ended up in a Walmart in Kingman Arizona for the night. Cyndi said she had heard that spending the night at Walmart was a road trip rite of passage and she did not want to miss it. We were ready to settle in for the night, but first things first, food, cards, and then sleep. We were ready for another day.
—*Love to all, Valerie*

I have hit the wall and am actually going to bed before midnight. We have been staying up late and playing cards. Only two games tonight. Yesterday was mostly Arizona - no rest stops in Arizona. I am going to write them a letter.

Last night we slept at a Walmart in New Mexico. We stopped to sleep and picked a spot for Shera to go out and do her business. It was muddy because we had gone through a downpour. She wrapped her leash around the bushes and I had to go out and untangle her. Well, in we both went with muddy feet. I saw a little mud ball and quickly picked it up, so she wouldn't step on it and get it all over the carpet. Turned out it wasn't mud - yuck. So, we did the best we could and this morning everything was put in plastic bags, including Cyndi's flip flops, and all was tucked into a bin under the motor home. We will sort it out in Arkansas. We traveled through NM most of the next day. They have nice rest stops but Cyndi was having so much fun driving she didn't want to stop.

We are now in Amarillo Texas. They do have rest stops but it consists of a covered picnic table and that is IT. Cyndi as never been in NM or Texas, and she says, "New Mexico is gorgeous!" The entire sky the whole day was completely filled with beautiful thunderhead clouds, lots of red rock formations and more. We went through about three short, but heavy rain storms. Saw lightening, heard thunder. So exciting! They would last about 10 minutes. High winds, too. The temp wasn't bad, so Cyndi did think of her Harley buddies, but decided the high winds would have been a little much on a bike. She has dubbed it "Sooo, exciting in the motor home." When we got to Texas, the sky cleared to pale blue, the wind died down, and everything turned flat.

Cyndi has done some off and on freeway driving, but if it looks like it might be difficult I take over - like when we have to stop for gas or go through residential areas. Today, we stopped for gas and I thought we might not have room to turn around, so I had Cyndi get out and help. I didn't have room, so for the first time on this trip I had to back-up at an angle. Oh dear! Cyndi was able to direct me, and we *finally* got everything going in the right direction. We got the gas and Cyndi got back in the motor home grinning from ear to ear, and exclaiming "Isn't this the best day ever!" For her it was sooo exciting, but I was worn out.

When we hit Texas, Cyndi decided she was hungry for a steak. We over-shot the runway and ended up in Oklahoma. I'll bet not many people can say that about Texas! We found a steak house and had filets and huge baked yams. Yum!

We shared the driving and part of the time we went through patches of rain and high winds again. When Cyndi stopped driving at one point she had been clenching her jaw so hard, trying to keep the coach in a straight line her teeth hurt. It was getting late, but we were only a couple of hours from home, so I decided to go all the way. Cyndi would have liked to spend another night on the road, but I was headed for the barn!

We hit highway 412 and were going very nicely when it decided to split. No sign telling us what to do and the GPS was un-characteristically silent. We took the wrong fork and ended up on the "scenic route", a narrow road in the dark, Arkansas dark! We drove for about a half hour. When Cyndi started seeing a house here and there she exclaimed in surprised "People actually live here!" The GPS finally found her voice and got us back on track. More adventures!!!! We got in about 1 a.m. and Martha was up waiting for us, wine glasses in hand.

When we got in late last night, I thought it best to go to a shopping center and unhook the car from the motor home under a bright light. The remote wouldn't work to get us into the car, where the keys were, so the car was unhooked and abandoned. We went home. Thank goodness it was only a dead battery. We gave the car a good shock and she decided to go right on home! —*Love to all, Valerie*

August. I have been home for a week and a half now. We had company the first few days we were here, but we are on our own now. Martha and I are making steady progress on the "getting settled" stuff. We have spent 5 days moving furniture around upstairs. I know this because Martha is keeping track. She is expecting me to spend at least that many days downstairs when all of her boxes are either unloaded or have found a storage spot. Martha has a "Thing" about chairs. Never met one she didn't love and want to own. I asked her to please refrain from any more purchases until we figured out if we have room for the ones she already has. With that in mind, we went out together and bought two. They are small recliners that fit our short torsos. It took us 3 days of moving every single piece of living room furniture, many times, to find just the right place for them. A redoing of the hearth room happened at the same time. It turned out our new grouping took up the spot where the love seat had been happily residing for 1 & 1/2 years but it has taken the move in stride.

The day before yesterday we left the house with a *LIST*. There were 9 items to be accomplished. We dropped off 3 large bags of socks at the church. David had lots of socks that will now be keeping the feet of the homeless warm. He had lots of underwear too, about 70 pairs that cannot be recycled. Now I ask you, if you had neither, which one of those items would you rather have?

Then off to the bank and the Nail Salon. We were headed down the road to get some more items scratched off the list when my car refused Martha's request to *hurry* into some fast-moving traffic being led by a very large truck. Then the engine warning light came on and that little screen that likes to dispense advice, you don't even have to ask for it and it is plentiful, also came to life. It informed us that "Engine power has been reduced". We already knew that! We went towards home, and a place that I knew fixed cars, only to learn that (Bad news) I had a drive train problem that they could not work on, but, (Good news) was still under warranty so it needed to be taken to the dealer. We went home to get David's car, to follow me to the dealer. Once we were home, we both decided the car could wait for the next day. We were pooped.

My car was delivered to the dealer the next day. We got the rest of our errands done, and stopped for a wonderful steak dinner. We were too tired even to make toast.

We picked up my car and as we were making our way home, our friend Ron called to tell me he had just had his car detailed, it was a great job and involved a $15.00 off coupon from the mail. We had both cars and were right around the corner. Who could resist? Especially since I had been telling him that David's car was in need of some serious cleaning. I told the guy to take his time. I was in no hurry. Tomorrow? Naw! Let's make it the day after. That was yesterday. I had already decided that it was going to take an act of congress and some pretty tough enforcers to get me out of the house today. Color me resting. —*Love to all, Valerie*

Dear friends and family, today I took some time to sit down and read all the condolence cards that have been sent to me. It is heartwarming to know how much my MB was loved and remembered by you all. So many of you recalled little bits about David that you were kind enough to share, it meant the world to me to read all your messages and words of comfort. I would like to once again thank Cliff for the wonderful Memorial Dance he put together. I thought it was a great party and tribute to my MB. I enjoyed a Margarita and used several Kleenex but the couple of hours I spent will stay with me as one more memory of my wonderful life with David. — *Love to you all, Valerie.*

50 years ago, I missed my cousin Mary's wedding. I was recovering from the birth of my first child, a happy event that had happened just a few days earlier. When I learned there was to be a 50th anniversary party, I called and invited myself. I received an enthusiastic "Yes, come", and started making plans.

Now, I had never made flight plans on the computer before. How hard could it be? We have this small airport and Santa Rosa has an even smaller one so making flights is a bit tricky. No big planes land at either one so at least 3 planes are involved. Add to that the fact that Santa Rosa is only serviced twice a day and only by Alaska Air, and you see the beginning of my dilemma. I had a plan. I would go through the list of flights and pick the route that took the least time. When I found one that only took 9 hrs to get there and 8 hrs to get home I booked the flight.

The party was scheduled for the 14th so I was going on the 13th. I wanted to be there with time to spare. I had a 1:30pm flight and Martha got me to the airport in plenty of time. There was only one lady in line ahead of me, but she did not look happy and was taking an awfully long time, grumbling about connecting flights and baggage not making the proper transfers. I was wondering what her problem was and getting a little antsy when she finally was finished, and it was my turn to step up.

After wishing the attendant a good morning and introducing myself, he responded with "Sorry Mam", the folks in Arkansas are so polite, "Your flight has been delayed". My first thought was, "No big deal. I have a 2-hour layover in Denver". A good, but as it turned out irrelevant, thought. The plane was having technical difficulties in another state and it's time of arrival was to be determined much later. I was given several options, none of them getting me to Santa Rosa before the next day. I chose option #5 which was to return home and come back the next day to take a 6:00 a.m. flight. Martha was called, and I was picked up and returned home where I promptly took a nap. Flight delays are so tiring.

I set my alarm clock and the alarm on my iPhone, for 4:00 am and was in bed by 11:30. I woke Martha up promptly and we were off again. The agent told me to hurry right to the plane and to have a good flight. I was all smiles as I boarded the plane, took my seat, and headed to the party. We sat for a few minutes and were then told there was problem with the wing defrosters and we would have to fly lower, so more fuel needed to be taken on. 45 minutes later we taxied out to the end of the runway, sat for a few *more minutes*, and were then told there were other technical problems. We would have to return to the boarding area and deplane. It was 7:30.

Once again, I was given a series of options that would probably not get me to the party in time. When told I had been trying to get to a 50th Wedding Anniversary Party for 2 days, and was now sure to miss it, the ticketing agent went in to overdrive. San Francisco was offered as an alternate destination. The agent assured me it was only 60 miles by car once I got there. He obviously has never driven in the San Francisco area and I obviously had forgotten how bad it could be. A call was made to my son-in-law Scott. Even though it was 5:30 am in CA and I had awakened him from a sound sleep, he said he would come, to San Francisco and pick me up.

A lady in line asked if I was considering moving back to CA where things might be easier. I told her no, but I was starting to see the benefits of flight insurance. Does that kick in if they can't get you off the ground and to your destination in 2 days and you miss the reason for the flight?

I was switched from United Air to American Air, yeah howdy, I'm a frequent flier with them. I went over to my new airline and spent my 2 ½ hr. wait time trying to take another nap. Did I mention that flight delays are tiring? Finally boarded, and once again at the end of the runway, the pilot came on to explain that the weather in San Francisco was quite cloudy and we would have to sit and wait so we could be layered in. Just as I was about to scream "Just kill me now", he added that it would only be for about 7 minutes.

I went to Texas, got my connecting flight and was on my way to the party. I was pretty sure it would still be going on when I get there. The 50th Anniversary Party was well under way when I finally arrived. But, my wine was chilled, and the food was yummy. I had a great time. Valerie

My flights home were not uneventful. I was dropped off at the airport and went to the check-in podium. Ticket counter would be a grand name for that small dais. The very nice young man there started frowning and asked me for my itinerary while explaining that all my return flights had been canceled. He asked if I had had any problems getting out of Arkansas. Well, yes, *a few*. The next sound he heard was a small voice, coming from the general direction of me, saying, "I think I'll just cry". "Well" he said, "I can get you back on your original flights from Santa Rosa to Las Vegas and from Denver to Arkansas but the one from Vegas to Denver is now full". Then he inquired, "What would you like me to do?" *I managed to keep the first 3 or 4 retorts (Golf words!) to myself.* He was, after all, *really trying* to help the little lady in distress. I opted for Vegas. I have friends there who have asked me repeatedly to visit so a night in Vegas could be a good thing. In Vegas, I made my way from departures to ticketing. Not a short trip. The ticket agent was almost as irritated as I was that some nincompoop had canceled my flights. "I'm not sure how, but I am able to do this. I got you on your original flight" she said. "Lucky for you, it's running late. However, you are going to have to run for it if you want to make it". Still not a short trip!

I had my carry-on, thank goodness for wheels, and a backpack stuffed to the gills with things a girl needs if she is going to be traveling through 3 airports, and 2-time zones for 9 hours, a book on CD, the sweater I was crocheting, a pillow, a blanket, a snack or 2, to just hit the highlights. I asked in what direction I should start running and the answer was "Go that way and pray you get through security quickly". I took off running, ok, jogging. I was hoping no one would have the bad form to jump in front of a 69-year-old grandmother huffing and puffing her way through the airport to make her flight home. I made my flight, I got into Arkansas at the correct time and my sister Martha was there to pick me up. A fairytale ending? —*Love to all, Valerie*

I am home, and it is *HOT*. This is so unusual here. I was thinking, possibly out loud, while I was in CA that the hills were so brown, that it never looks like that in Bella Vista. Well, the sound you now hear is me, eating my words. I am watering every day to save the lawn, a thing almost unheard of in this neck of the woods. The saddest thing though is that it is too hot and dry for the birds. We see, maybe, 4 birds a day. 2 small Woodpeckers and 2 Cardinals are hanging in there with us.

The fact that we had *rain* this morning was the hot topic at Mahjong, that and the fact that Valerie was back. It has been a year since I last played with the group and the fact that I was so warmly welcomed back was most heartwarming. Oh yes, and I won $4.00! —*Love and hugs, Valerie*

September. Our drought is at least temporarily over. We had some rain yesterday and tonight we had a thunder storm. I went out to let the dog in and called for Martha to come out. In the distance the lightening was so big that through the tree tops it actually looked like sunset for a second. When we first went out the storm was not quite to us and it was sooo still. The trees were not moving at all. Now I have really experienced the calm before the storm. We stood out there for about 10 min. while the storm came our way. It found us. The wind and rain were ferocious and the thunder and lightning a thing to behold. I have never seen lightening so big and bright. It was awesome. —*Love, Valerie*

This week we joined the church. The "Powers that Be" met with four of us at 0 dark thirty, retirement time (8:45 a.m.) and the first thing was pictures. Martha was not happy about having her picture taken, but had no choice. They put her up against a wall, so she asked if they would be taking only one pose, the answer: "no". After the first pic was taken she turned to the right for a side shot. The session folk may be checking for similar photos in the Post Office now. They had told us ahead of time that they would be asking for our history, I was worried that if I told them my history they wouldn't let me join. Luckily, they meant *ONLY* our religious history. Saved! They voted us in, yippee!

The next morning, at church, we stood in front of the whole congregation, were sworn in, and were whisked off to a reception line. I have never been in one so long nor shook so many hands. We got lots of hugs too. It was awesome, and very heartwarming. We were so worn out by all of this that we went home for much needed naps. Martha is making sure I don't wrap myself up in my blankie and let the world go by.

Tuesdays, we are now taking clogging lessons. I definitely need the exercise. Saturday, we have a play, Hitchcock's "The 39 Steps", and early next week we are going on an outing with the Welcome Club. Oh my, I think I need another nap.

Toy painting takes up Monday afternoons. David was part of the church's toy making group before we officially moved here and was very pleased when I joined the painting party. I am also using up lots of the yarn I brought from CA to make sweaters for the outreach project for kids in need. It is going to get cold here sooner or later. David, who moved enough nuts, bolts, nails and tools to start his own store, was quite amazed that I wanted to bring all that darn yarn with me. He would like what I am doing with it now. It's OK to look now David. —*Love to all, Valerie*

October. I saw 3 A.M. today. I saw it the only way it should be seen, from the night before. It didn't seem as fun as it did in my Wild Child days, but I got a lot done in those wee hours.

There was a Big DON'T LOOK DAVID, as I climbed up on the desk, twice, to attach a longer chain to the ceiling fan. It is on the same switch as the light. It was on, and I was getting cold. Martha did the "David" thing this morning though. She scolded me for climbing up there without her in attendance to cushion my fall.

Shera has a new job. Protecting us was not really keeping her busy enough. When we let her out to check out the area after dark she has decided it is her duty to go across the street and pick up any socks the children who live there may have left in the grass. The first time I saw one of the unidentified globs on the porch, I left it for morning and better light to see just what it might be. Actually, I do it every time. It has been over a year since she brought home the Armadillo carcass but THAT is something my leaky old memory does remember.

We have not been happy with our Cox "Bundle" so we made the change to Direct TV for cable and AT&T for Internet and phone service. Direct TV went smoothly, and we are happy with the remote and the picture, in that order. Learning a new remote is quite taxing. The switch to AT&T was not so smooth. We had NO service for days. Yesterday, after 2 hours on the phone, I now have service, but Martha does not. Apparently, a wireless adapter will solve the problem, so it has been added to our never-ending list of errands. I, however, am enjoying the new, faster service.

My sister Cyndi and her husband Larry will arrive tomorrow. They are bringing my Mom for a visit. She is 91 and pretty much wheelchair bound, so it is pretty brave of all 3 of them to undertake this journey. They will be here for a week and we are excited. Please pray that all goes well. People always notice that I look just like my mom. When visiting her in various care facilities folks would take one look at me and tell me where she was. Carol the caregiver put it succinctly. When meeting my Mom, she exclaimed, "Shit Valerie, it's the same face"! —*Love to all, Valerie*

For anyone who might have been wondering, Clogging is harder than it looks. I was ready to use my age as a factor but some of the ladies in the advanced class just before ours have more than a few years on me, thereby shooting that excuse down in flames. So now the blame goes to the previously mentioned long list of errands that keep us too busy to practice. Yea, I'm hanging on to that one for dear life. Feeling good today in Arkansas, —*Love to all, Valerie*

Two words... Road Trip! My boy's, Don and Larry, and I are off to see the Dallas Cowboys play. Monday Night football baby! Don is the one who went with me to CA after David's funeral. We hadn't been on the road very long when he came forward with some news. "I had forgotten how interesting it is to use the bathroom when the coach is in motion" Shortly thereafter I was tooling down the road and had to tap the brakes. Larry (the rookie) had been on his knees visiting with us and the next thing we knew he was doing a face plant into the drinks on the console, all this *before* the Margarita's. I had the coach filled and was ready to go when they got here. Well, almost. I had to round up some clothes, and we had to stop for food and beer. I already had 2 bottles of Margarita's in the coach. We are on our way.

We are in Oklahoma watching Sunday Night FB. David and I had never been able to get the TV to work in the coach, but my boys were able to figure it out in about 5 min. We have had food and drink and Football is in the air.

We KOA'd the first night; Margaritas and meatloaf were on the menu. The next morning, we were having breakfast and Don looked at his watch and said, "We have done it again". Here we were, getting on the road. It was 11:30.

The second night we were in the parking lot at the new Dallas Stadium. We were surrounded with tailgate BBQ and music. We got settled and made our way in to the stadium. The game started off great and ended great but the bit in the middle cost us the game.

The tour of the Stadium, at 11:30, of course, on Tues. was impressive. Tons of pics were taken. We had our pictures taken on the 50-yard line STAR. While we were waiting in line a young man got on one knee in the Star and proposed to his girl. It was too sweet for words. We got to poke around in the players and the cheerleader's dressing rooms. And, I got pics of Larry, on the field, throwing a pass and kicking for the extra point, neither of which will compromise his present career choice. Love you honey. :)

VALERIE KATZ

We were on the road, heading for home around 4:00 pm. Our Rookie is getting wise; when we are tooling down the road now he chants, "No breaks, no breaks". What will people think if he is doing another face plant on the dashboard? My answer? They will think, boy, that guy is traveling with some really fun relatives. You need a sense of humor on these trips.

We are KOAing it again tonight. Don found one on his iPhone. I was a little dubious when there was no KOA sign at the freeway exit. Don said not to worry. It was right there on his phone. I typed an address into my traveling friend, the GPS. She had quite a few things to say about our situation and was summarily disconnected. It turns out that that particular KOA had lost its franchise, and forgot to let Don's iPhone know... so was no longer in business. There was a new one at the local Casino, so we stopped for chicken and garlic bread to take with us. I told Don I would figure out how to turn on the oven while they checked in. Having spent many a year in my house growing up he said, "Perfect, the smoke alarm should just be going off." I'm sorry to say he wasn't far wrong.

We are settled in, Margaritas have been flowing, and families have been called. Don said he was going to set his alarm for 7:30 in the am. Larry and I agreed. He could pull in the slides, head for home, and wake us at 11:30. We are having a great *ROAD TRIP!!*

As promised, Don was up at 7:30 on Wed. and Larry joined him. They unhooked the coach and took to the road. True to my word, I remained in bed until the coach was in motion. We stopped at a Love's Truck Stop for breakfast, gas, and a new windshield wiper. The boys washed the windows and the coach's very dirty face and installed the wiper.

The road we were on was quite bumpy, so I was having a rough time playing my video game on my iPhone. I was sure I had paid for a much smoother ride but since I had my feet up and was resting securely on my laurels, I guessed complaining would be very bad form.

Larry decided he wanted to take a turn at driving. I was riding shotgun and Don was in the back resting. Pretty soon here he comes, **Don**, "Did you guys pass the 540 interchange?" **Us** "NO" **Don** "Are you sure?" **Us**, now not feeling quite a 100% sure, "No, we don't think so". **Don**, now pointing at his iPhone, which was giving my GPS a run for her money in the know-it-all department, "Well, it looks like you did about 30 miles ago." The boys had taken umbrage with my GPS's directions and had turned her off. I turned her back on and she immediately sided with the iPhone and said it was time to recalculate and turn around.

Larry did a great job of handling the coach the rest of the way home, even getting it on to our road, a very tight squeeze, and into the driveway. We were 3 tired but very happy souls. I just got back from dropping my boys off at the airport. I'm so sorry to see them go but will remember this as one of my favorite road trips. *Love to all, Valerie*

November. We are as set up as possible for the big yard sale this weekend. I hope it doesn't rain as the garage is not big enough to hold all of our goodies. I put an ad in the Bentonville newspaper to run from Thurs - Sun. Tools, electronics, DJ equipment and more. Hope the ad brings in tons of folks with full wallets and big vehicles to haul it all away. We have sold $200.00 already and there is not a dimple of a hole to be seen. Oh… it will be *so* nice to park in the garage and be able to put things away in the house and the garage. *WE HAVE STUFF!*

We had the yard sale for three days. 7:30 am to 5:00 pm. We are pooped. Since I had the most "Treasures" I got to spend the most time in the garage guarding them. People who wanted to haggle on Friday and Saturday were informed that prices were firm until Sunday.

VALERIE KATZ

Friday, after the sale... I came in, threw myself in my chair with the massager on my back and Martha brought me dinner and wine. I spent the evening repeatedly putting lotion on my hands. They were doing excellent imitations of sand paper. I was putting Neosporin on my nose. It seemed to think that Yard Sale meant, "Gotta Run", and it was a little raw from all the blowing.

Saturday, after the sale, I came in, was served dinner and wine and immediately fell asleep. I woke up at 8:00 pm, got right in bed and didn't arise until it is time to get ready for the sale on Sunday. I don't know about the rest of you, but I prefer the crack of 11:30 to the crack of dawn any day.

Sunday, the last day! "If it's still here, make me an offer". There wasn't really much left, I was ready to deal and so was Martha. Things that were large or bulky were especially marked down. We were tired and didn't want to have to move any big stuff. I was again served dinner and wine by Sister Martha.

Before you get too "Oh my, isn't she the spoiled one" on me, I must make a small clarification. Martha and I have a deal. I make the smoothies in the morning, which I did every day of the sale, and she makes our salads for dinner. However, serving me in my chair, and pouring the wine, just may have been a little above and beyond. Neither one of us wants to do it again, *EVER!* It was a lot of work and we are *RETIRED.* —*Love to all, Valerie*

The week after the sale was a manic one for me. I could not leave for California until the garage had been totally finished. All storage areas were gone through again. I, very briefly, thought we might need another 'Sale' but called Helping Hands instead. We didn't have near enough time to address the idea of packing.

Thanksgiving in CA, we are all over it. We will leave on Sat. and be there in plenty of time for Martha to bake pies at Cyndi's house on Wed.

THE NEWS FROM ARKANSAS

Things went a little awry. We went and got the coach on Fri. A.M. I stopped for gas on the way home and discovered that the one set of keys, the ones that are never, ever, supposed to leave the coach had done just that. They are the ones with the only key for the gas tank. I searched the coach to no avail. So… instead of packing, I drove to the next town to have keys made.

Today, my new rookie, Martha, and I loaded the coach and took off. Did we make it by the crack of 11:30? No. By the time we got on the road, approx. 3:30, it was just "We better get started." In our defense, this is the first road trip I have taken without either David or one of my boys to help with the heavy lifting. However, we were on our way. We were about 20 min. from home when I discovered I had left the phone charger at home. We were just getting to the AT&T store, so we pulled in. Now, if you lived in our town you would probably be shaking your head about now. Getting to the AT&T store means going around a few stores, huddled together, surrounded by a one way, one lane driveway with two very sharp turns. This was no place for a 35-ft. motor home pulling a car. But a girl can't travel all the way to CA with a dead iPhone. I need it for navigation and to keep the GPS in line. Mission accomplished, we were on our way again. About 15 min. later, with the setting sun's blazing glory shining in my eyes, I realized that I had also left my glasses at home. Not good news for my new co-pilot. "Oh, well" I tell her, "we won't be driving after dark, so we should be just fine".

Again… Part of a new Rookie's journey is the overnight parking lot of a WalMart. Our good friend, the GPS, who was already hoarse from the constant "Recalculating and U-turn" messages she had been delivering almost non-stop since we had left the house, we wanted to take a different route and had not asked her permission before hand, got her revenge. Not only was the WalMart she took us to quite a way from the freeway, it had gone out of business. I pulled over, asked the iPhone for help, and we were on our way again to a nearby RV Park. By then it was very dark, and the road was un-lit and narrow. The Rookie did a great job of helping me find the driveway, thereby keeping us from ending up in a ditch.

Ah, a great first day. It's an adventure. I can say that now. Even though Martha beat me at cards, I got my glass of wine and am ready for bed. The alarm is set for 6:30 A.M.

It is now Monday night. The trip is going well, and we have an internet connection, so I can send the "News". We are doing well and will be in Canoga Park by Wed.

We are on the final leg of our trip. We spent Tues night In Needles CA. Not the best of choices as it turned out. We had stopped in Kingman and had the coach washed. The nice gentleman tried to discourage a stop in Needles with "You might want to go on to Barstow. There really isn't much in Needles".

Well, we had it on good authority, we were, after all, *3-day veterans* of The Good Sam's Club, that there was a RV Park there and we would reach it just as the sun was going down. We did. We got settled and hooked up... So far, so good. Then we hit the bump in the road. As it turns out, Needles has no cable company. No, none! A non-issue under normal circumstances, but this was the final night of Dancing with the Star's! We had been congratulating ourselves on our perfect timing. Dancing with the Star's final one night, and Canoga Park the next. A perfect plan... not so!

Oh yes, in answer to your question, we did try the antenna. We even had the nice lady from the office come and show us just were a small opening in the hills allowed a signal to penetrate the area. She said as far as electronic goodies were concerned, if you didn't bring it with you, you don't have it. She was able to get 4 stations for us, none of which had Dancing with the Star's or anything else we recognized.

A call was made to sister Cyndi. When we explained our problem, she said "Needles! You should have known better for crying out loud!" She promised to record it for us anyway. My family will be greeted on Thanksgiving with a warm "If you saw Dancing with the Star's, don't tell me. I haven't seen it yet!"

Wed. when I checked the valves to see if any dumping was necessary, the reply was "Are you kidding. You will be up to your ankles in something quite unpleasant if you don't take care of business now." I did. So today is the big day. Happy Thanksgiving all! —*Love, Valerie*

December. The day after Thanksgiving the coach needed water and propane. I had learned my lessons. This was going to be a piece of cake. The water went well, no splashing in the air or on my head. As for the propane, I was sure I remembered how to pull in and get the job done. Not so, I pulled in the wrong way and on the wrong side. Just pull in and turn around the man gestures. No English being spoken here. Not even Spanish for which I know a few words, and a few gestures of my own. I couldn't even say "35 ft. and in the back of a gas station sir?" By the time I figured out that he wanted me to pull out into the street and try again I had already started my 8-point turn. He was of no help, being of the wild waving and unknown gestures variety. Then, he wanted me to tell him where the propane went. Now, how would I know that? I always pull up, someone puts the propane in, and I pay and am done. I got my keys and went to help. The propane is in the large compartment, which for safety has no lock on it. Not in the little compartment, with the lock, that, to my surprise, has a radio and jacks for hooking up who knows what electronic gadgets. Every day an adventure, and never too old to learn... I hope...

The week after Thanksgiving was spent in Ventura. I was able to see my mom daily and visit with my sisters, and get my hind quarters handed to me nightly playing cards with them. I also, was there, in town, not in the hospital, for the birth of my niece Heather's baby. She and her husband Tom are adopting. They have gone through the whole nine months with this girl. Dr. Visits, those little black and white pictures of little Makenna's in vitro progress and several false alarm visits to the hospital. She is adorable and I'm quite sure well worth the wait.

When I left Ventura, I needed it all. A dump station, gas, and propane. I knew where to go. I knew what to do. I knew how to pull in to get the job done. The only thing I got scolded for this time was not checking in before dumping. Apparently, since this is a densely incorporated area, the process is limited, and they can only help so many each day. Duly noted. With all that said… I do love this RV and am having a great time. —*Valerie*

Our travels and travails continue. That beautiful new mirror I had installed on the right side of the coach just before we started out is a thing of the past. At this point in time, what is left of it is laying right at my feet, along with my faithful companion, Shera. This time I did it up big. I not only knocked my mirror off completely, but just so it wouldn't be feeling lonely laying there on the street, I knocked off one that was minding its own business, just parked there, on the street, on someone else's coach. Narrow street, traffic, on the way to the dump site, and then to pick up a grandchild from school, I didn't stop. I went back the next day, to make nice and confess only to learn I was wanted by the police for hit and run. Insurance companies have been contacted and, hopefully, police have been informed and my picture taken off the wall at the post office.

The black tank, the one with the really smelly stuff in it, wouldn't close properly, so I was moving the coach, just a little bit, to clean up the driveway, and pulled off the end the extension cord connecting me to the house. I was heading to Orange County to see my daughter and her family, so without a backward glance, off I went. I could deal with that problem upon my return.

If you are not plugged in, nothing in the coach is working. Now, on some level I knew that before I went off for my visit. I knew it on a more direct level when I got back. Everything in the refrigerator was a messy thing of the past. That includes the ice which I sort of needed. A glass of wine would have been very welcome about then.

Fixing an extension cord of that size turned out to be more of a job than I could handle. After several try's and vain attempts to find one to replace it, and with the tears beginning to fall, I called my motor home/dance friends Roz & Chuck and they said to come right over. Chuck fixed the cord and Roz fixed the wine. Getting a little tired of the "Live and learn" part of the trip but really having a great time.

Yesterday was perfect weather, in the 70's, with good friends, Richard, Kathy and Bob on hand to play golf with. The front 9 produced a 60 something for me, and everyone was kind enough to not bother me with any details about the back nine score. Suffice it to say, I had a wonderful time and got a lot of bang for my buck. —*Love, Valerie.*

CHAPTER 5

Arkansas 2011

February. On Saturday I was enjoying the afternoon on the deck. It was almost 80 degrees and spring was in the air, very unusual for January in Arkansas.

Today, it is snowing. The most I've seen since we moved here 2 years ago. That is the exact phrase echoed by the rest of the residents of Bella Vista who have lived here for many, many years. Oh no!! Not the 2 to 3 inches *a year* that we hear is the norm. It is the worst snowstorm ever in our Village. We add that to the others, hottest summer, worst ice storm, most rain, etc. We seem to have brought out the biggest and the best. Since we don't get snow here, *uh huh*, snowplows are few and far between and there has not been one around here. It is 5:00 pm and we have not seen the mailman and don't expect to. It may be "Neither snow nor rain" etc. but not without the plow!

Yesterday while I was out running an errand I heard it might snow so on the way home I stopped and bought 6 bottles of wine. I wasn't even a Scout, but I am prepared! I found a Red that I like so have made the switch. Healthier? Who cares!!

We went grocery shopping 2 days ago, the propane tanks are full, and as long as we have electricity we can out last

the weather. I hope in a week or so I don't have to eat those words for lack of anything else to eat. Shera has been out to do her business, I went out on the deck to measure the snow and clear the snow off the bird feeders, so the birds will be able to dine. The newspaper, if delivered, is at the end of the driveway and we don't really care what it has to say today. As you probably remember; Valerie will never move from So. California and she for sure does *NOT* do snow. Live and learn.
—*Loving it in Arkansas, Valerie*

We are still watching the snow melt and taking pictures of the first real winter Martha has ever experienced. Having her here, living with me, was David's idea and is just one of the wonderful and caring ways he is still looking after me. I miss him so.

I like to inform my friends in CA that the weather man here in Arkansas actually knows what the weather is going to be and do, unlike the ones in CA. I always considered the weather report in CA as little more than an educated guess that had a 50/50 chance at being correct. Our weather man said we were going to get 2 to 3 inches of snow overnight. In the morning we had 10 to 12 inches and it was still snowing to beat the band. By the end of the day we had 18 to 20 inches. I am willing to cut him some slack as this was a record breaker. However, when I report this to my distant friends, I will only mention the record breaking part. The report of a few inches will stay with me in Arkansas. Las Vegas isn't the only place that keeps its secrets.

My darling Shera was gone for quite a while one evening. The next morning, I found a good sized pile of "Who knows?" on the floor in my bedroom. It was painfully obvious that Shera had changed her mind about eating it, after it was too late. Not taking any sass from Shera, I got rid of it.

The next day it snowed. Shera went out again, and again was gone for some time. When she returned she had brought another "Who knows?" back with her. It was too frozen for her to eat. If she thought I was going to thaw it out for her she was VERY much mistaken. I brought her in, told her "thank you" and "what a good girl you are", and got the pipe wrench and a large kitty litter bag. The litter bag was for the "thing" and the pipe wrench was to push it in to the bag. It was the first thing I saw that I thought was sturdy enough to push a frozen item approximately a foot in diameter and 2 to 3 inches thick into the bag!

I got an e-mail from my sister Cyndi today. She thinks she knows what it was! She wrote "A possum is a flat animal that sleeps in the middle of the road." Also found frozen in the back of the house apparently. Who Knew?! *Love to all, Valerie*

It is 7:00 pm and I am just now getting to my morning smoothie. Had to be in Rogers at 9:15 this morning, that's like going from Woodland Hills to Newbury Park, about a 20 min drive, but without the traffic, so I grabbed an apple and some grapes and got in the car. Those were followed by almonds, very good for you. The fact that they were covered in dark chocolate was just a bonus.

Next stop, Church. This was the day to meet the Blood Mobile and make a sacrifice to the Vampires. After the deed was done, their instructions to me were to go home, rest, not lift anything, and have a good lunch. Two slices of toast, one covered with an egg, the other with cinnamon, also very good for you, and sugar. Yum! —*Love to all, Valerie*

I had quite a scare this weekend. On Friday I left the house about 8:45 am and didn't get home until 4:30 pm. Now I needed a potty stop ASAP and I was pretty sure Shera, who had been home all day and confined to the house, needed one too. Without much more than a passing glance, we quickly passed each other through the garage and proceeded to take care of business. When I returned to the front yard to get her, Shera was nowhere to be seen. After much calling and whistling I called the neighbors to see if maybe she had gotten in their garage. She hadn't, and she was gone all night. I got a call from animal control early the next morning. Shera had been their guest all night at the "Hotel with the bars on the windows". She was howling, something I have *never* heard her do, and was ready to go home. Apparently, she was unhappy with the accommodations. An outside doghouse with no heat and no comfy 4-inch-thick bed. And right next to several other similar establishments with noisy guests who kept her up all night. She got no sympathy from me. I hadn't slept very well either and Martha is in CA and couldn't even hold my hand! Since she was a first offender the $25 ransom fee was waived. If not, it was coming out of her allowance! Let's see, bloodletting, lost dog, my sister gone. Yep, we have another Country Western song in the making. —*Love to all, Valerie*

March. It is 3:30 in the morning and I can't sleep. Too many thoughts running around in my head I guess.

There was a notice in the church paper on Sunday about a Sweetheart Dance being held in April. There are notices posted all over the Village about it. It is at the Yacht Club and is Black Tie optional. Wouldn't David have loved that? He loved to put on his Tux and his black and white shoes and go out and strut his stuff. I would have loved being on his arm too. We did make a lovely couple out there on the dance floor.

April hosts the anniversary of my son David's passing and my 70th birthday. And now I have lost the diamond out of my engagement ring. I know my David is up there watching over me and wishing he was here to hold my hand. This for sure is not a Don't Look David day.

I am going to CA to celebrate my big day with my family. That is something to look forward too. I sent my family an e-mail a while back reminding them it was one of the big ones. "It's number 70, and I just know you will want to throw me a party!" —*Thanks for listening, Valerie*

April. I have been to CA. It was a short trip. Just in and out for my birthday. My kids put on a great party for the big day. There was a 10-minute slide show, complete with music, of my life from early teens to the present day. That was followed by a "Roast", things that were tucked away in the memories of those present and resurrected for the enjoyment of all. It was all in good fun, and, there is a video I can't wait to see. I can't remember what everyone said! Well, I'm 70 now!

I flew, so there are no coach stories. That meant the dog had to stay home. Martha?? I was feeling quite badly about her not being able to attend, *until,* we were talking to our new doctor and she informed him that I was the really, really old sister. I then announced that I wasn't feeling so bad about it anymore and that she was uninvited!

There was quite a storm going on when my plane landed back here. I told Martha that I really appreciated the thunder and lightning show she had ordered for my arrival. However, the storm is still going on.

I got home on Thurs. Fri. night there was a tornado warning. Now, they pretty much go around us as we live in a hilly forested area, but I did get a little uneasy when we got a phone call from the local weather service telling us to go to our "Safe Place" right away!

On Sat. there were flood warnings and on Sunday there were warnings of both tornados and flooding in the surrounding areas. We are quite brave and are not afraid :)

Today we went in to Bentonville for our Dr. apts. Instead of going home the way we went (the back way) we decided to take the highway and stop at the recycle center. The area around Hwy 540 is now a lake! We took some pictures of the tops of some ball washers on the golf course. The water is so high the tops are all you can see. Anyone know how to golf from a canoe? We had to go back to Bentonville to get home as the regular route in to Bella Vista is closed due to flooding and an unsafe bridge. The light show in the sky is still going on and it is still pouring. It doesn't look like it's going to stop any time this week.

In other news, we have some birds building a nest on the deck. I was watching them work, from my hiding spot in the house. Both birds were rounding up really good nest stuff. It didn't take me long to figure out who was the "He" and who was the "She".

He, had gotten quite a large item in his beak and wanted to make sure no one was watching just where he was going. He hopped around the deck for a good 5 min. Finally losing patience, *She,* hollered something that I'm pretty sure in bird speak meant "O for crying out loud, stop hopping around and deliver the %$#& thing." He was so unnerved by this he dropped his large find back on the deck. He had had his instructions however and picked it up and delivered it with great haste.

Tornados! Floods! I don't know about pestilence, but we have enough food not to be concerned about famine. *We still love it here.* —*Valerie*

May. For those of you who have called or written wanting to know if we have blown away or drowned, the answer is "Not Yet!" On the night Joplin took such a big hit the weather service called us 4, yes 4, times telling us to take cover. We feel this area is pretty safe, so we kept the news on and watched the minute by minute reports. We had our priorities straight. We were very concerned that it would interrupt our taping of the Tom Selleck, Jessie Stone movie. It did! They are rerunning it here at midnight on Saturday though, so all is well.

It is time for the trees next to the power poles to be trimmed on the road to Bentonville. Apparently, it is taking a little longer than was initially expected. None of the men are too keen on being way up in the top of the trees, in a metal bucket, using a chain saw, when the wind is blowing a gale, it is pouring, and the lightening is turning night into day. Go figure.

Still safe and loving every minute of it. —*Valerie*

June. It has been a tough few weeks. May 28th, David's birthday, and yesterday the first anniversary of his passing. I had plans. On his birthday I planned to do two of his favorite things. Take Shera to the dog park and go out for a steak dinner. But you know how plans go. My Granddaughter Jennifer graduated from High School, so I was in CA on his birthday. I hadn't told Shera of my plans, so she was not all disappointed.

On the first anniversary of his passing I planned to have the party he always wanted, all our new Bella Vista friends with me making my BBQ ribs, lots to drink and real cloth napkins, of course. The party was just too much of an undertaking for me. What I did was put on the hat and dress I wore when we got married and walked down the steps he had installed out back so we could take salt blocks to the deer.

I scattered his ashes out there in our own little forest and took one last walk with my Master Builder, Wonderful Man, and fiercely missed Husband. Carol, his much-loved caretaker and my sister Martha were there with me. Then the three of us let David take us all out to dinner. I ordered for David, a steak, baked potato, and asparagus. I also ordered his two favorite drinks, a shot of Dewars Scotch and a Strawberry Margarita. I did him proud I think... I drank and ate it all. We toasted him and told him we would love and miss him always.

> *Thanks to all who have reached out to me on this day.*
> *Valerie*

July. It has been in the 100's here for over a week. Martha will be home tomorrow night from her 2-week trip to CA. Hope it has cooled off some by then or she may not get off the plane. I have been walking Shera every night since she left. We don't go until around 8pm so the sun is on its way down. When we get home 2 things happen immediately! She gets her cookie and I get my shower! Shera, now being empty of anything that might need a trip outside goes to bed and I don't see her until the next morning. My next move is to get myself into my P.J.'s, and some wine into my glass. —*Love to all, Valerie*

It was Friday night in North West Arkansas. The lure of dinner and Karaoke at the Moose Lodge had been once again presented and was looking rather good. Country fried steak, mashed potatoes, gravy, green beans, salad, bread and butter, and dessert. Home cooking delivered with a smile, and all for the sum of $9.00. Even I couldn't resist. It was time to get out there. For a year now I have been resisting the invitations of friends to join them for an evening at the "Moose". Too many "David" memories were in the way. But, it was Karaoke Night, something David and I had never participated in, so I thought what the heck, let's do it.

Our "Sunshine Group" so named it appears, as the evening is traditionally opened with a spirited rendition of "You are My Sunshine", was 8 strong and full of enthusiasm. Then came the bump in the road. It turned out there was a small dance floor in the Karaoke room. I was not expecting there to be dancing and that really threw me for a loop. As I was trying very hard to keep it all together, a nice gentleman came up and asked me to dance. Now my mother brought me up way too polite to turn him down and hurt his feelings, crying and wiping my nose on his shirt would have been an even bigger no no, so out on the dance floor we went. A nice slow two-step, sort of like when I was first learning, back in the 80's.

I heard my friend Louise ask her husband Ronnie if he was ready to leave. "No, we're going to stay and close the place tonight" was his response. Now that doesn't mean the same thing here as it does in California. That doesn't mean 2 a.m. It's more like 10:30 or maybe even 11:00! After a 30-min drive and we were home. It was 11:15.

It was a bit of a breakthrough I think. I didn't feel like crying anymore and I had a really good time. I have been trying to do better about getting "Out there". I joined an 8-week grief workshop and I have played Mahjong three weeks in a row now! Two steps forward! Aren't you proud? Your reporter hasn't sent out much "News" this past year as there hasn't been much news to share.

Watch out! I may be finding my voice again. Love, Valerie

August. I start my big adventure today. 4 days in CA (hot). Then off to Australia, 6 days in the Rain Forest and the Great Barrier Reef (warm & moist) and 6 days in Sydney (cold). If you are wondering why the weather update... I am limited to one carry-on bag! Lots of thought went in to this. 2 plastic bags that you squeeze the air out of did the trick. It's all in there. What it will look like when I spring them loose will be fodder for later news.

The flight was full and there was no more room for carry-on bags. So, they made me check my bag (no charge) which is quite heavy due to the over packing I mentioned earlier. How lucky am I!

When you get through with security, if you go left there's an escalator that takes you down and back to the general population. If you go right, there's an escalator that takes you down to where my flight takes off. I went left. I had to go through security again.

Now let me explain about security at XNA. It's a very small airport so when I had gone through the first time there was no one in line. Now I have to go through a second time and there are *two* people in line. The nice lady looks at me smiles and says, "Went the wrong way didn't you". I smiled back and said "yes". When I got to the lady who shoves your bags through the x-ray machine, she also smiled and said, "Went the wrong way didn't you". I said, "I can see by the comments that I'm not the first one to do this" She laughed and said, "Oh no, not even close" When I got to the gentleman in charge of the scanner he smiled "Went the wrong way huh. Hand me your hat again".

As I was gathering my items and putting my shoes back on, the nice lady from the x-ray machine came bustling up and said, "Now when you go through that door be sure to go to your right this time". Point taken! I put on my shoes and went to my right / flight. Has anyone seen my keeper?

The flight was delayed 2 hrs. which meant my son Larry would be picking me up after midnight, but I am on my way!
—*Love to all, Valerie*

Seeing my Mom was a priority so Kalyn (age 12) & I visited her on Sat. Kalyn was playing with my iPhone and trying not to be bored to death. I had warned her. This day is all about Great Grandma and would involve sitting in her room, probably watching Martha Stuart for hours and visiting. She wanted to be with her grandma so off we went. Well, she took some not so very flattering pictures of me and great grandma, and I'm thinking "Oh well, no one will see them". The next thing she says is "Do you know who Susanne Bango is?" As my eyebrows shot up into my hair line I inquired, "Why!?" "Oh," said Kalyn "I posted the pictures on Facebook and she commented on them." She was then informed, quite calmly, really, that you shouldn't post other people's pictures without telling them first. She is a smart girl. She then said, "Oh Grandma, I thought you looked so pretty". She will live to take pictures another day.

The annual Birthday Bash was on Sunday. Don & Debbie were wondering about getting a water feature for the day as the kids are all getting older. Then came the question, "What about Mom?" As the giant double slide with a wicked turn at the bottom was going up Don said, "Oh Mom is never going to get up on that". Well, she did, many, many times and I have the very, very unflattering, but hilarious pictures to prove it. Debbie has been warned about posting them to Facebook. —*Love to all, Valerie*

Australia! We left the Morefield's house @ 6:30 pm. 29 hrs. later here we are, at the Cape Tribulation Exotic Fruit Farm and B&B. Aussie Land! The pilot on the first flight said the flight would take 14 hrs & 3 min. He stressed the 3 min several times. What's three min. to me? Take your time, I'm in business class! All the comforts of home!

Our cabins are in the Rain Forrest and when you are there you see nothing but the forest. We wanted to go to the beach. Our host said "Take the shortcut but be sure to follow the blue ribbons. Don't go on until you see the next blue ribbon, or you will get lost. We kept our eyes on the blue ribbons! We got to the beach only to find a sign that said "Don't go in the water. Watch for Crocodiles! If you are launching a boat watch even better and hurry!

Allyson, our hostess, said "The park service puts those signs on all beaches. There's really no danger. They are like American lawyers, worrying about getting sued. Go ahead and swim". I hope she's right! We found a place to eat. Then the trek back in total darkness. Luckily, we had heeded the "be sure to take the torch (flashlight) with you" warning. We were tired and in bed at 8. We slept till 7 the next am.

As promised, breakfast was served on the deck at 8. Fruit course first, then French toast, bacon, bread, yogurt and croissants. We won't be going hungry!

I had been told that there would be some hiking at one stop in the Blue Mountains. We walked miles every day at our first 2 destinations, 90% of which were on uneven surfaces or going up and down lots and lots of stairs. I was getting fit! As we stood looking into the abyss, a beautiful abyss by the way, I looked across from us and *WAY* over on the other side I thought I saw something moving. I asked the man standing next to me if those were people over there. "Yes!" he said, "Are you going there?" I looked to my son-in-law Kevin and he shook his head yes. The man looked at me, shook his head, and said "When you get there you better go right and not left. If you go left, you may die." Good to know.

We started down. There was a stairway of sorts all the way down. Someone who thought (and rightfully so) that future enthusiasts might like to see this beautiful canyon in the Blue Mountains from the inside, carved these steps out of the rocks. Kevin has offered "You will use one set of muscles going down and another set going up." This is great news as by the time we got to the bottom, approximately 1& 1/2 hours later, my leg muscles were quivering and begging for mercy. My right knee had started to hurt like there is a knife stabbing it. These were facts that I was keeping to myself. I asked to go on this trip! I had promised my daughter when we were making our way down that I would *NOT* start to cry and hyperventilate like I did as a teenager trying to climb out of a volcanic crater in the Grand Canyon. Unfortunately, I had to also tell her that my equilibrium hadn't been all that hot for some time and I might need a hand to steady me on some of the narrower parts that had no handrails. No, I'm not kidding. *WAY* up on the cliffs with no handrails at times!

We start the climb up. Some ladies coming the other way stopped to tell us that we had done the easy portion of our hike and we were about half way up. Kevin found a tree branch and offered it to me as a walking stick. I think he saved my life right there and then. I was starting to need help. Another group told us about a half an hour later that we were about half way up. Another half hour later we saw a park ranger working on a sign. "What's that you're working on?" we asked. "Oh" he said, "this is the half way marker". My daughter Denise informed him in a tone of voice I'm pretty sure she learned from her Mother, that we had heard that 3 *times already.*

The steps aren't getting any easier but as we get to the "You've got to be kidding" portion of our climb, my knee decides to take mercy on me and stops hurting, temporarily. My arms, that have been hanging by my sides, acting like they are just along for the ride, now need to get busy. I need both of them to help me, where there is actually a railing, to pull my tired carcass up the stairs. As I'm sitting on a rock while Kevin takes pictures, OK, taking a brief rest, a group of people pass us and a gentleman that has got to be at least 10 years older than I am, just breezes right past us. I tell my hiking companions "He's Just showing off". Pretty soon, as we make our way up the hill, he comes back. He's got a thin walking stick. He says I don't need to carry that great big thing; I just need a little one to steady myself. I thank him, but I'm leaning pretty heavy on my stick, so I stay with it. We find a few more sticks along the way that he has scattered like bread crumbs.

I have to stop for a few minutes as I can't seem to catch my breath. I tell Denise and Kevin "The good news is, if I die you can have me cremated and carry me home in a little box. You won't have to ship the body". Kevin says "Yes, but Don will kill me." I'm thinking "Yes, and Larry will be helping him". (Those are my boys!) Denise is having none of my attempt at humor and offers, "No one is going to die here today!" We resume our climb.

Kevin points to a sign that indicates the path to an easier trail. I tell him, "Ugh, we spit on the easier trail!" We continue, with smiles all around. Well, I think there were smiles all around. By now I am spending most of my time looking down at where my feet should be next.

We made it to the top! The adventure took us a little over 4 hours. First stop, the toilet! I dropped down on the seat. I'm not sure I will be able to get up and I can't reach the door lock. I'm wondering how the heck I will get out! Of course, I did get up.

The views, the waterfalls, the beautiful birds, a wonderful sight to behold! I wouldn't have missed it for the world! It's sort of like when we went white water rafting. You are nervous and a little scared at times, but the rush and excitement of completing the adventure is awesome. I loved it.

There was a café at the end of our hike. As we were getting something to eat Kevin read us the info on the hiking trails. Trail one: Challenging 2 to 3 hrs. Trail two: For the experienced climber, lots of steps, 3 to 4 hrs. (That's the one we took). Trail three: Be sure to have your Will in order before you go. A great adventure!

In Australia a bottle shop is the code for liquor store. I found a bottle of Jansz champagne in one and thought "What a great souvenir!" (Jansz is my Mother's maiden name and my sister has taken it as her last name) We drank the champagne, no sense taking it home. Martha doesn't drink champagne, and I put the bottle in my suitcase. Somewhere between Aussie land and home it disappeared. Bummer, doesn't come close to what I was thinking when I unpacked.

The Australian GPS that Kevin purchased for our trip was much more polite than my U.S. model, with one exception. The phrase "you are exceeding the speed limit" seemed to be on the tip of its tongue. After hearing it several times and disputing the findings, Kevin handed the offensive device to Denise and asked her to "Make it stop!" She did, with remarkable speed.

The Game! We went to an Australian Football game. My thighs were still screaming at me over the trip to the bottom of the known universe. Our seats were in the very top row of the stadium. The stairs were not the normal 8-inch rise. They were at least 12 inches. I took a look up and thought "Oh dear".

I took it one step at a time, grabbing on to a seat back and hauling myself up.

The game was the most fun I have had at a ball game ever! The play never stops. There are 15 men on each team. More than 5 steps may not be taken when holding the ball without bouncing it, bumping it to another player with the heel of the hand, or kicking it. With a football! There are also 6 officials on the field running forward and backward like gazelles.

Then came halftime, "Were going down to get some beer Mom, want to come." Down those stairs and then back up again!? I didn't think so. I said I was fine and they offered to bring me some wine. A deal made in heaven. After I got the wine I was somewhat concerned that it might make a trip down necessary, but what the hell you only live once. All those folks were on the field, running back and forth. Their efforts were not in vain. Our team won 112 - 86. Lots to cheer about and I did!

We went out to the Great Barrier Reef for 2 hours of snorkeling. We opted for the wet suits and were happy to have them. There was still the sound of teeth hammering together all around us. We saw whales on the ride out and swam with the fishes and turtles. The coral was absolutely beautiful. What a great experience. That evening we went to dinner at a local pub. We had seen the sign saying there would be entertainment that night. There was a man singing, Bluegrass? Sure sounded like it to me.

The next night at an open-air market I got a Chinese massage. Then we walked across the street and watched the end of a movie, in the park. Just like in the Wedding Planner!

On our last night we went to the Sydney Opera House to see a comedian. Where were our seats? The very top row! By then my thighs had stopped screaming at me, My Sherpa, Alex, helped me steady myself across the row to my seat. I am on the mend. What a great vacation!

Getting home... Delta to LA, on time, no problems. Delta to Atlanta, a 2-hr. layover with a 4 hr. delay and 4 gate changes. Ugh! Delta to home, all in all 30 hours. But home at last!

Samantha wanted to know what was the first thing I going to do when I got home. I told her I was going to sleep for two days. I told Martha I was going to take a sleeping pill. Normally I would take 1/2 or 1/4 but I was going to take the whole thing with 2 Advil and go to bed for those two days. She said "Don't get carried away. Remember, you signed us up for Meals on Wheels and it starts tomorrow." —*Oh dear... Valerie*

I am back from Australia and have promised myself I will go up and down our stairs at least 10 times each and every day! You are probably wondering why. Well, let me tell you. For three years I have been sitting around North-West Arkansas like a slug. I got ready to go to Australia with my family by walking the dog, for one whole month, around our neighborhood, three cul-de-sacs. It might sound like a lot but in reality, takes a whole 15 to 20 min. depending on how often the dog wants to stop. The trip has awakened some of my muscles. I will try to keep them from nodding off now that I am home. —*Love, Valerie*

September. Once a month Martha and I go somewhere with Ladies Day Out, a part of the local Welcome Club. Today was the day. We set our alarms, we got up, and we got ready. We forgot one very important item. They are redoing the road leading to our meeting place. It is a 2-lane road, so all traffic is stopped on the one lane they are working on and the other one gets to go. I have been caught in this before and read an entire chapter in my book waiting for my turn. Not a good thing to forget. Due to the delay, we were 15 to 20 min. late and everyone was gone. A gentleman came out and asked us if we were waiting for some ladies. He said they had already left for Fort Smith. I asked Martha where we were scheduled to go. She keeps our appointment book. Her reply, "An old whore house that is now a Museum" "Did we pay for this trip already" I asked? Since the answer was "Yes", it was time to hit the road.

We got on the freeway, set the cruise control for 80, and called our friend Ron from church. We ask him if he knew the name of our "destination". He said no but that he would call around and see if he could find out. He ended up having to call the church office for the info. They got on the internet and came up with a name! "Miss Laura's".

We then called 411 for the phone number for the Fort Smith Chamber of Commerce and got the address. My son-in-law Kevin handles the iPhone account. "Kevin, it was really a necessary 411" We had already tried the Garman GPS app on my phone and gotten all the museums around Bella Vista, but we were going to have to get much closer to Fort Smith to find the "Museum" we were looking for.

We tried the GPS in the car, no luck, then the iPhone GPS and Google, better luck. We had used all our life lines, but we got there! I'm sure my David was watching from above, happy he had left me that phone, feeling proud we could figure it all out, and laughing his keester off. Since we had been driving so fast we actually got to our destination before some of the other ladies. The tour of the "Brothel" was really fun and interesting. Before we left we were given a Sheriff's badge, a sticker that said we had been to Miss Laura's and a certificate from the health department that said we were "Healthy" and could resume our work at this "House of Prostitution". Then we walked over to Bobby's, a diner that was in a very old railroad car. It was a hamburger place so, of course, we decided on a Reuben Sandwich. The burgers looked great, but the Reuben was good too.

While everyone else went back to their cars to drive to our next stop, we decided to walk. WE had a ½ a Reuben to walk off! (We shared the sandwich). We were walking, we took the long way around (Not exactly on purpose) and we still got there at the same time as the rest of those ladies☺

We then got to ride on an old trolley car. When we stopped to change direction we all had to change the direction of our seats. The backs were on some kind of hinge, so we took hold of the backrest and pulled it over, so we were all facing front again. The gentleman who was giving the tour was quite funny and told us about the accidents he had had while driving the trolley. He then asked for volunteers to drive. There was a spot that went by the Veteran's Memorial Cemetery (The irony of the place was not lost on me) that was safe for amateurs. When he noticed my hand was up, Martha said, "My hand was up first!" He said we could wrestle for it, but I graciously opted out.

When it was Martha's turn to drive she asked a young boy that was there with his family if he would like to drive instead. The smile on his face said that she had made his day. She asked me later if I would have done that. "No" I said, "I wouldn't even have thought to!" The ladies in front of us were laughing when they overheard our conversation. Martha leaned forward and said, "She's wearing black because she's the bad sister."

During a stop on the trolley ride the lady who organizes these outings stood up and said she wanted to thank Martha and Valerie, the two ladies who had so kindly volunteered to help with these outings in the future. I whispered to Martha "Did you volunteer me for something!" she said, "Just stand up, I'll explain it to you later". Bad sister indeed!

We were dropped off at the History Museum, Drugstore and Ice Cream Shop. There were 19 of us and only one lady taking orders and making the ice cream deserts. She was a true Southern Lady, kind, friendly and unhurried. The place was absolutely adorable. It was a very old pharmacy with lots to see. In the Museum proper there were old fire trucks and all kinds of stuff from the Civil War. It definitely deserves a trip back to see the rest.

I have an app for my phone that allows you to dictate stuff and e-mail it. I have been using it to take notes on my travels, so I don't forget the little things worth remembering. On the way home, I did some dictating. You need it to be REALLY quiet or you get some very funny stuff in the translation. Martha and I call it 'Siri speak". Here's some. Good luck. It's been a long day, time for my wine. —*Love, Valerie*

> *Mike said we were going to see old rock. Wyatt called several places and then finally called the church and ask if anybody there knew where the old horny housewives...*

October. Martha and I depart today on our much-anticipated trip. The Castles on the Rhine! Fifteen days gliding down the Rhine and Danube Rivers. We found out about this adventure through our Sisters Club. There will be 24 going from Bella Vista. Our first stop will be Amsterdam where we hope to visit the town where our Jansz Grandparent's came from.

Our time in Amsterdam was not as plentiful as we thought it was going to be. Two half days is all we had, so going to see the town where our grandparents came from will not be an option. By the time we got to Amsterdam from the airport it was about one in the afternoon. By the time we got to the ship we were tired from traveling, and looking forward to a little rest. I spent a good deal of that time trying to get my iPhone to work, with no luck. I guess it just needed a nap and some time to catch its breath. After dinner when we came back to our room it was working quite nicely.

After a shower, a nap, and (OK, let's all say it together) a glass of wine, I was ready to go out for our emergency meeting which is mandatory before you set sail on any cruise ship. This one was different. No sitting around in uncomfortable areas with orange life jackets on. No! We sat around the lounge sipping complimentary champagne and eating yummy little snacks while listening to the safety check.

I heard someone in our group talking about their medicine cabinet. I was thinking to myself, "They must have a suite! We don't have a medicine cabinet!" I have a thing for medicine cabinets. :) When we got back to our room I noticed our dressing table area had a large mirror with a handle on the bottom. I pulled on it and low and behold, there was the medicine cabinet. It's huge! It now holds some very important medicine. Two bottles of wine! Others were asking, "Have you tried to open your window?" We have not. The view from our window is at water level. We can see just fine thank you. There is a step up to the bathroom. I figure by day 13 or 14 I will remember it's there and stop stubbing my toes!! The weather has been absolutely beautiful.

So far, so good!

A few notes on our river trip. My curling iron had a bit of trouble with the power converter. As I used it, it kept getting hotter and hotter. I was oblivious to this so as I was getting to the end of my hair prep it took matters into its own hands and burned 1 1/2 inches off the right side of my hair. I, being right on top of my game, didn't notice until I had burned off a second section. So far three of us have tried to rectify this little dilemma. I have lots of hats and I will wear them. ;(

On our last night in Vienna we went to a concert. It was just for those of us on our ship. We had a warm greeting of champagne as we entered. The evening consisted of a small orchestra (9 pieces: 3 violins, 1 viola, 1 bass fiddle, a piano, a flute, a clarinet, and a percussionist). They were joined by 2 dancers and 2 opera singers. The music was wonderful, the singers were fabulous. The dancers... another story altogether. I realized as I was watching them that I had watched way too many nights of Dancing with the Stars. I was analyzing their performances as comments and numbers the judges might be giving them swam in my head. Suffice it to say the scores would have been in the 3 to 6 range and the comments would have been bleeped. I just stopped looking, closed my eyes and listened to the music.

While we were in Germany, they were celebrating the day the Berlin Wall came down. There was a 3-day Holiday and lots of festivities. One evening we went into town to enjoy dinner and a tasting of "New" wine. Apparently "New" wine has quite a kick. There were 3 different wines offered. Now this was not the usual tasting. They filled our glasses and left the bottle. I had made a deal with Martha at the beginning of the trip. When free wine was being offered she was not to refuse it, she hardly drinks at all, but was to graciously accept it and when my glass was empty I would trade hers for mine. All in all, a good deal I thought. During out appreciation of one of the bottles Martha spilled her glass. And she was the sober one! The next day I was glad she had as the wine did have that kick!

There was entertainment too! A gentleman sang and playing the accordion. A lady sang with him. There came a time in the evening when patron participation was asked for. The gentleman wanted to know if I could yodel. We were on our 3rd bottle of the vino and I gave it my best try. Amazingly enough, he said I needed more wine!

Martha and I are going through our "Bucket List". This trip was on it. The Panama Canal has been on mine too. However, we went through 69 locks on this trip and the Panama Canal has been scratched! We met a fun couple on the trip who we exchange e-mail and addresses with. I assured them they had a place, once occupied by the aforementioned Canal, on my Bucket List.

When we got home our time was upside down. We were in bed the first two nights at what we thought was 7:30 pm. and up at 4 am. It took us a week to get on the correct timeline. Then we discovered our clock was 1 hour fast and we had been

going to bed at 6:30 PM. Daylight savings time! The weather was perfect, the cruisers were a hoot, and it was a great trip.
—*Love, Valerie*

December. It's Dec 4th and time to head for CA for Christmas. Day one was a bit of a challenge. Martha had a schedule. None of this "crack of eleven thirty" stuff for her. We were on the road before 9:30! We had been packing the day before and I had failed to properly turn on the refrigerator. We stopped for a bite to eat and discovered that the Blueberries had started to defrost and had run (not a dainty stroll but a mad dash) all over the refrigerator and the floor. Blueberries again, some folks never learn.

We ate. Martha volunteered to drive while I cleaned up. She started driving; I had forgotten a cup of coffee in the microwave. It turned over and spilled all over the microwave and the stove. (Insert very bad golf words here!). A second later, another bump and turn, and Martha's bottle of iced tea came flying off the table and flew open. There was now coffee, blueberries, and iced tea on the floor, the stove, and the refrigerator. I was just finishing cleaning up that awful mess when Martha called "Valerie, look out the back window at the car. As I was crawling over the bed I heard an awful scraping sound. I decided I didn't need to look and hollered "Pull over!" We did, only to discover that the car was now only attached to the coach by the cables! We were almost done with the re-hooking up of the car when I *almost* stepped over the cables and did a "Face Plant on Hwy 40"! (Always looking for a new Country song.) Next stop, the hospital. I had 3 X-ray's each of my right knee, my left wrist and my left shoulder. Good news, nothing broken. While I was waiting to have my lip sewn up, I commented to Martha "This better not be a dry county, I didn't pack any wine. "By the time we were done, the pharmacy in the hospital was closed (closes at 7). When we got to Walmart their pharmacy was closed (also closes at 7) so no pain med's until morning and, adding insult to injury, it *IS* a dry county, so no wine.

We decided to pitch camp in Walmart's parking lot only to discover that the generator, while being quite ready to sing a happy tune, had no intention of turning over and making itself useful. I know for a fact that It did not get any of the before mentioned liquids spilled on it and therefore has no excuse for its bad behavior. No generator, no microwave. So, Martha had some nuts. I had an upset stomach so wasn't hungry. We had had enough fun for one day and went to bed around 8. I must confess that my prayers took on a less than normal thankfulness. I said that the traveling mercies I had prayed for had not exactly met my expectations and could He do a little better on day 2.

Day 2, although not as physically challenging was none the less a bust. Martha went into Walmart with my prescription at 9. It took them until almost 11 to get it ready.

Next stop, getting the generator to work. We went to a place that said, "come on down" only to wait until 5:30 for them to even look at it. They said something about the gas level. "Should I get some?" I asked. "I checked the propane level". "Oh no, if it's powered by propane you should be fine". They worked on it for about an hour and said sorry. They couldn't get it to work. I would have felt a whole lot worse if they had charged me for the 6 hours I had been sitting there!

Martha had decided on about hour 6 to get out the manual, and sure enough, if the gas gauge goes below 1/4 tank the generator won't start. On to the Flying J, they have everything, propane, gas, a dump site, overnight parking and a nice fellow who knew something. He filled the propane, I filled the gas, and we spent the night. The good news, we found another Walmart that didn't sell wine, but, believe it or not, sold pre-packaged Margarita's. We went to bed happy.

Day 3 was, for us, uneventful except for one little thing. The levelers are having some sort of a family fight and the ringing and dinging just wouldn't stop. Our dog Shera is in a delicate state of affairs. We just got an electronic fence for her and every time she hears a beep she thinks she is going to get a shock. She was shaking so hard her teeth were in danger of rattling out of her head. There was only one thing to do. I pulled off the freeway, got out my trusty Philips head screw driver, and removed the assembly for the levelers. Hi five? We drove for 11 hours, made up some lost time, found another Flying J and went to bed. Margarita happy again!

Another easy day. We needed to take on fresh water and empty the tanks, so we pulled into an RV park tonight. Martha jumped out of the RV so fast she missed the office and walked right into a private residence. The good news (besides the hysterical laughter) was that the only one home was a small dog that just wagged his tail at her. What does Martha have to say about this? "It said welcome on the door!"

In answer to some inquiries after sharing a photo of me from the face plant, no, I did not get this eye from beating the tar out of the first guy who wouldn't sell me some wine, nor did Martha and I take on some Biker Dudes.

Also, David's cousin said our adventures made his trip to Fort Lauderdale seem pretty tame, so Martha said she wanted to travel with him from now on. Should I be insulted?

Now for some good news, gas is under $3. The insurance company will pay to have the 2 teeth that took a hit in the fall, and are sitting back in the cheap seats, brought back to the front row. And, I am feeling much better today. —*Love, Valerie*

CHAPTER 6

Arkansas 2012

January. We are on our way home. 2 days so far and it has been the usual for us. The crack of 11:30 was but a dream. We left Simi Valley at 2:30 pm and headed for Banning, the farthest we thought we could get before dark. In our defense, it had been raining all day and that did slow down the packing process a bit.

My sisters arrived from Ventura and we were transferring Martha's stuff to both the car and the coach when Donald whispered in my ear, "Mom, Martha has a piece of furniture in Cyndi's car!" In answer to my question "What is it!" he said he didn't know but he was headed for the tape measure to make sure it would fit in my car. As my friend Charlotte would say, "Oy Vey!

The car and the coach, now loaded to the gills, off we went. As we were pulling in to the RV Park in Banning it started to snow. We were assured it wouldn't stick. Setting up the coach we couldn't get the lights to come on, our friend and travel companion, the GPS informed us she no longer had power, and the generator only groaned slightly when asked to pitch in.

After much anxiety, OK, full blown panic attack, and several phone conversations with our dear friend Elden, power was restored. The mechanic who had been working on the coach in CA (and who I am pretty darn sure had padded the bill) must have turned off the coach battery switch. David would have known to check that first, so this was a, Don't Look David, moment. My brain is still vacationing in the South of France and refuses to come back until I get a grip!

It poured all night and I hardly got any sleep. Good News: It was no longer snowing. Bad News: I wasn't sure we were out of flash flood danger, not that we had any reason to believe we were *IN* flash flood danger, and thoughts of beating the crap out of the previously mentioned mechanic, made sleep almost impossible. So, we are off to Phoenix to see our niece Adrienne and her new baby. —*Wish us luck, Valerie*

We were headed for Tucson when out of the blue I got an idea. "Martha, we should stop in Tucson and look at motor homes." I had looked at them with son Don while visiting in Simi Valley. I really wanted one a little shorter and easier to handle. I had looked at new and used and hadn't seen one I would trade mine for. It is 10 years old and all the little things that could go awry were doing so, and my Master Builder isn't around to fix things. *So...* we found a wholesale dealer and fell in love with a 2006 Dolphin. We spent 2 extra days in Tucson completing the deal and now are on our way again. P.S. We were, after all, almost out of gas and propane, and the coach, having been lived in for many weeks, was now in need of a good cleaning. It was time for a new one! Since neither one of us smoke we couldn't blame it on dirty ash trays. ;)

We were headed down the highway, Martha driving, me in the back unpacking and organizing our new, and sparkling clean space. Martha hollered for me to come up front as some man was waving and gesturing at her. I looked around and one of the tow bars had come lose and was flailing about bashing my CRV in the face and making a real mess. One of the bars holding the tow bar to the coach had come disconnected. (I really must figure out how to make that **not** happen again!) We searched the basement compartments and came up with something to hold it together, temporarily. We drove a few miles to WalMart. They didn't have the part and the salesman had given up trying to help me when I found a very large padlock and asked the salesman if it would be strong enough for the job. He said yes, so the tow bar is padlocked in place. We were a little worried about it so no book on CD for the rest of the evening's journey. We had to keep an eye and an ear out for trouble. The headlights work so much better on the Dolphin that I didn't mind driving after dark to make up some time.

Things have been too quiet (Yea, right!) so we are spending the night in Roswell New Mexico. Maybe some extraterrestrials will spice up our night. We *REALLY* hope to be home tomorrow. It's been almost 2 months! —*Love to all, Valerie*

Not being able to get inter-net service, or achieve warp speed, we did not make it home yesterday. We finished our book on tape and put the sound track of Camelot in the CD player this afternoon. The final notes were playing when we pulled through the Highland gates and turned on to our street. Sunday, 3:30 pm, and we are home, our own little Camelot.

Thanks for traveling with us and praying for us. Valerie

It's 10:00 am and I am making our smoothies. While putting the blueberries back in the freezer, I neglected to make sure the zip-lock bag was indeed zip-locked. Out they poured into the top bin and then on to the bottom bin. Blueberries again! I'm going to stop buying those ornery little troublemakers. And those little suckers stain! I was distressed, but not quite enough to call forth any "golf words". You know the ones you can't say in front of the grandkids. I decided I would get right to the job. Before they started to thaw and got more apt to give the freezer a permanent purpled hue. I would scoop them up with the ice scoop and just pop them back in the bag. I mean, it couldn't be dirty in there. All you ever do is put frozen food, straight out of the freezer in the market, and directly into the freezer at home. Right? Not so much... The first scoop was instantly redirected to the sink. I'm not sure just what was in the bottom of the bins, but it was not pretty. After removing everything, I tried to clean up the mess. The blueberries were thawing fast. The bins had to be removed, no easy chore I can tell you. The top bin is in there permanently! No doubt! After about twenty minutes of huffing and puffing I gave up on it. It's wire and could be dealt with. (Still no golf words)

The bottom bin took at least that long, and it took two of us to accomplish the task. It also took two of us a good five minutes to figure out how we got it out, so we could get the darn thing back in again.

My little ray of sunshine afterward, was just that. The sun came out. My reward for leaving out the golf words I'm sure. I was able sit on the deck, my favorite place, and drink my smoothie. You've got to take the "Rays" where you find them.
—*Love, Valerie*

February. Who would have thought it would come to this, the highlight of my day? "Oh goodie, Shera went to the bathroom in the yard!" But that's how it is. When we got home from California, we came in through the garage. When our neighbors came to bring us our mail, Shera went out onto the front porch to greet them. She took one look at the electronic fence flags in the yard and refused to go out again. I knew she was serious when she pooped on the rug in the hearth room, twice!

My days have been filled with trips to the dog park in the middle of the day, then around 9:00 PM back in the car to take her away from our street to someplace where she'll do her business. If she is not happy with the location I have selected for the evening she will get on the floor of the car, turned her back to me, and get a look on her face that I have become quite accustomed to. The one that means, not here mom!

The weather here has been beautiful which has been a bonus under the circumstances. So, I spent a couple of days out in the yard, sitting on the rim of my new flower bed, throwing cookies and liver treats around me so that she would venture off the porch to get them.

That strategy has been working quite well. We still go to the dog park because she loves it so, and it's great exercise for her. However, she will now go willingly out into the yard to do her business. Well, 4 feet into the yard anyway. I'm going to put the flags back up next week and then we'll see how it goes. This is me, full of optimism.

I have cut my hair, quite short. As you may recall, I burned a hunk of it off while on our cruise. After returning home I decided "Why not?" I hadn't cut my hair that short since 1976. I only remember the year as I had my brother cut it for me in anticipation of a 4-week recovery from surgery.

After 7 weeks on the road, we, my hair and I, came to an agreement. I wouldn't ask too much, and it would do something that I liked. I was OK with this pact, but found my new "Do" just so, so. A change of color would perk things up a bit. I decided on keeping the same color on the top and turning the hair from my temples down a reddish brown.

I selected a color and went to work. I put it on, washed it out, and dried it. The color was perfect... if I wanted to look like Raggedy Ann's mother. Two more trips to the store for new colors, and the growing fear that my hair might start falling out, resulted in a not so horrendous color. All in all, I like the look, and will continue to sort out the color.

It's a good thing Shera has had a change of heart as today it is snowing. Snow!! That means a Pajama Day! —*Love, Valerie*

April. Martha and I have the motor home in the driveway and we are getting ready to hit the road. *NO!* Not with my face this time. We needed to get it ready, gas, propane, water and more importantly, to charge my electric toothbrush and new electric wine opener. The trip preparations hit a bump when the wine opener charger could not be found. The search was launched! The sheets are not on the bed, the ice cube trays are not filled but after several hours of searching, the charger was found. Martha mistakenly suggested using the old manual one. *HAH!*

The search did, however, forestall the inevitable "Where the heck did I put that" portion of the trip. I had already found most of what we needed. :) The coach is new to us and by the time we got home in January, I honestly didn't care just where I put things.

So, we will be off to visit friends in Missouri, and visit the birthplace of Martha, Pella Iowa.

Wish us luck. You know we're going to need it. *Love, Valerie*

June. It's the end of June in beautiful, temperate, Bella Vista, AR. On Thursday it was 104!! We left Friday morning for California. It's got to be cooler there. We had a few stops to make on our way out of town, so we didn't get started any earlier than normal. The inevitable crack of 11:30.

We made it to Oklahoma City and beyond without me taking a nosedive on to Route 40. I didn't think it was necessary to even up the two sides of my mouth. I wasn't above a little bribery in convincing the car to stay put. I promised the car that if it would just hang on to the back of the motor coach, not be flailing around and disengaging itself, I would get her nose fixed when we got back to Arkansas. After getting herself loose two years in a row and getting banged in the snout by those heavy steel bars coming from the Coach, her face is pretty banged up!! And she's so vain!

The only automotive malfeasance came from the Coach. We like to listen to books on CD whiles traveling. After only one disc the darn thing decided she wasn't into that story, or any of the other ones we had brought along, so she just stopped working.

We were getting into Albuquerque around 6:30 P.M. so I called Best Buy to see if we could come in and get a new player installed. I was willing to go in, pick out a new one and spend the night in their parking lot if necessary. I mean, we were spending the night in Albuquerque any way. Their installation guys work from 10: A.M. to 5 P.M. Now, those hours sound like the kind of hours I would have liked to work, when I worked, but they were **not** working for me in this situation. Tomorrow will be another quiet day with no one reading to us.

We had a hard time finding the KOA. Finally found a parking enforcement gentleman who helped us find our way. That was after he informed us that, we *for sure*, couldn't stay in his Sam's Club parking lot!

We got signed in and were headed to our spot to open the wine. Martha said, "Sis, look at the speed sign." It said the speed limit was 6 1/8 miles per hour. Yes, 6 1/8. We were too tired by then to go any faster anyway. Keep us in your prayers. You know we need them. —*Love, Valerie*

Well our trip continued in what for us seems to be the norm. On Sunday when we started out, the rear camera wasn't working. We drove all day without it. This is not good!! Then we noticed that the refrigerator had turned off too. I was driving along, thinking about that, and remembering we were once again carrying frozen blueberries and what a mess they make when left to defrost in a motor home. So, I pulled over onto an off-ramp. I remembered seeing a fuse that said Refrig so I went looking for it. I found it and I have fuses! I replaced it and "Yea Howdy" it worked.

The next day, Monday, we stopped to get gas. This gave me some time to think. Never a good idea on the 4th day of a trip, standing out in the 100-degree heat in Needles CA. Today we would be getting to our first destination, my son Larry's house, to drop off Shera, We would be going through some pretty gnarly interchanges. Tough in a car, never mind a motorhome pulling a car, and not something I wanted to do with no eyes to the rear! Maybe there was a fuse for that too!!

We then started the "Changing of the fuses" debacle. Let me explain something first. With my stash of fuses is a fuse tester. Unfortunately, I don't have any idea how to use it. Also, I couldn't see a number on any of the fuses (bad lighting) and had been thanking my lucky stars that the one I used for the refrigerator had not blown the panel! I hadn't been able to see a number on it so I had just stuck with the same color.

I decided the thing to do was to buy some more fuses, so I would be sure of the size, and go from there. I asked the clerk how to tell if the fuse was good. Explanation received, I set out to take care of the situation. I replaced 2 bad fuses and the rear camera was still not working! At this point I was thinking bad golf words but was keeping them to myself.

There must be another fuse panel! I found it, under the steering wheel area, almost completely hidden and not so very easy to get to. Actually, almost *IMPOSSIBLE!* So I got out my trusty pliers and went to work, pulling each one out, checking it and, after buying more fuses because they were not the same *size*, replacing 2 bad ones.

The rear camera was still not working, and neither were the windows or any of the dash dials. Now not only could we not see behind us, we couldn't roll up the windows, remember how hot it was, or see how fast we were going, or if we were running out of gas! Golf words were in danger of becoming audible!

THE NEWS FROM ARKANSAS

A little good luck found us right then. There was a fix-it shop right across from where we were busy trying not to panic. There was a very nice man who restored the mess I had caused but still no camera. We looked through the Ford book and the Winnebago book. The only thing it said about the camera was where it was and that it had 2 settings, on & off. This I already knew!

I got on my iPhone and started making calls around the country until we found someone who could tell us where the power to the camera came from. We were on our way again.

While I was busy with this problem, Martha took Shera for a walk. She made a small error estimating the safety of a certain step and down she went. She looked like a turtle being flipped onto its back in slow motion. I don't remember if she asked me not to say that in the "News". I'll ask her right after I send this. She has some pretty good bruises including one that she says covers the whole left cheek of her bottom. She won't let me take a picture for the "News".

We also discovered if we reset the radio (anywhere from 1 to 8 times) we could get it to play our book

For those of you who have wondered why no plans have been made to see you, this trip is mostly about our Mom. We put her on Hospice care on Wed. and I am spending most of my time with her. We call her the Energizer Bunny though, so she may recharge.

All your prayers must have been working. We are now safely parked in Ventura with all systems working. *Love, Valerie*

During our stay in Simi Valley I was shopping. Among my purchases was a bottle of wine. I know no surprise there. The surprise was that I was carded! Yes! They asked for my ID! *NO, NO, NO,* it had absolutely *nothing* to do with the fact that they card every living soul who buys alcohol in Target!

However, it did help to inspire me to ride the Manta rollercoaster at Sea World with my granddaughter Kalyn. You could tell how fast we were going by the way my hair was standing straight back. She hates the picture, but I laugh out loud every time I look at it. *Love, Valerie*

September. I have been very busy since I got home at the end of July. Here are the highlights.

There is a beautiful Veterans Memorial here in Bella Vista. On Sept 8th we celebrated the completion with a very wonderful and moving ceremony. I was there to honor David. I had purchased a tablet in the final wall for him. There are 4,848 tablets honoring veterans from 23 states.

Between the June/July draught, and the dog, my front lawn was all but dead. I decided to get some Astro-turf. After getting the estimate, ($13,000.00!) and picking myself up off the ground, I decided that I would settle for a strip down the driveway and put rocks on the rest. Low maintenance! That's my goal!

My Altrusa ladies service group delivered 1600 dictionaries to all the 3rd grade classes in the 4 towns around here. I personally delivered 150 to the third graders at the Gravette School, six classrooms of eager learners. We are also busy getting ready for a spaghetti dinner and 40 table card party fund raising event. I'll be glad when those are done. I am also redoing the hand book, doing all the fliers, and newspaper articles for the club. Someone told them I could write!

Martha is still working very hard getting ready for the craft fair. I am now helping her put some beads on the bags. You know how I love bling!

Take a nap for me. I don't have time. Love, Valerie

October. A note to my children... I have some news that I am now ready to share. I have a beau. His name is Bob Edney. He is wonderfully kind with just enough ornery to make him fun. I think he is very special and he thinks I am too.

We have golfed, danced, laughed and cried together. He lost his wife last year. We both feel very lucky to have met. When discussing this I told him I thought we were "Shot in the butt with luck to have met". After clarifying that that was indeed a *good* thing, he agreed.

I'm happy, Mom

November. Today has been a long and interesting day. I went in to get a regular haircut that usually takes me about one half hour. That was at 9 AM. I didn't get out of there until 1:20 PM. I was having my haircut and got to talking to the girl about hair color and how much she would charge to do the job for me. She was kind enough not to point out how much better it would probably look if she did. We did the long No bleach version. I sat and read my book, which I have on my iPhone, for several hours. But the color wasn't right when we were finished, so the hair was re-washed, and the bleach version was done. By then my phone had a dead battery. So, my darling sister Martha was called, and she brought me the charger, so I could continue to read while this process was underway. Well, she was only 5 minutes away. ;) So, there I was, the day already half gone.

Next stop the RV lot. I had a dead battery there also, so we went down and jumpstarted it. Then into town to have the battery checked. It is now 1 o'clock in the morning and the darn thing is still charging. I hope that it won't have to be replaced.

While we were there getting that looked at, I had them look at the left front headlight. It had stopped working on my last trip to California. After much testing and checking it turned out that the reason it wasn't working was the fuse that made it work was missing, probably, residue from the fuse debacle on my last trip to California. Apparently, I took that one out and forgot to replace it. The gentleman at the repair shop however was quite impressed with the fact that I knew where both of the handbooks were and that I could find them quickly. He was also impressed by the fact that I had a plethora of fuses, both large and small, for him to choose from. I didn't bother to tell him just who was responsible for this mess. No need to bother his busy little head with those trivial facts.

Tomorrow I have an appointment with a dentist In Joplin Missouri, an hour's drive from here, but it's where the insurance company has decided I can go get my teeth fixed. The teeth that were injured when I fell on Highway 40 last December. I have to claim part of the responsibility for the delay. Well, maybe 70%, for not being diligent, but it certainly is time to get them fixed. I hope this dentist turns out to be satisfactory with the insurance company. The last one wasn't, and I need get the work done. So here I am at 1 o'clock in the morning getting the news out, having a little glass of wine and a Snickers peanut butter bar, hoping to get some sleep. It's a one hour drive tomorrow and I have to be there at 8:45 AM!!

My friend Bob said my hair looks beautiful and it was worth all the time I spent getting it done but I really should sleep sitting up in a chair so as not to mess it up. Well, I am sitting up in a chair but obviously I am not sleeping.

It is now the next day and it has been a really good one. The old dentist said I needed at least 3 root canals. This new guy said, "Not so!" I don't need any. A BIG high five to the insurance company for sending me to MO. (It actually hurt to say that.) Next stop for my teeth, braces. They really must go back to where they belong. They don't meet in the front and I am a little weary of eating stuff through the side of my mouth.

The coach does not need a new battery!! —*Love, Valerie*

November. It was the middle of Nov. and it was time to get plans made for my trip to CA. I normally like to be there from Thanksgiving to Christmas. Martha, my usual traveling companion had decided she didn't want to be gone so long so I made arrangements for her to fly out on Dec 10th. My new beau, Bob, had lost his wife the day before Thanksgiving last year so this year was an extremely hard time for him. I decided to stay in Bella Vista and spend the holiday with him.

He wanted to do something completely different and un-thanksgiving-like, so we went to a local casino. The only thing even remotely Thanksgivingish was the big turkey dinner. We had a great time. Then it was time to get the coach ready and hit the road.

Apparently, there is still no one but me who thinks me driving out to CA with only my trusty iPhone and Rottweiler is a dandy idea!

Martha tried to enlist Bob's help by telling him she was very worried about me making the trip alone. She drove that point home by telling him I was not a good driver and that I was stubborn and hardheaded. Although I thought her assessment of me was a *little* harsh, it seems to have done the trick and Bob has decided to make the trip with me. Good news. I want him to meet my family.

The left front headlight on the coach was out so we took the coach to Bob's brother's work to get it fixed. While we were there I was told the tires had dried out and were something to think about. So, *I'm* thinking... when I get back from CA. The next day I took the coach in for servicing and a checkup. I'm sure glad I did. There was a seal that had decayed and had to be replaced. Good thing they saw it. It was right over the bed! "Oh, and by the way", they said, your tires are dried up and you should think about having them replaced. Should we draw up an estimate?" I'm still thinking, "After CA" but an estimate wouldn't hurt.

Let me tell you, Bob had other plans! The tires were dangerous and should *NOT* be driven to CA or anywhere else except back to the RV place for new ones. Hey! They had lots of tread! What did I know? The coach got new tires and our trip was postponed a few days. —*Love to all, Valerie*

December. The first night out we pulled into a Walmart, put out the slides, and poured some drinks, Rum and Coke for him, Vodka and cranberry juice for me. We got ready to enjoy our evening. I tried to get the TV to work so we could watch a movie. No luck. After 30 min. of trying I noticed that despite having the generator on the microwave wasn't working nor were any of the electrical plugs that usually come on when the generator is on. Oh dear! No coffee in the morning and no heat that night were my first thoughts. Heat also comes from the batteries so at least that wasn't an issue. I called my friend and my "I'm on the road and need help" buddy, Eldon. He had lots of good advice, none of which worked. Then a man from another coach came by. He knew more about coaches than we did. *Not a tough job to top that.* He spent about 45 min crawling in and around the coach to no avail. However, he and his wife were very nice and invited us into their coach to see all their renovations and new do-dads. So, the evening wasn't a total loss. ;)

The next night we pulled into a casino and while we were hooking up I saw what the problem was. This is the fourth coach I have traveled in. It is the first one where when you unplug from an outside source you have to re-plug it into a port in the coach. If you don't, nothing works! I felt both relieved and astounded. Relieved that no costly repairs were needed and astounded at my stupidity for not remembering this very important step when we left home. I do make user errors, but I usually don't make the same mistake again. Everything is now working, and we are moving right along. All's well that ends well, or so I hope. Keep us in your prayers!

Day 3, coach wise, was uneventful but the evening was a hoot. We decided to stay at a Pilot truck stop. Bob was driving and over my frantic "No not there and what are you doing?" He backed, yes backed, the coach and the car into one of the parking places. We had a grand view of all the trucks coming in, getting gas, and either going their merry way or parking. We poured some wine and settled in to observe. I didn't know Bob had some training and expertise in backing those BIG RIGS into those slots, but he did. The commentary was most entertaining. "Oh yea, he's good. Oh no, he'll never make that. Watch out for that guy!" Two glasses of wine and a Snickers ice cream bar and we were ready to call it a night.

Day 4 was humiliating. I wanted to go to a little town called Quartz Hill. I had grown up there and wanted to show it to Bob and see for myself the changes. So, when the GPS said to turn left, I went straight. Bob was concerned about me disobeying the GPS but I told him I knew where I was going, not to worry.

The wind was blowing, the dust was turning the sky grey, and we were driving in what turned out to be uncharted territory. I was lost. Here we were, parked on a road, too narrow to turn around on, that looked like it just went on forever. **BOB** "Maybe you can turn around in that field." **ME** "It looks too soft." **BOB** "Do you want me to go check?" **ME** "Oh, would you?" So, there's Bob, walking around in the howling wind and blowing dust, checking out the field.

He came back with this advice. "I think you can make it, but once you start through the field, don't stop!" To the sound of

"Don't stop, don't stop, and don't stop" I made the turn. We turned the GPS back on and with no more arguments from me we headed for Simi Valley.

We got to my son Donald's street and unhooked the car. Its batteries were dead, an inevitable side effect of towing a CRV. Donald said no problem, his street was all downhill. So, we put Bob behind the wheel and gave the car a shove. He negotiated the corner and glided to a stop. "Don't worry about the car" I said. "I brought my mobile jumper cable thing and we can start it with that." Unfortunately, it turned out that these wonderful little gadgets have a life span of about 4 years and the 4 years were up. It now needed to be replaced. Ugh, let's think about that in the morning...

In the morning I turned on the generator and started a pot of coffee. Half way through the pot the generator stopped working. "What happened?" inquired Bob. Oh, I knew what had happened, I remembered. If the gas tank gets below 1/4 the generator will no longer work. Bob's repeated requests to stop for gas had been overruled in favor of waiting till the morning when we could go to a station near Donald's house where we could dump the black and grey tanks, and get gas and propane. All in one easy stop. I called Donald. "We need coffee and jumper cables." He had the coffee. I sent Bob for the coffee while I got the coach ready to go.

On the way to the gas station Bob mentioned that he was hungry. "There's a McDonalds right on the next corner. I'll stop and let you out for breakfast and pick you up when I'm done." The man made a wise choice. After inquiring if he could bring me anything, he jumped out and went for it.

Donald and Debbie were kind enough to host a get-together with my son Larry's family, so I could introduce them all to Bob. After dealing with the coach we went shopping for a new jumper cable system and were the last to arrive.

Bob dubbed the trip "An interesting and exhausting experience." I was hoping the trip would go without incident but that would have been something of a miracle for me. Hmmm, better late than never, all's well that ends well. I think I need of a new mantra.

However, the day was not over. Thinking (always a mistake) that the trip to Ventura would charge up the car batteries, I decided to drive the coach and have Bob follow in the car. I realized right away that I didn't have my glasses. I pulled over and started a search of the coach. I called Don to see if he had them at the house… Nope, not here. Bob called from the car to see what the matter was. "Nothing" I said. "All's good." I set off again. I've driven this route many times. I could do it without my glasses.

I see a green sign, I start to turn, the freeway? No, the Presidential Library. I forge ahead. Another green sign, I turn right. I still don't know where we are, but it was not the freeway. Bob calls again. (Did I mention that it was after dark and raining?) I tell him I don't have my glasses, I can't see, and he will have to drive the coach and I will follow him.

He programs the GPS with Cyndi's address and we are off. We are in constant contact via the cell phones and he tells me where the GPS is telling him to get off the freeway. That's too far, I think. So, I tell him to get off at the next exit, to get behind me and I will lead the way to my sisters. He makes a valiant effort to deter me, but I prevail. After making the turn to Cyndi's house, I go a mile or so and realize I'm not where I think I am. OH NO! I can't tell him I'm lost again. I just can't. The phone rings. "You're lost aren't you" says my honeys voice. "Yes" I answer meekly. "I thought so" he says. "The GPS keeps saying recalculating and getting farther and farther from our destination" I get in behind the coach and follow.

When we get to Cyndi's house I say, "This is Bob, the sweetest, kindest, most patient man in the whole world and I don't deserve him. I need a stiff drink!" Proving my praise was justified, he went back out to the coach for the vodka and cranberry juice. We got to talking about some wonderful Mexican food we had had on our journey and Larry, Cyndi's wonderful husband, said he was hungry for guacamole and proceeded to get out 5 avocados and make fresh guacamole. He even went to the store for fresh chips! So, there we were, at 9:30 PM, at the end of a trying day, safe and sound, having drinks, eating a wonderful snack, and laughing. —*Life just doesn't get any better than that. Love, Valerie*

It's Day 5 and we are on our way to Orange County to introduce Bob to my daughter Denise and her family. My Son in-law Kevin went all out. When we got there, we were greeted by the smell of bacon cooking. Bacon, one of my favorite things! The family greeted us too. :-) Kevin and my granddaughter Samantha had a treat in store for us. The first course was cinnamon persimmons and figs, cut in half, topped with bacon and goat cheese and cooked in the oven. Yum! That was followed by a salad with candied pecans and cranberries. Samantha served course three, a 4-cheese pasta, and that was followed by scallops and Brussels sprouts cooked with more bacon. I'm not describing it properly, but it was a feast!

Day 6 found me taking Bob to the airport for his trip home. He had not flown since 9/11 and was unprepared for the changes. We went early, and he invited me to come to the gate with him, maybe have a snack. I informed him that I would not be allowed past security. He was carrying some items that caused some concern for security, so he had to go through twice. He told them he hadn't flown in about 20 years and didn't know the rules. Then he told them he was from Arkansas. He said they all had a good laugh and sent him through. I'm going to miss him...

It is now day 7 and we have gotten the news that my Mom is in a coma and it is just a matter of time. The rest of my trip

is on hold. Pray that God takes her, so she can be with her Mother. She has made it plain that that is what she wanted.
—*Love to all, Valerie*

God did take my mom. She has gone to be with her mother. I can just picture them, hugging and laughing at the joy of being together. There are no arrangements to be made. My Mom had donated her body to the UCLA Medical School and she has been whisked away. I have been grieving and saying my goodbyes to her for some time now, so her loss is easier for me to accept. Goodbye Mom. Give my love to my Davids
—*Love, Valerie*

CHAPTER 7

Arkansas News 2013

January. Martha and I are home. Was the trip home uneventful?? "Well, of course not." We needed new tires, again!! When we had the "new" tires put on in AR the bozo that put them on put the front hub caps on upside down, lucky for me, so we couldn't get to the tire stems to check air pressure. They just didn't look right. I had asked about the tire pressure when I picked up the coach. They looked low to me. They are at 50 lbs. they told me, just where they should be. (I know better now!) Bob and I checked all 4 tires and bumped them up to 60 lbs. My son Don tried to get the hubs off the front tires and couldn't, again lucky for me, so he took the coach down to Americas Tires where he was told they were not the correct tires for the coach and it was dangerous to drive on them. They could blow! We had only gone 1600 miles on them already!

I called Camping World in AR and they were great. They called Americas Tires, checked out the situation, gave them the corporate credit card, and told them to fix the problem. I spent a few hours at America's Tires, Camping World sent $1,200.00, and new tires with 80 lbs. of pressure were on the coach. We needed the big ones!!

The second morning of the trip home we got up to find the coach batteries dead and the generator not coming on. This was a new one for me! I tried the engine and that came on. We tried to pull the slides in and "Thank you God" they did come in. "Oh, we'll drive this morning and that will charge them up" I told Martha with more certainty than I was feeling. What I was really thinking was "Golf Words!"

We drove all morning and the generator, and the batteries were still in the "Were on vacation" mode. It was time to call Eldon... again. It appears the "Live and Learn" portion of traveling in a motor home has not yet come to an end. Eldon informed me that the battery boost button works on the generator also... And it does! The generator came on and I immediately turned on the microwave and made myself a cup of coffee. A girl has to have her coffee... and her priorities.

Another thing that had not been working all morning was our new radio. We were in the middle of a very good book! It turned out that the button that turns on the radio is right next to the battery boost button. I gave it a little push and yippee, the radio was working again. I must say, the radio not working was causing many more "golf words" than the fact that the generator wasn't working, and we had no microwave! Priorities again.

Not wanting to be left out of the excitement, the backup camera stopped working. HA! I've got its number. It's 5! A new number 5 fuse and we were ready to rock and roll.

The new tires delayed our departure, so we had to hit the road hard. We were up early, on the road, driving after dark, and stopping for the night in truck stops. Debbie had made us a BIG bowl of mac & cheese to sustain us on our journey. I warmed it up and ate it while Martha drove, and she did the same while I drove. It was raining most of the time but were not rookies anymore. We took it in stride and prayed we would not get snow.

I had missed Bob & he had missed me. He told us to call when we were close, and he would go to the house and turn up the heat and order us a pizza. He knows how to keep us moving!

So, today is the first day of a new year and we are taking it easy. There is a light dusting of snow coming down now which is wonderful and beautiful, now that we are no longer on the road. I'm spending the day at Bob's, so I won't be tempted to clean or unpack the coach. When learning of this tactic of mine Martha announced that she had opened the slide for the bedroom and gotten her toothbrush. Her plan for the day, to brush her teeth then go next door to get the mail. Atta girl! Happy New Year to all, —*Love, Valerie*

March. Oh dear. I fear this trip is going to be just like the rest of our trips, *eventful!*

This is not our usual trip, no motor home. We are moving Martha to Mesa Arizona. She had been working on the plan for some time. Her preparation work was meticulously made. She had spoken to U-Haul and they had assured her that a 17-foot truck would move a two-bedroom house. Arrangements to pick it up on Wednesday, March 20 were made and carried out.

The movers arrived, took one look at the truck and said it might be too small. They would go ahead and start and hope for the best… uh oh! The plan had been for Martha and I and all three cats, in three separate cat carriers, to be in the cab of the truck. I had been asking everyone I knew to pray for us. Hard!

The truck was NOT large enough. A second U-Haul was needed to tow behind the first one and someone was going to have to drive the car.

Thursday morning rolled around. Martha and I got the cats into their carriers. I got the books on CD's set up for her. "Well Sis" I said, "good news. We are right on time, it is the crack of 11:30!"

Bob was there to see us off. He asked Martha if we were going to trade off driving the vehicles. She said "No, the cats would drive Valerie crazy" She was correct! One of those cats didn't shut up for 3 hours! Martha hit a bump; the CD player fell on the floor, the book turned off, and the cat shut up. Martha decided to do without the book.

I have never traveled with cats before. Apparently, you can't stop by the side of the road, put on their leashes and tell them to do their business. (It always works with Shera) Martha explained to me that cats get up in the morning, eat, poop, and sleep for most of the rest of the day. A piece of the old cake.... She forgot to tell the cats.

One of her cats didn't make it to the motel. It did its business in its carrier. (Ever smell cat poop!) Martha picked up the offending feline, tucked its head under her arm, took her in to the bathroom and gave her hindquarters a good scrub! The cat spent several minutes hopping around and shaking her tail at us. We spent the night at a Motel 6. I am pretty sure it was one of the *FIRST* in the line, but they did keep the light on for us. Still smiling, —*Valerie.*

Leaving last night's aged abode, one of the cats clawed a hole in her carrier so two cats were put into one. After driving couple of hours one of them asked for a potty stop. How?! I don't know, but I took Martha's word for it. It was the same one that had received the impromptu bath the night before, so Martha pulled over and let her out of the carrier to ride free hoping she would use the litter box that was placed on the floor. By the time we stopped for gas two cats were running loose in the cab of the truck and no one had used the litter box. I was quite happy at that point to be alone in the car.

When we arrived at this evenings Motel 6, (At least 3 decades newer than last night) the loose cats were not in the mood to get back in the carrier. After about 20 minutes of chasing them a very tired Martha was seriously thinking about leaving them in the truck for the night. She finally got hold of one, put her in her carrier and exclaimed "I'm not moving again until I'm down to one cat!" Me? I don't think I ever want to do it again!! As we were leaving to go get something to eat, we hollered through the door to the two cats inside the room, "If someone comes to steal you we will not pay the ransom. We will be down to the required one cat!"

We found a nice Route 66 Coffee Shop and shared a meal. For desert I had banana hot fudge Sunday and Martha had sweet potato fries. It had been a trying day.

Looking forward to Arizona. Love, Valerie

PS Sending the News from the road is *still* tricky!

April. My friend Charlotte and I are on our way to Barcelona. On the 5-hour flight from LA to New York we had a snack service. A very cold cheese and turkey (I think) sandwich which we had to pay for! 5 hours and not a proper meal service! We are cutting them some slack though as we were not charged for the luggage we checked. Mine alone may have sunk the Titanic.

Now we are on the 2nd leg of our journey. We applied at the terminal for up-grades but were informed that all business and 1st class passengers had had the poor form to show up. Snack time on this flight included complimentary wine. Now we're talking! I'm not sure just how many compliments I can get but I intend to find out!

Our dinner was a choice of chicken or pasta. We chose the chicken which turned out to be a very good choice. The roll was as cold as the earlier sandwich had been. I balanced my entree on it to warm it while I ate my salad. I decided not to use the time-honored approach invented by my son Donald of putting it under my arm for warming.

This flight will be an 8-hour journey, so naps may be in order. If we had gotten into 1st class, I would already be in the prone position. *Love to all, Valerie.*

They woke us up on the plane and served us warm, (yes warm!) croissants, orange juice and coffee. We got off the plane, picked up our luggage, and went to meet our ride. We went to the sign that said, "Drivers waiting area" and there was no driver there waiting for us. He must not have seen the sign. Charlotte called the number on the transfer that we had, and no one answered. She tried again, And again. Then at my suggestion she called our travel agent... Apparently it was almost midnight in California, so we woke her up. I for one was not the least bit sorry... We were hanging around an airport in a foreign land with no help in site!

We ended up taking a taxi to the hotel. The hotel is beautiful. It's an old hotel with bunches of charm. The gentleman who came out to open the door for us was dressed in livery, was very, very, polite and took our luggage. It was very early in the morning here, so our rooms were not ready and wouldn't be ready for several hours. They put us in a temporary room and said we could stay there until our room was ready.

A snack and 2 rooms later we were finally settled in. We both took a nap, for most of the rest of the day. I finally got up and told Charlotte I was going to take a shower. "Now!" she said. I said "Yes." and when I came out in my PJ's she said, "Aren't we going to get some dinner??"

After some conversation we decided on room service. We had a yummy meal along with vodka tonics. We're ready to hit the hay again. Traveling seems to be more tiring than I remembered. —*Love to all, Valerie.*

We have boarded our ship and are ready to spend the next 7 days cruising the Mediterranean.

Charlotte and I are making friends everywhere we go. We seem to be having money problems. We haven't gotten any euros so today in the middle of our shore trip we wanted a cup of coffee. I gave the tour guide a five-dollar bill and she gave us four euros. We looked at the menu and it said we could get a cup of decaf for €1.3. I said we wanted 2 Cups of decaf. He came out with these giant, (for Europe), cups of coffee and said owed €6.5. When I explained we only had 4 he gave me a *LOOK* and repeated his request. We added $2:00 U.S. He came, picked up our funds, and left. He was back at warp speed to repeat his request for payment. Oh dear! It still wasn't enough. We added 2 more U.S. dollars. At that point he smiled, took the cash and left us there looking and feeling pretty dumb but laughing.

In Barcelona when we took the cab to the hotel the cab driver didn't have a credit card machine and was looking quite upset. Lucky for us, the doorman could see that there was a problem and came out to pay the fare. Like I said, making friends everywhere.

It's cold, windy and the water is quite choppy! We are on the ships tender. The captain (obviously inept) anchored the ship out in the ocean therefore making the tender necessary. I had to wear a scarf to keep the wind from blowing my hair completely off!

We were starting to wish we had stayed onboard today. Then we got to San Rafael. A little town about 40 minutes from Cannes and it's absolutely beautiful. The only thing we have seen more of than castles and churches is cranes. The whole French Rivera is being restored! We are staying on the ship for the next two days. No outings. Need a little rest.

All the drinks on the ship, including alcohol, are included in our fare. A day of facials and massages are in order. *And* we have procured six decks of cards. Ah yes, life is good!

We have our plans for today. Sleep in, have a late breakfast, and find some place to put our feet up and read. The first 2 parts of the plan went so well Charlotte had to check her watch to see if my "Good Morning" greeting to a fellow passenger was correct or if it was, indeed, afternoon.

I just glanced over at Charlotte and it appears she has gotten the nap portion of the day confused with the reading portion of the day.

We have been doing some shopping. Next to us in port are some beautiful yachts. Charlotte has chosen a blue yacht and I will have to make do with a white one. I believe it comes with a captain. I can easily afford it. I won $69.00 playing roulette last night!

First let me say that the Internet service is terrible! I'm going to try one more time to send this.

This is the day I have been waiting for. Monte Carlo, Monaco! The Casino! Mon Deau! I have been practicing my French phrases. I can Mercy bow cups with the best of them now! But for me it was not to happen. I am here in my room, with a Z-PAC and I have been Nebulized! In English that means antibiotics and a mask allowing me to breathe medicated mist. The doctor said to sit up, eat fruit, and drink lots of water and herbal tea. To add insult to injury, alcohol is off limits. The good news was that the movie "The America President" was on TV today. It's one of my all-time favorites. I'm still looking for a bright side.

It's the next day and I'm not feeling better. Don't know when I've felt so rotten. Back to the medical center. The doctor asked me something that sounded suspiciously like. "Do you always look like this? I was nebulized again, got 2 X-rays of my chest, and had blood drawn. More souvenirs! I get to take the X-rays and medical forms home in the hopes my insurance company will pick up the bill. Stop laughing!! So now I sit here waiting for Charlotte to return from her outing and hoping like crazy she is getting good pictures. Forget it. The doctor said I should lie down and now and I'm starting to get grumpy. I'm turning in. —*Ugh, Valerie*

It has been a long and tiring trip home. I am still sick and waiting to board yet another plane in Los Angeles for the final flight to Bella Vista. My flight has been cancelled and I am huddled on a seat in the airport. When I look up, I see my son-in-law Kevin. He comes over to me and I say. "Believe it or not Kevin, I feel worse than I look". And believe me I looked terrible. If I hadn't felt so rotten, I would have been insulted that he had the nerve to recognize me in that condition.

As it turns out we were both experiencing delays. Kevin took pity on me and took me to the Admirals Club where he is a member. He got me a hot drink and a snack and said he had to go catch his flight. "Oh Dear" I said, "Do I have to leave the club?" He assured me he had explained my situation to the nice man working there and he would keep track of my flight and let me know when it was time to fly. Many thanks to Kevin, his mother would be so proud. —*Love, Valerie*

It's Thursday morning. I've been home for whole week. It must be time to hit the road again... On Wednesday I had my hair done. Then I had a brainstorm. Uh oh! While we were on vacation Charlotte had worn a shower cap to bed to keep her hair from getting messed up. I decided to try that. I donned a shower cap from my overnight case and hit the hay. I got up Thursday morning and raced to the mirror to see how this had worked! Apparently, you're supposed to make sure the shower cap is dry on the inside before you put it on your head. I looked like someone had attached a wet Brillo pad to my head! I plugged in the curling iron and got to work. It doesn't look like the hairdresser did it, but it'll have to do. My friend Bobbie will be here in a couple of minutes! We are going to the 3-day Altrusa Conference. This will be a first for me.

I had packed the bare necessities. Bobby on the other hand had packed four bottles of wine, all open, previously sampled for safety sake I'm sure, snacks, playing cards, and little paper plates. We were ready to hit the road!

Bobby was driving and had decided to take the back way. She had our destination programmed into her GPS, a very polite version, that doesn't disgustedly say "Recalculating" but rather says "Please make a legal U-turn" when you've deviated from her desired route.

When we had been on the road, failing to follow her instructions, for so long that the GPS was no longer speaking to us, we stopped for directions and a cappuccino.

The directions went something like this. "Go back out to the road and turn right. You'll get to the top of a hill and see a beautiful valley. Keep going until you come to a traffic light, I think the name of it is Cherokee something. Go through the town and the road will dip and go under some railroad tracks. Right after that, and just before the Easy Mart, make a left turn. I don't really know the name of that street either." Believe it or not, we took those "directions" and headed on down the road!

Tucking the location of quite a few casinos away for future use, and taking at least one more wrong turn, we eventually got to the Embassy Suites in Norman Oklahoma. We went into the hotel and started checking in for the conference. The ladies said they did not have our money or registration! We called Carolyn, who was in charge of sending in our papers, to find out what had happened. No answer! The nice ladies said not to worry; they would take care of us. They said they only had two spots left for dinner would we mind being seated with the Honor Guard gentlemen. "Oh no", we said "That sounds just fine". So, one half hour later we had our credentials, we had our name tags, we were ready to go! That's when we discovered that we had all but joined the D.A.R., The Daughters of the American Revolution. We were at the wrong sign up table. Altrusa was down the hall. That meant no dinner with the honor guard either. Drat the luck! I had better luck at lunch the second day. They had a 50-50 drawing and I won $250.00!

During opening ceremonies, our own club President donned white gloves and carried in the Arkansas Flag while the delegates sang the Arkansas State song. Luckily, the words to all the states songs were printed in the handbook. Everyone seemed to already know the one for "Oklahoma".

This was my first conference of any kind. It was enjoyable, informative, and exhausting. There was a reception afterwards which Bobby and I decided not to attend. If it had been an open bar we might have been interested, but since it was not, we went back to our room, got in our jammies, and made ourselves comfortable.

On Sunday morning we got up, had our complimentary breakfast and headed down the road. We made a couple of stops on the way home, at the previously mentioned casinos, where I won $50, and we were still home before dark. All in all, a grand weekend. —*Love, Valerie*

September. Bob has wanted to take me to Hot Springs Village for five days of golf. I have been out of town a lot so we had decided on this is the week. We were up at six, yes six AM, and out of the house by seven. Bob's been packing for several days. Therefore, the Tequila for the margaritas, the chips, snacks, and of course the golf clubs were ready to go.

Northwest Arkansas had been experiencing some heavy rainstorms. It looked like it was clearing up, so off we went, straight into the *HEART* of the storm. Now, Bob does not carry an umbrella in his car. I carry two in mine, but a fat lot of good that was going to do us. We got settled in our lovely cottage overlooking the golf course and took off to the market. I grabbed a small towel to put over my head to keep the rain that was still sprinkling, off my hair. A golf Vacation! That deserves an all-American dinner. So, we bought fried chicken, corn on the cob, and watermelon, with apple pie and ice cream for dessert.

While we were checking out of the market it started to pour. The box boy asked if we were from Hot Springs Village. I told him we were from Bella Vista. Bob said, "Don't we look like locals?" The box boy said "No, but because of the flooding a lot of the roads are being closed." It seems they have had 9 inches in 3 days!

I put the towel over my shoulders and a plastic bag over my head and headed for the car. I opened the door, wondered where the doggie bag had come from, I knew we hadn't left anything in the car, and looked up to see I was facing a very large dog! Luckily, it was a nice dog and I was faster than him or her. I got the door closed to that car and went around and got in the right car! After all, all sedans look the same to me and I was half blinded by the bag! Dinner was delicious, and we ate so much we can hardly move. Just one of my normal trips! More fun tomorrow! —*Love, Valerie*

June. The summer of 2013 has come and gone. There were no motor home trips to entertain the troops with, but it did have its eventful moments.

At the end of June, I flew out to CA to pick up Sara and Kalyn, my 2, 13-year-old grandgirls, for an open-ended visit. That's right, they were invited to come and stay as long as they wanted. Yes, I can hear you all asking, "Has she lost her mind??" My mind has been in the lost and found too many times to count so let's not go there again.

We were off to a good start. The plane was on time, our seats were all together and Kalyn, our quite nervous first-time flier, had failed to hyperventilate. Who could ask for more? To my surprise, the girls did not want to share a room. Luckily,

I have 2 rooms downstairs, so it was not a problem. It actually turned out to be a blessing.

After a fun day of grocery shopping and bowling the girls had had enough of me and retired downstairs. I was upstairs resting. Big surprise, not as young as I once was. The next thing I knew there were tears, and unkind things being said. I'm a pro... I know how to handle these things. I sent them to their respective rooms and told them to stay there until the next day. Like I said two rooms? A blessing! They called their fathers.

The next day was more bowling, the girls baking cake, lots of giggling, a great time being had by all. We ate, and the girls bid me farewell and were off downstairs. It was then a repeat of the night before including the calls to their fathers. Those calls were followed by return calls, to me, from the fathers. I kept reassuring the dads that their darlings were, in fact having a wonderful time and had been sent to their respective rooms to get a good night sleep. I said I had half a notion to take the phones away from them. "Oh, we do that at ten each night when she is at home" replied one of my boys. Eureka!

At ten the next evening when the girls were heading downstairs I put out my hands and asked for the phones. The hue and cry were loud and long, but I got the phones. The answer to "But why Grandma?" was. "You have a wonderful time with me, and each other, all day. Then you go downstairs, get tired and grumpy, and call *MY BOYS* and upset them and I won't have it!

On the fourth night I asked for the phones. "We haven't had a fight in two days grandma. Can we keep our phones? Please, please, please!" I relented; I let them have the phones, along with this warning. "If you make a call to California and upset my boys you won't see those phones again until we get to the airport and you go home!" They never had another quarrel the rest of the 2 ½ weeks they were here. What they won't do for those phones...

We did more bowling, went to the pool, and went to the Water Park. The Park was in Hot Springs, a little over 3 hours away so we had an overnight at a motel.

As it turns out, we have a drive through zoo here. Now those who stay up late also arise late so, with the exception of the Hot Springs trip, we never got an early start. When we got to the Zoo, the lady said to go see the babies first because they get put to bed first, and then we could make a leisurely tour of the park. We did just that. In between those two things Kalyn and I took a ride on a camel! It wasn't even "Hump Day"!! Sara didn't want to have anything to do with that dirty beast, but she did agree to take our picture.

The animals were great; we saw a fawn just after it was born trying to get its long legs under it. We took pictures of many animals with their noses pressed up against the windows of the car. Then I saw a mother doe actually giving birth! The car was stopped, the engine turned off and three very excited girls settled in to watch. It was a great time to be sitting there. The animals were migrating to their evening resting places and we watched the parade go by.

It then occurred to me that we hadn't seen anyone else for a while. "You know girls, it's getting kind of late. We should go". The "But the baby hasn't been born yet" replies stopped and were replaced by "Let's go grandma!", when I added, "We don't want to get locked in here over night" "What will we do if we are locked in grandma". "Oh, don't worry, if push comes to shove, we can call 911". Ever looking on the bright side. Plus, I have traveled with me before…

We were indeed locked in. Luckily, they hadn't locked the restrooms because that's where grandma went first! By the time I came out, Kalyn had looked up the website on her phone and called the owner to tell her of our plight. "Well how did you get in?" the owner wanted to know. "We've been here all day" Kalyn told her. "I'll be right down" was her reply.

When she got there, she asked if anyone had told us that they close at five. "Well, no", came our answer. It was seven o'clock. "Well girls" I said, "You probably don't read the "News" I send to your parents when I am traveling, but believe me, this is what traveling with grandma is all about. Always an adventure.

The second wave of grandkids was soon to arrive, along with their "other" grandmother. I had one week to rest. —*Love to all, Valerie*

> ***A note from California:*** *You are the only person this could happen to!*

July. When my grandchildren, Alex and Samantha were here at the end of July with their other grandma, Betty, we went for a nature walk at Tanyard Creek. It was 100 degrees and we had no map. We took that walk in 2009 when Samantha and Alex were here with their parents and I'm pretty sure Kevin, my son-in-law, had one. We had been walking for what we all agreed was "Long enough!" and were having a difference of opinion on the correct direction out. Betty asked what we would do if we couldn't find our way. "Oh, don't worry" I said, "I could call Bob and have him come over to the parking lot and blow the horn until we show up." We found our way and didn't have to make the call, but I think it might have been a more fitting conclusion to one of my adventures if we had. —*Love, Valerie*

November. The end of 2013 is right around the bend. The weather here has been un-predictable. Two weeks ago, we were playing golf in shirt sleeves. Today it has barely gotten to 30 degrees and snow flurries are forecast. I hope we don't get too much "Weather". I have two trips to get ready for.

I am preparing for the trips. I will be pampering myself! Well, maybe not on Monday. That is the day of my colonoscopy. But on Tuesday I have a 90-min. massage at 10:00 a.m., at 1:15 p.m. I get my hair done, at 1:45 p.m. I get my nails done and at 4:00 p.m. I meet with my insurance man. (Not a good idea for me to hit the road with my insurance in question.)

My sister Cyndi said it sounded like fun but wanted to how I could my get my hair done a half hour before I got my nails done. Well. it only takes her 15 minutes from start to finish to do my hair. Remember I don't have very much of it. Also, my nail lady is very understanding.

Thanksgiving was another new adventure for me. No California. Last year we went to a casino! This year we went to Carbondale IL. This summer when Betty, came for a visit bringing with her "Our" grandchildren, we spent two days here in Bella Vista and then another two in Branson. I guess the visit went well. She invited me for Thanksgiving. Denise, Kevin, and the kids were going to be there! Bob and I went and had a wonderful time. Twenty-four Morefield's gathered for Thanksgiving dinner on Thursday and on Saturday we went to the farm where Betty grew up for a wonderful meal attended by about double that number.

Five members of my family have birthdays on Dec. 1st. One of them is Samantha so we went to Betty and Bob's for brunch and the Happy Birthday song. For us it was time to hit the road for home. We stopped at a gas station that had cranky pumps. The first one we tried wasn't working at all! Bob had some trouble paying at the next one. It kept asking for his ZIP Code and when he entered it, it didn't believe him, and would ask again. He finally had to go inside to pay. The lady in there called him babe so many times he was getting ready to break into the Sonny & Char song "I've got you Babe". But they had gas, coffee, cappuccinos, and restrooms so we left there happy.

Since we left home on Wednesday, Bob has driven about 800 miles. He's getting tired of it I can tell by the increased speed, increased changing of lanes, and increased impatience with people who are not going as fast as he would like, or at the very least getting out of this way! That noise you just heard in the background was him shouting "Aw come on now, Tattletale!!!" His frame of mind was not improved by not being able to get the Kansas City Chiefs football game on the radio. I told him I would download the NFL radio site to my iPhone. "Is there a charge?" he asked. I told him "$.99 but please do *not* tell my kids I'm spending their inheritance in such a frivolous way."

Now that Bob had past all those pesky people, I had to inform him that I needed a potty stop. He says he's "Not happy" but he's smiling so everything is okay. I hope! Surprise, there was a line, mostly women. When the last gentleman left, I decided to take the road less traveled. I went into the men's room. One of the "Accommodations" was broken but lucky for me it was the one where you have stand up to do your business. I guess I better pass up coffee on this stop.

There is a new Mexican restaurant about two miles from our house. We are quite taken with the quality of the food and the size of the Margaritas. We stopped there and ate, drank, and watched the end of the game. The Chiefs got their keesters handed to them which was bad news for Bob but good news for me. That made $3.00 I won over the weekend! Next… Pick up the coach and get ready to drive to CA for Christmas! Happy Thanksgiving Everyone! —*Love, Valerie.*

December. On Dec. 6th my son Donald will fly into Arkansas. He will arrive at 2:30 p.m. and we hope to be on the road to CA, in the motor home, no later than 3:30 p.m. Will we make it? I'll let you know. It takes 3 1/2 days to make the trip, barring any unforeseen delays. Who Me? And Donald wants to be back at work on Tuesday. A road trip with my son! Yippee!

The weather here was beautiful, the day before yesterday, yesterday and today. However, they are forecasting snow in Bella Vista on Friday. Tomorrow we're supposed to get icy rain and by Friday 2 to 3 inches of snow!! Taking off in the motor home! *Not* looking like a good idea.

It's been snowing for hours. The trip has been delayed. Plan B looks like me flying out there and flying back sometime in January ;(

My son has been called. I will cancel his flight. Alma has been called. She will watch Shera for an extended time thru January. Plan B is being arranged.

Yay for us!! American canceled the flight so the miles will be put back into my account. They even refunded the $5.00-dollar charge for, "Who knows what". The snow is still coming down with a vengeance. Except for the change in plans for my trip, I LOVE it!!

After sending a picture of the snow to Don, he said it was beautiful and my Grandgirl Sara. would love it. He suggested I FaceTime with her the next day and take her out to see it. He then reminded me that she's 14 and sleeps till noon." My answer? "Remember I'm 72 and I sleep until noon also."

We have 7 inches of snow on the driveway. "Bob the Brave" took my car out for a spin. I have all wheel drive and he thought it might make it up our little hill, out of the cul-de-sac, and up the steeper road to his house. There was no shoveling. He just backed out of the garage and went home! My little car had no problems at all. It scurried up, over, and around. I won't be paying for snow removal this year. I'll just get in and go. A good thing too, there is a Mahjong game I want to go to on Monday! —*Love to all, Valerie*

Since my trip to CA was delayed due to the snow, taking the coach was no longer an option. The coach had been un-winterized and parked in the driveway before we left for IL. The gentleman at Camping World was sure I was mistaken (crazy) when I had asked to have it un-winterized in Nov. The trip to CA was explained and the job was done. Now it had to be undone.

THE NEWS FROM ARKANSAS

A new date for departure was set. I made my flight plans for Dec. 16th. Thinking there would be no stories to write about on this more conventional trip. My baggage did not get lost; it was at the baggage claim before I was. Yippee.!

As I was exiting the terminal, I saw the Budget shuttle bus leaving the curb. I hollered, jumped up and down and waved. It did not see me. A good thing too, getting my paperwork out so I would be ready when the next bus came, I discovered I had rented from Alamo.

Alamo has a policy I was unaware of. You must have a confirmed return flight in order to rent a car with a debit card. I have 3 debit/credit cards and none of them would do. Could I call for a credit card number? No, the person must be there in person, with the card, to sign a contract! I explained... I had rented the car for a month with no real return date. I was here to see my children and grandchildren for Christmas. How long I would stay was still in question. By now I was speaking to a third person, the *supervisor*. (David would have been so proud.) He explained "The Policy" to me one more time. He wanted to know if one of my children could come over and do the honors. After telling him that one lived at the far end of Simi Valley and the other one in Rancho Santa Margarita, his comment was, "OH, the far ends of the earth." I turned on my blank, I don't know what to do now, sorrowful look and keeping eye contact with him, just stopped talking. After a few minutes of that he just smiled and said he was going to make an exception this time, and to please remember this for future visits. I picked out a bright blue (So I would be able to spot it right away in a parking lot) Nisan Versa, and was on my way.

There was a stalled car on the freeway, so I was going 10 miles an hour in 6 lanes of the 405freeway. So, I was able to check in with Bob, turn on my Kenny Rogers Christmas album, and resurrect my Christmas spirit. —*Merry Christmas to all, Love, Valerie.*

On New Year's Eve I decided to take a walk. I have been eating too much junk food, and anything else I could reach, so wanted to get some much-needed exercise. First, I took all the snacks that were in the motor coach and threw them in the trash! Then I decided, a walk to get my nails done was just the thing. Not really sure how far my destination was, about a 25 to 30-minute drive, I grabbed a bottle of water, some tissues, my back pack, and prepared to leave.

When I told my daughter-in-law Luz of my plans, she wanted to know where the nail shop was. "OH, on Ventura Blvd. just before Fallbrook." was my reply. As her eyebrows shot up to her hair line she asked if I had my phone and if I was sure I wanted to walk as that seemed like an awfully long way. I think she wanted to ask if I had lost my mind, but she just told me to be careful and call if I needed anything. I didn't get the earliest of starts, probably around the crack of 2:30, but decided to stop at Walmart and refill some prescriptions that had to be transferred from Arkansas. BIG surprise! It took me a lot longer than I thought to get that done, and I ended up leaving Walmart without my prescription.

When I walked out of Walmart it was dark! These short days are really very annoying. Then, much to my surprise, and yours I'm sure, my stellar sense of direction had deserted me and I took off for the nail shop, in the wrong direction. After wandering around in an unfamiliar neighborhood for a while, I found Fallbrook, a street I was familiar with. I looked at my phone to check the time, only to discover it was almost 6:00 pm. I was tired. I figured it was about another 1/2 hour walk to the nail shop whose closing time was 7:00 pm.

I called Luz. The conversation went something like this. **Me** "Honey, can you come and pick me up?" **Luz** "Sure, where are you?" **Me** "On Fallbrook." **Luz** "Fallbrook and?" **Me** "Hmmm, I'm not sure but it's past Walmart." **Luz** "Mother, I need the name of the cross street." **Me** "I can't see one from here.

I'll cross over and try to find one." I found the name of the street and she was on her way. She called from the car... **Luz** "Are you past the fire station?" **Me** "Yes." **Luz** "Are you past Oxnard?" **Me** "No not that far. Stop! You just passed me!"

When I got in the car she grabbed my backpack, tossed it in the back seat and announced "Mother, you're in time out!" At that very moment, my phone rang. It was Larry. "Hi Mom, your GPS broken?" he chuckled.

Happy New Year! Love, Valerie.

CHAPTER 8

Arkansas News 2014

January. I got a text complete with pictures of Bella Lane this morning. Bob wanted me to see the snow. I sent a picture of me, in straw hat and sunglasses, enjoying a drink and snacks at a little spot overlooking the ocean. I'm visiting with Denise, Kevin and the grandkids and we were having a lovely warm day.

Still trying to get some exercise, we took the dog for a walk a couple of times. In this neighborhood there actually are places along the sidewalk where, if you have had the poor form to venture out without the proper necessities, you can stop, get a plastic bag, and stash your doggie trash, in a provided receptacle. When I'm feeling cheeky I call this area Yuppyville. It is quite a lovely place.

I first used the term when my daughter informed me that my grandchildren, who I think were in the second or third grade, were required to learn a foreign language. Being less than a ½ day from the Mexican border, I assumed it was Spanish. Denise said that that was what she had thought too, but they were learning Chinese. I started to laugh and said, "Chinese! Of course, they are, you do live in Yuppyville after all."

I'm having a marvelous time, but Bob and Bella Lane are calling. I will be glad to be home. —*Love, Valerie*

February, Spring is in the air! The trees are starting to bud, flowers are coming up in my garden, it was light until almost 7:00 pm last night, soon I will be drinking Margarita's on the deck... Oh yes, and when I got up this morning, it was 24 degrees. And yet, I still love Arkansas! *Love, Valerie.*

March. I had an adventure last week. I didn't have to get the coach out, didn't have to pack, and didn't even have to leave town. All I had to do was drive a few miles to my friend Bobbie's and pull into her driveway. The problems started when I was backing out of her driveway. I felt a crunch and heard a car horn start to blare. I had backed into a gentleman who was driving his nice, white, Ford 450 pickup truck. You know, one of the really nice ones, with four doors. I got out of my car and went around to see what I had done. I apologized and told him I was so very sorry. His answer? "Well didn't you see me?" At that point Bobbie came out of her house to see what was going on and volunteered go back in the house and make a copy of my insurance card.

I followed her. She was upset because of the way the other driver was acting. I said, "Well Bobbie, I just ran into his car!" She said "I know but we've already called the police. They said they'd be right here." Oh dear... I hid in the house with Bobbie until the police car showed up. The police arrived. The other gentleman, whose name was Keith, pointed at Bobby and said she wasn't even in the accident but was trying to put her two cents worth in! The policeman gave him a stern warning and said that nobody was going to be fighting here. I told him not to worry, he wouldn't have to get his night stick out and beat us. The policeman was doing his due diligence. He wanted names, addresses, insurance cards, and just to make sure we were who we said we were, birth dates. I believe I may have whispered an unkind remark to Bobbie about the fact that I was 12 years older than Keith, but he was really looking the worse for wear.

After all was said and done about the accident, the policeman invited me to the back of my car and asked, "Do you see anything wrong with this picture?" It seems my tags were overdue. A year overdue! He said if he had seen it parked somewhere, he would have had it towed. I guess he figured I had, had enough trouble for one day so he just gave me a warning and told me to take care of it, pronto!

I called Bob and he offered to go with me. I started looking for my registration. Lucky for me, that was one thing the officer had not asked me for. I looked in the car glove box where I assured Bob, I always put it. Not there.... Bob wanted to know if I held title on the car and if so, where was it? Ah ha! The safe! I quickly found the little piece of paper I keep the combination on. I have not committed that piece of information to memory. Three times around before the first number, change directions, three times around before the next, change directions, then two times before the third, or something like that. I only get into the safe two or three times a year. I need what's left of my mind for more important things. Like finding the pink slip for my car which was not in the safe! Bob decided to call the revenue office and plead my case. They said to bring me on down.

When we got there, they asked me for my registration. As I was trying to inform them of my plight, my mind was very busy packing for that trip to the South of France it always takes whenever I am confronted with a tricky situation that has me flummoxed. Bob took over answering most of the questions. Their next question was "Are you sure that's your plate number? We don't show that license number for any vehicle at all." Bob went out, paper and pencil in hand, to check it out. Folks, it's a personalized plate, 4MS VAL. Even with my brain on its little vacation, I knew that.

"When did you buy the car, and did you register it for your personal property tax?" were the next questions. The blank look on my face said it all. Oh, how I wish I could go on vacation with that traitor, my brain.

When you buy a car in CA the salesman goes to the DMV and your registration comes in the mail. It's a done deal!

Not so AR! After the dealership has done "who knows what!" and has handed you a stack of paper you are quite sure caused the demise of a whole tree, you have to check back in a week, or so, and return for some official paperwork. That little piece of information was not mentioned in the hour it took to finalize the deal. Then you must go to the Revenue Office, register your vehicle, and pay the personal property tax. I learned that only three states have a personal property tax! Lucky me...

Next stop, the dealership. Oh yes, they had my paperwork! They had it neatly filed away and were happy to give it to me! It was, however, too late to go back to the revenue office.

Eight AM the next day, my phone rang, "Is this Valerie Katz?" "Yes" I say. It was the officer from the day before. "Ms. Katz, what color is your car?" "It's a light greenish color" I reply. "Well" he says, "The license number 4MS VAL belongs to a 2010 red Honda CRV, not a 2012 green Honda CRV." "Yes, yes", I say. "I transferred it from my 2010, I'm going to take care of it today!" He gave me his version of "See that you do" and hung up.

I had a dental appointment, in Joplin MO! I started to hot foot it over to the Revenue office. Then I realized if I went there first, I would be late for my dental appointment, so I made a quick U-turn and dumped a full cup of coffee onto the passenger seat. Oh dear....

I made my dental apt. Things at the Revenue Office went smoothly. My car seats are black, so the stain does not show.

Now, here is the irony. When I traded in my 2010 CRV, I didn't really *need* a new car. I usually keep my cars until there is a darn good reason for a new one. The things that sold me on getting a new one were, (1) having Blue Tooth technology, and... (2) having a backup camera so I would be less likely to back into anyone!!

Forget bringing my mind back. I'm going to join it in the peace and quiet of the south of France. —*Love, Valerie.*

April. My iPhone... I now tell folks that I don't know what I would do without it. It holds my life in its sim-card. Can I come out and play bridge or join you for lunch? What are the flight numbers for my trip to CA? When is that hair appointment? I ask my iPhone and out comes the answer. It has been giving me some trouble lately. It would only take pictures when it was good and ready, sometimes not until the next day. It's conversations with the Bluetooth in my car were sketchy, and it was dropping data off my calendar. I don't know how many times in the past couple of months I have said to Bob, "Honey, I know I put that in my phone calendar, but I just can't find it!" Someone needs to knock on my head and find out if I'm in there!

Yesterday, after an important event, I was downloading pictures to my computer. Pictures, I had taken, but not seen, as my little friend would not show anything but those tiny thumbnails, and it quit! In its defense, I will say, it did give me enough of those pictures to write the press release I need to post before, it expired.

Sooo, today being such a beautiful day, I will not be sitting on the deck with a cup of coffee, getting some much-needed rest, and watching the birds. I will head to the AT&T store to get the up grade my son-in-law Kevin has been telling me I could get for the past year. Oh, how I wish I had listened. One and a half hours in the AT&T store and I am the proud owner of the iPhone 5s.

It did not go smoothly. After several attempts to prove me wrong, Steve, the AT&T guy, agreed with me, the phone was indeed, dead. He said we couldn't even get my information (MY LIFE!) off of it. You will all be proud of me, I did not cry... I did, after taking a few minutes to just shake my head, ask him, "What about my cloud". That is where, I've been told, your data goes if you remember to save it. I had saved my contacts! He pulled them up on his computer. We needed it to contact Kevin. He handles all cell-phone data and up-grade matters.

Steve had several ideas on ways to purchase a new one. My answer to these questions was as firm as the one about getting the phone in the first place. "We have to ask Kevin." When Kevin didn't answer Steve's call, I used his phone and called Denise for help. "Did you try to text him" she wanted to know. *I can't, my phone is dead.* She handled the problem and Kevin called Steve.

The new phone was slow to complete its up-loading. It wasn't until I was at the beauty salon for a cut and color (that appointment I remembered) that It chimed in and gave me several voice memos. Of the six that were there, only two were distressing. I had made a promise to a friend to do something with her last night and had made arrangements with another one for lunch today.

I have some fences to mend.

Every time I go to CA I learn something new about my phone. The best... how to talk, text and e-mail by talking to Siri.

I'm leaving for CA on Sat. I was distressed about the 2 layovers I had to take, therefore making my trip last the whole day. Not anymore. I will take the day trying to coax my brain into coming back from its vacation and trying to remember how to relax. —*Prayers for my sanity please, Love, Valerie.*

May. My Mother's Day Trip 2014, I'm going to CA to see my daughter Lili and her husband Scott, who is my second cousin.

THE NEWS FROM ARKANSAS

No, no, it's not like it sounds. Lili was married to my son David and when he died, she took his place in my heart as my daughter. Scott was a 45-year-old bachelor and his dad liked to say he never had any luck finding a wife until he met one at a family reunion.

So, there I was, making arrangements to fly out to CA to see them. They now live in central CA, so I don't normally see them on my trips to see my Southern CA family. It was their turn! I was using my frequent flier miles for the trip. The flights are difficult. Our little airport is small and has just gotten its second runway. The one in Santa Rosa, CA is even smaller than ours.

When the American Air mileage lady and I were done making the arrangements she said my lay-over in Los Angeles was too long (no argument here) so it had to be considered a destination and 3 frequent flier trip miles were required. My "You've got to be kidding, this *is* taking place all in the same day, isn't it?!" seemed to get her attention. She said for $150.00 I could purchase the "hop" down to Los Angeles and save those miles. Wonderful! Now I could see all my children! More plans to make.

Denise said she would host a Mom's Day party the following Sat. Things were taking shape nicely.

I started my journey at 7:00 A.M... Twelve hours later I was in Santa Rosa. Arkansas to Chicago; flight delayed because traffic too heavy over Chicago, change of planes and terminals because big planes and little planes can't use the same runways. Not to worry, I had a lay-over that gave me more than enough time to accomplish this. Chicago to Los Angeles; a similar adventure only his time from large to small planes. I was now running a little behind schedule, but Lili was not disturbed. They are only about 15 min. from the airport and monitoring my arrival was easy. There is only *one* flight into Santa Rosa at night. I was on it.

VALERIE KATZ

I was packing for my flight back to L.A the next day when I got a text from American Air. Your flight has been cancelled, call this number to reschedule. "Oh Dear."

My little "hop" from Santa Rosa to L.A. was rescheduled... It would require an early morning trip to the little airport to get a voucher for a 2-hour bus trip, *with* a change of busses, to the Oakland airport, and a new flight on Delta to L.A. The day had only just begun, and I was already bushed. I took a nap.
—*Love to all, Valerie*

My time in CA seeing kids, grandkids, sisters, brother and friends was wonderful. Sister Martha was in town visiting from Mesa AZ. A big bonus! I did not have my motor home, so I was sort of living out of the trunk of my rental car, dirty clothes in, clean clothes out. The bag that was holding all things pertaining to my face and hair, and my PJ's, were carried in to wherever I landed that day. It was working surprisingly well.

Unfortunately, when I was doing some necessary rearranging in the trunk, I laid the keys down and when finished, closed the trunk with the keys still in it. I was at Don's house and not one of us had AAA, so I called my insurance carrier. They said they would be happy to send someone out, but they don't cover rental cars.

It took the gentleman a good 20 min. to get the car unlocked, all the while delivering ominous warnings about anti-theft safeguards and the probability that breaking into the car might disable the trunk latch therefore making the whole process moot. Lucky for me, this was not the case, *so*, many $"s later I had my keys.

Then, looking for something in the trunk (vitally important I'm sure, but for the life of me I can't remember what), and getting ready for a very quick lunch with a still working friend, I did it again, this time at Larry's house.

In panic mode I called Luz to see if she could come home and loan me her car. She was busy taking daughter Amanda to work and picking daughter Kalyn up from school but agreed to come and drop me off for my lunch date. She then picked me up and found a neighbor, who did have AAA, and I once again had my keys. —*Love to all, Valerie*

It was Baseball Nut time again at the Baskin Robbins ice-cream parlor. It is a vanilla ice-cream with a raspberry swirl and cashew nuts. Yummm! Unfortunately, they only have it three months out of the year.

While Mary and I were shopping in her quaint little town she mentioned there was a Baskin Robbins. We went in and while *she* was picking out two pints to share with the folks at home, *I* was inquiring as to the availability of my favorite flavor. The answer was yes! Mary had made her decision and the nice lady was waiting for mine. "I'm trying to decide on one scoop or two" I said. "If you get two the waffle cone is free" came her response. "Well then, two it is" came a very quick response from me. Mary said it was too bad we had purchased the ice-cream, or we could stop for lunch. "I'm eating my lunch" I said.

This was the start of a Baseball Nut journey... once with Mary, once with Denise and her family, twice with my brother, and a whopping six times with Larry and his girls. It would have been seven, but I played Mahjong one night so had to miss it. I always got the free cone too. No Baseball Nut with Don's family. Debbie made Dutch Apple pie and cinnamon rolls. I was getting worried about being able to get into my jeans for the trip home, but Debbie said not to worry, they would throw a Mumu over me.

"When is your flight home Mom/Valerie" was a common question from family and friends. "Sat. the 31st" was my reply. Friday night I retrieved my suitcase from the trunk of the car along with the things I had shopped for, must haves to be sure, I *was* flying, and dirty clothes. I didn't want to carry all that heavy hair and face stuff, so I packed all but the bare essentials in my check-in suitcase. My flight was at 12:30 pm so Larry took Kalyn and me to breakfast and bid me goodbye.

I turned in the rental car and headed for my flight. I dragged my new suitcase a long way before arriving at the proper place to check it in. It is the first trip that I had used my new suitcase and I was very excited to have one that swivels in all directions. Mine did not. It wasn't crazy about the thought of tipping and being pulled either. It is going back!

I got to the nice ticket lady. I gave her my driver's license and she started looking for my flight. "What flight are you on?" was followed by "Where are you going?" and "What airport do you fly into?" Uh oh! My flight had already left... the day before. Oh Dear, time to re-book my flight. I could leave that day if I wanted to spend $600.00. Or I could us 25,000 frequent flier miles, the lesser 12,500-mile seats had already been spoken for. Not liking either of those, I could re-book the next day, no charge, but with one lay-over in Dallas. I took Dallas and asked if I could check that darn suitcase. I think she was feeling badly for me by then, so she was very sweet when she delivered her answer, "Sorry, security you know."

At that point all I wanted to do was book a room somewhere and sleep until my 7:00 am flight the next day.

As I was searching for the rental car pick-up spot I heard an announcement for the fly-away bus. I had forgotten all about that mode of transport! I caught the bus and called Larry for a ride back to his place. After his first "You've got to be kidding me" came "You did this for more Baseball Nut didn't you."

I was not going to get into my suitcase! I stayed in my clothes and retrieved my pajamas from my carry on. Along with Larry I arose at 4:30 am for yet another trip to the airport. I had put my pajamas back in my suitcase in the trunk but forgot to zip it up. So, when Larry pulled it out my clothes went flying. I did make my flight.

As we were making our approach to my lovely little airport, I looked out the window at the rolling green fields and all the beautiful green trees and thought, "My Ozarks, I'm home". — *Tired but happy, Valerie.*

July. I have been to CA again, a short trip, just 8 days. No travel problems to report. I have been putting on weight so when I got back home, I was going to join Jenny Craig, (a weight loss system) and try to get back into my clothes.

Here is part one of the problem. Bob is like a Jewish Grandmother, eat, eat, Valerie. It's good for you. My friend Charlotte, who *is* a Jewish grandmother, sent a text to me while I was still at the Los Angeles airport. *"Call me when you are on your way. I have cereal, donuts, wine, and West Wing. Luv Char."*

We both believe West Wing was the best show on TV... *EVER*, so when we get together, we eat, play Mahjong, eat, and watch West Wing. I was to be at her house for 1 night. She had purchased 2 cinnamon rolls, 2 apple fritters, 2 glazed donuts and 2 filled donuts, one with raspberry and one with lemon. My first question was "Are we having a party? And the second one "Are you crazy?" A moot point for sure. Here is part two of the problem. I ate my fair share and we finished off the rest for breakfast. I have lost *all* good judgment. —*Love to all, Valerie*

Twenty-four hours at the Katz house...

July 27, 10:30 pm. Bob says goodnight and goes home. I do my "Getting ready for bed" routine. (This seems to take longer the older I get.)

11:15. I'm off to bed. Early for me but I must be up at 7:30 for a doctor visit.

11:20 Alarms start blaring all over the house. I think it is the burglar alarm and can't understand why it won't stop when I turn it off. Shera is freaking out!

11:25. I figure it out, get the ladder, and try to take the battery out of the carbon monoxide alarm that I think is the ringleader.

11:30. I call Bob and put Shera out on the deck.

11:35. I get the battery out of the alarm and the clanging keeps going. I test the battery and it is dead. I don't have a spare! I always keep a spare!

11:45. I call Bob to ask him if Casey's is open 24 hours. When the answer is yes, I tell him I am going to get a replacement battery. Good News! He is already on his way over and will stop and pick one up.

July 28, 12:00. a.m. Bob arrives with the battery, we put in the new one, and it makes absolutely no difference. The clanging continues. It is very hard for us to communicate as the noise level is unbelievable and someone has her hands over her ears.

12:10 to 1:00. The only thing that will stop the noise is to disconnect the alarms; no easy feat as they are hard wired and have batteries. We first unplugged them from the walls. Still clanging. Then we went around again and removed all the batteries. There are 7 of those critters in this house and they are loud! Peace was restored, and Shera was coaxed back into the house with the promise of a cookie.

1:20 I'm feeling a little woozy and Bob thinks we should call and report that we have had this problem with the carbon monoxide alarms. I call 911 and get the Bella Vista Police Dept. who redirects me to the Fire Dept. I am told to go outside and wait for them.

1:40. Bob goes home to get 6 more batteries. We needed those little square ones and he has a bunch of them at home.

1:50. The fire department shows up, checks out the house, no carbon monoxide. Bob returns, batteries in hand. The wonderful Firefighters want to make sure all is well before they leave so they put all the new batteries in the alarms and reconnect them to the walls. "God Bless Them."

2:30. Bob returns home, Shera and I return to our beds. Yee gods!

9 am I go to my new gynecologist. In the course of her "Exam" she asks about my vaginal estrogen ring. "How many of them do you have in there?" "Oh, just one." is my reply. "May I take it out if I put it back in?" she wants to know. I am puzzled but say it's OK. I'm telling you; it was just like one of those little cars in the circus when all those clowns come out of it. She proceeded to take 3 of those rings out of me! "I don't know how that happened" I say. "I take one out and put a new one in." "Well" she laughed, "I think you forgot to take one out a couple of times." My only clue as to how that happened is a couple of times, I decided to do without them as they are quite expensive and must have just left the old one in there. No wonder they have been so hard to insert!

10:30 pm. It is once again bedtime. Bob goes to wash his hands and says, "Honey, there is no water pressure." He checks around the inside of the house, no problems. He goes out front and there appears to be a broken water line and the water is gushing out.

10:45. I find the phone number for after-hours water problems. My call goes through to the Bella Vista Police Dept. I hand the phone to Bob and he explains the problem. Names and addresses are asked for. "I'm Bob Edney" he says, "but this is my girlfriend Valerie Katz's home". "Oh yes" she says "*I think I talked to her just last night...*" She will call around and get us some help. Bob and I spring into action. The coffee maker is filled with water and an extra pitcher is filled. Never a dull moment...

It is now almost 3 am. There is still much going on out front, but they are on their own. I must get some sleep. The alarms just wanted me to know they needed new batteries. Bob say's we should change them every 6 months. I think once a year should do it. I'm not asking Shera for her opinion. I would be up on that ladder constantly! —*Love, Valerie.*

September. It's the start of a new week. Yet again, I am over scheduled. I promised myself when David and I moved here that I would not let that happen... so much for grand plans.

We had two visitors to my Altrusa Club meeting last month. One introduced herself the way most of the ladies tend to do. "Hello, my name is_____. I'm a retired school teacher, business woman, etc. and I can't wait to get started!"

The other one said "Hello, my name is_____. My husband and I moved here and retired. My goal is to sit on my deck and drink coffee. Ah yes, (Substitute vino for coffee) me too. *Love to all, Valerie*

November. It was time to get ready to go to California. Since I was going to have to be gone for quite some time it was very necessary to take the coach. The weatherman kept threatening snow so not wanting to have a repeat of last year, (winterize, un-winterize, winterize, make flight plans), I didn't bring it home until the last min. Bob was going with me and my last min. plans to un-winterize it myself wasn't going over to well with him. He and Minnie went to Camping World to get the job done.

The coach (Minnie) was an absolute necessity because of the length of my visit. My return being undecided except for a two-week return, by air, for a cruise Bob and I were taking in Jan.

I need to take my lovely Shera with me and that seems like it's going to be a problem. She is having a little trouble getting around and it's going to be hard to get her in the coach. She weighs 80 pounds and I for one can't lift her. Bob and I have been talking about building a ramp to help me get her up the stairs. Lord knows I have enough trouble getting up and down them myself. —*Love to all, Valerie*

Today Shera went to be with David. She was having trouble getting around. I took her to the vet on Tuesday. The vet looked her over, checked all her blood stuff, took all kinds of tests and gave her some more pain medication for her arthritis. Wednesday, she kept getting worse. Thursday morning, she couldn't get up at all, so we had to lift her and carry her back to the vet. We left her there for a while and the vet called and gave me a list of things we could do for her. Then she said something about quality-of-life. By then I was crying. She said I could call her after I had a chance to think about it. I got dressed and went right down there and we put her to sleep. The vet thanked me for coming in, putting her down and not putting her through anymore trauma. The vet and the two girls that always work there and I were all sitting on the floor around her and they all gave me a hug and told me to take my time. I'm going to have her cremated and scatter her ashes out with David's. —*Love to all, Valerie*

We are ready for the trip to CA. At 11:25 we were 40 miles from home. It has been the "usual" beginning of a trip for me. Bob is dealing with it all in surprisingly good fashion. We made it to Clinton OK. Oklahoma?

I tried to get a movie going on an old laptop I keep in the coach only to be reminded it has no speakers, therefore no sound. Then I tried David's old DVD player, only to get spinning noises and a notice that there was no disc in the player. My somewhat insistent response of "Yes there is!" had no effect what's so ever. Bob was in bed waiting for the movie. By the time I switched to my new tablet he was asleep. I hooked up my ear buds, tuned in Netflix, and enjoyed a Kevin Spacy TV show I had wanted to see.

Believe it or not we were back on the road at 8:00 AM. Bob was not going for that crack of 11:30 stuff. He said I could continue sleeping but it was time to hit the road. I got up and made coffee! Bless Bob! The first 1 1/2 hrs., he was driving in fog. The wiper on the driver's side was useless. I was making a list of things to get at the first gas station!

VALERIE KATZ

Bob says he didn't know there were hurricanes in New Mexico, but we sure had to fight our way through the wind to get gas! My hair hasn't been blown back like that since I went on the roller coaster with Kalyn!! They said it was blowing 55 miles per hour. We were heading right into it. Minnie was wolfing down the gas!!

We decided to stop for the night at a casino. Really enjoyed the prime rib and margaritas! Even better, I won $150.00 on a slot machine!! Bob picked it out for me, put in $100.00, and told me to have fun. When I got to $200 I cashed in, gave him back his $100 and put my ill-gotten gains back in the machine. Got up to $180.00 and when it wanted its money back, I cashed in at $150. By then I had gathered quite a crowd. Both the slot machine and I had gotten pretty loud. Clang, clang, yahoo!

We were on the road today at 7:30. No fog but 2 patches of snow flurries! I found the weather map on my phone, so I could tell my pilot that we would be driving right on through in about 1 1/2 hours. He kept on driving; wiper blade still iffy.

We seem to have an LP gas leak. The alarm had been going off and on for 2 days before I found the problem light, near the floor, below the refrigerator. Bob took the cover off, looked it over and disconnected the darn thing. I'm still alive and the coach hasn't burst into flames, so I guess it's OK. I need a few other things looked at so will try to locate some place to have the Minnie looked at. The alarm would have been driving Shera nuts if she had been with us.

When the small things happen, fog, snow, propane, wiper blades, wind, Bob just looks at me now and says "I know... It's an adventure." I'm trying to get caught up with the news. — *Wish me luck, Valerie.*

The reason for the prolonged stay is my son Larry and his wife have been living in the home I brought my family up in and have owned for 40 years. Larry has a very long drive to work so he wants to be closer and cut his drive time by about 3 hours a day.

A very good plan to be sure. Therefore, we needed to get it ready to sell! Larry and I rolled up our sleeves and went to work.

The house is in escrow! We must have done a good job sprucing it up. The first people who saw it, put in a bid $15,000.00 over the asking price. SOLD! Larry wanted to know if we should wait for more offers and a bidding war. That would be a great big *NO*.

Larry has found a place, and it looks like that one is in escrow too. Yippee! —*Love to all, Valerie*

My car got hit when it was parked on the street while I was off dumping the Minnie's tanks. The Honda looks like someone tried to pull her nose off so she's in the shop and I have a rental car. When she went off down the road on the back of the tow truck, she looked smug, like look at me, I could be a float in the Rose Parade. Don't kid yourself. She still has that long drive back to Arkansas being pulled by the Minnie. She'll get her pretty new nose mussed up!

The coach needs some electrical work which I was hoping to have done when I got back at the end of January. However, the electrical cord decided to short out and a neighbor came to the door saying there were sparks flying out from under the coach. The end of the cord had burned completely off! If those motor homes catch fire the only thing to do is RUN!

I thought I would have to have it taken care of right away, especially since finding a new heavy-duty cord was not working out at all. Then I remembered my son Don had one I had given him when he bought my previous motor home from me. So, I drove right over and borrowed it… back.

Do I dare hope for speedy and uncomplicated escrows?? —*Love to all, Valerie*

CHAPTER 9

Arkansas News 2015

January. I'm on my way back to CA from the cruise. I'm trying to use the 3 1\2 hour layover that has now been upgraded to 6 hours, to good use getting caught up on The News. There is a lovely bar with very little business, so I don't feel like I need to stir my stumps to a new location.

About the cruise, it was a seven-day cruise, left Galveston on a Sunday afternoon, return to Galveston the following Sunday. Of the seven days there were only 3 where we stopped so people could get off and do touristy things. That might not have made some folks happy, but me, I love the cruising part. I could be on the ship the whole time going in circles in the ocean and I'd be perfectly happy.

However! The first stop was Falmouth, Jamaica and it was the highlight of the trip. My sister and I went zip-lining. The Zip Trip started off with the guides taking every single thing that we had on us, (except our clothes, thank goodness!}, away from us and had it all stowed away in lockers. That included our cell phones which we had planned to use for picture taking. Then we took a large four-wheel vehicle up a mountain on what could only loosely be described as a road. On the way up one of our guides said, "We have five zip lines for you today and two surprises." That line was delivered with a lot of good-natured, and suspicious, mugging and back slapping.

The longest of the zip lines was 600 feet and the next longest one was 580 feet. After our first three zips we were confronted with the first surprise. A straight drop down, 90 feet! The second one was 45 feet, still high enough to make that step off the platform and the plunge down, pretty exciting. I must say a little squeal was heard from me when I stepped into the abyss on that first 90-foot drop. Yes, yes it was straight down!

When I told my son Larry about it he said, "Mom what stopped you?" "The ground" I replied. The guides had a system that slowed us down before we hit bottom!

There were people there taking pictures, so we did get some which I will share with you. Martha and I agreed, it was the highlight of the trip. Bob, not being inclined to hurl through the trees suspended on a wire, decided to forgo the adventure. —*Love, Valerie.*

February. It is now February 13, *Friday the 13th*. Except for that two weeks home to go on the cruise with Martha, Bob, and a bunch of my friends from Bella Vista, I have been in California since the week before Thanksgiving. I'm getting homesick.

I came to California to sell the home I raised my children in. That part of the trip has been bumpy. I took the escrow papers into the escrow office and they informed me that there were two liens on the house, one from 1994 and one from 2001. Now I know I paid those liens off a very long time ago. Would you believe it! Now they want me to prove it!

Poor Bob has been called into service. I don't know how many times I've called him and said, "Honey can you go by the house and get into my file cabinet again because I need…" and then the list would be endless. He's been so sweet sending me mail pouches every week. He usually sends them on Friday, so I look forward to Monday when I get mail from home.

Bob was called and once again asked to go to my house and go the file cabinet. I needed him to dig out the "Variel" folder. He found it and bless his heart overnighted the whole file to me. There was one all-important document that was greeted with great enthusiasm. It said, "Congratulations you've paid your loan in full". That took care of one of the companies. The other one is very old and had been passed to several lending companies, none of which would give a layperson the time day. I recalled that in 1994 I was making all home loans through my son-in-law Kevin. He was making loans for people like me who didn't really qualify for loans from the higher-end mortgage companies. I secretly called him my "Loan Shark". When I sent him a text about my predicament, he gave me the information on who he thought would be holding the paper, if there was still a paper to be held. I called the escrow lady, gave her what information I had, and put the ball in her court. She was almost as thrilled as I was that there was a paper forthcoming that said the larger of the two amounts had been paid off.

Now that they have noticed I am no longer a Mrs.; they need a copy of David's death certificate. I have one, I know where it is and lucky for me, Bob is still taking my calls.

The escrows are supposed to close on March 9 and the 10th so after getting everyone moved and settled in I'll be heading home! The really sad part of this journey is that I have been so busy with getting our house ready for the sale, escrows, house hunting and such, that I haven't had a chance to see any of my friends. But tomorrow I will make an apt. to get my nails done.

P.S. Just to show you how scrambled my brain has been, this is how I started this e-mail a few days ago. *"It is now February 12, Friday the 13th"*. I'm afraid I read it a few times before I saw my mistake.

If you are not still praying for me, please start. —*Love to all, Valerie*

March. Escrows! My daily mantra is "It's almost over"...

Bob, true to his word, sent me a copy of David's death certificate. Well, he actually sent me 3. Hoping to save himself a trip back to my house in case more were needed. Still a smart man...

When it got here I took it over to the escrow office. She asked me to sit down so she could discuss some other little things that were going on with the escrow. Oh dear... never a good sign. It seems that the reason the larger of the two liens against the house had never been cleared, even though I had that nice little letter saying I paid it off, was because when it was filed, two of the numbers had been transposed. Now it had to be researched and fixed but at least we know why. *Small comfort.* Fortunately, the other lien, the one that *was* a problem, was on its way to being cleared. I took that as good news.

When we got to the "clearing of the present title" conversation. She asked me if I could get David to sign off on the property. Now mind you, the death certificate was sitting under her wrist because I had already handed it to her. I was good! I *very* nicely pointed out that that was it right there on the desk. Her response was "Oh goodness, I'm so sorry. This has been a very difficult escrow." She wasn't telling me anything I didn't already know...

Kalyn was with me that day so when I got back out to the car I said "Grandma needs to go someplace where she doesn't have to use her brain. Let's go to the movies." If you haven't seen McFarland USA, stop doing everything, including reading this email, and go see it. The ratings gave it five stars which is the highest they can give but believe me it should get 10. Take everyone in the household! It's a family movie and it's fabulous. When we got out it was time for dinner. It was late enough that Larry was almost home, so we picked him up at the house and went and had salmon, broccoli, and a nice glass of wine. —*Love, Valerie.*

March 6 found me ready to take the coach in for repairs. I had my list. Hot water heater wouldn't work so hot water for face, dishes, etc. had to be heated in the microwave. The AC plugs on the side of the coach where I plug in my laptop and iPhone we're not working and therefore were a huge pain in my backside. Luckily, I was still plugged in at Larry's house so the fact that the generator wouldn't work was not an immediate problem, but I was pretty sure we would need it on the long drive home. The dumping of the black and white tanks, already not my favorite job, was made even more unpleasant by the fact that the seal on the black tank, the stinky one, did not seal properly! The carbon monoxide alarm which we had disabled before Thanksgiving because it wouldn't stop beeping needed to be looked at.

I hooked the car up to the coach, so I would have a ride home after dropping it off, put the address to Camping World Valencia in the GPS and hit the road. We had no trouble finding Valencia, we had no trouble finding the off-ramp, but then the problems started

As we were pulling up to a signal with a small Y in the road where right turns were too be made, my phone started to ring. That interrupted a turn right message from the GPS which of course the GPS doesn't take kindly to.

Since we were in the middle of not one but two cranky escrows, not answering phone calls from the escrow officers was not an option. Since that was who the phone call was from, I answered it.

By now we were just passed the entrance to that little Y in the road. It was too late to turn right and backing up was not only blocked by heavy traffic but was also impossible due to the car being towed.

I spoke quickly to the escrow officer, the light turned green, and I pulled through the intersection. How lucky I was! Just passed the intersection was a shopping center big enough for me to pull in, turn around, and proceed in the correct direction.

I pulled out onto the highway and when the GPS told me to make a left, I followed her directions. I followed her directions down a four-lane road which turned into a two-lane-road which then turned into a one-lane road. No! I don't mean one lane going in each direction, I mean one lane!

I was getting worried about the situation and golf words started creeping into my brain. Now we were up in the hills and out of any cell phone range, so the GPS had stopped talking to me and I could not call Camping World to find out where I had gone wrong.

I saw a couple walking their dog and stopped to ask, "If I keep going will I find civilization?" "Oh no" came the gentleman's response "that's a dead end up there".

Oh dear! After looking at my distressed face he said if I would follow the road all the way up to the end and veer left, there was an area large enough to turn the coach and the car around. I turned off the golf words that were bouncing around in my head and started praying instead that he was right. Good news, he was!

I did get turned around and headed back down the hill. When we got to where the two-lane road turned back into the four-lane road the GPS found her voice and informed me I should make an immediate U-turn. I was in no mood for her shenanigans and told her in no uncertain terms, and out loud, to *SHUT UP!*

While I was speaking to the couple with the dog I had said I was looking for Camping World and asked them if they knew where it was. They said "Yes, it was right there on the corner, you know, where you got off the freeway".

Oh yes, I knew. The one where I got the phone call, missed the right turn where the little Y was, and used the shopping center to get myself going in what I thought was the right direction.

Now Camping World is not a small entity. It's huge! The signs are huge! I missed them. I'm blaming the whole thing on the escrows!

Speaking to someone at Camping World seems to be a problem. I tried in vain to call them to find out where they were and why I couldn't see them from the Walmart parking lot where I ended up. It had taken me many, many unsuccessful tries to actually get someone on the phone to make the appointment to drop the coach off in the first place!!=

I drove through the Walmart parking lot, saw the signs for Camping World, and discovered it was on the other side of a barranca. A lovely, long, tree filled crater in the ground referred to in my lovely Bella Vista, by my friend Louise, as "The Ditch".

Now I had to figure out how to get over "The Ditch" and on to Camping World. Now I knew where it was, this was the second time I was making an attempt to get there. It should have been an easy thing to do! My friends, please, remember who you're traveling with.

The intersection that we are discussing was extremely busy. I made a left-hand turn onto the highway. Then I had to make another left-hand turn that looked like it was taking me back to the freeway. Then a right hand turns into a gas station for a turn around to go back out and make a left-hand turn to get back to Camping World. I was getting dizzy, but the end was in site!

Yes, I was going to make that left-hand turn. Then I looked across the intersection. The oncoming traffic was the off-ramp of the freeway. And there was a "no left turn" sign. Golf words!

Now what I needed to do was, in about half a block, cross three lanes of traffic, pull into a restaurant parking lot, turn around *again*, and get going in the right direction.

As you might guess by that time I was pretty sick of the whole darn thing and golf words were thinking about becoming vocal. I decided that when the cross-traffic light turned red I'd just pull out over those three lanes. What were those cars coming off the freeway going to do, run me over! I thought I looked pretty big out there in a motor home pulling a car.

That little maneuver worked. I went right at the little Y section, pulled into Camping World, and went in to introduce myself as the late Valerie Katz. Believe it or not, I was only about one hour late...

I gave the gentleman my list, we agreed on March 11 as a date for pick up, I gave the gentleman the keys to the coach, I unhooked the car, and went merrily on my way.

Little did I know that this was only the beginning of my troubles with Camping World Valencia. —*More to come, Valerie*

March 8, I received a call from Mark the service guy. He was asking for permission to spend more than the initial 1 hour requested to track down the electrical problem and to proceed with the repairs on the rest of the items on my list. That would be a big YES!!

March 11 came and went with no word from Camping World. March 12, and 13, the same. Not realizing I had been up to my ears in ESCROWS, friends and family wanted to know why I wasn't trying to get an explanation for this poor service from Camping World (CW). I called...

As I mentioned before, CW does not consider a ringing phone cause for any action on their part. I Left voice messages, also no cause for action on their part.

Then I remembered some advice from the Mr. Katz. "Ask for the supervisor!

Unfortunately, first you have to get someone to answer the %#£€¥% phone. I was now on a speed dial mission.

The *supervisors* name was Kevin. He also did not respond to the ringing of the phone but did return my call. After listening to my plight, he promised to have Mark summoned to his office so the 3 of us could get to the bottom of the problem. He promised to get back to me before the end of the day.

Much to my surprise and delight he called back in about 45 min. It was time for our 3-way chat. Kevin went over my concerns. Mark said he would check with his guys and get back to me. Kevin said that would be fine and that Mark should have that done no later than 5:30. Would that satisfy me? Yes, it would. 5:30 came and went. Kevin was called, and another voice mail was left.

Mark called and said he had been waiting for approval from me to get started. I reminded him of our conversation on the 8th.

I went to visit Don and Debbie and relayed this information. I also told them about the concern I had had when I left the coach in the first place. I had signed a paper that gave them permission to proceed with repairs without any more conversations with me.

"Mom", Debbie said, "Do you mind if I call them?" As my son Don says, "You don't want to have to deal with the Mrs. Crone". I dialed CW and handed my phone to her.

She managed to get Mark on the phone! Score 1 for Debbie! The conversation went something like this. "When will my Mom get her motor home back Mark. No, you already have her permission. Yes, you do. She signed the waiver to proceed when she left it with you. I want to know when my mother is going to get her motor home back! She is visiting us from Arkansas and you have all her possessions with no word when she will get them back!"

There is now pacing along with a loud voice accompanying this conversation. Debbie paced off to another room.

Soon she was back with the news that Mark will talk to his guys and call her in the morning. I was thinking "Oh dear, I know I've heard that before."

But Debbie said not to worry, she was on it. She continued to call, and Mark continued to stick with his story. Finally, she said she didn't want to hear that again. She wanted to hear only one thing. "When will my Mom get her motor home back!!"

"Well" said Mark huffily "if you're going to demand a day, how about next Wednesday."

I decided to call Kevin. After several attempts I final got a live person on the phone. As the lady was offering me the voicemail option, I interrupted her, and told her that, that would not do. I had been trying and trying and now I needed to talk to someone.

She put me on hold. When she returned several minutes later, she said, "They just don't answer their phones over there." (Welcome to my world.) However, she would pass my message along to Mark, Kevin, and the manager of the facility. Now we might get somewhere. I got a call. Your motor home is ready. Come and get it. It was Tuesday!

Mark was at lunch when I got there. I told the nice lady to hold on to the paperwork for a few more minutes. I would wait for Mark.

When he returned, I asked to check things out. The generator stayed on. There was no power to the coach, so the hot water heater and the electrical problems could not be checked. The coach batteries were dead. *Oh dear.*

One of Mark's guys was summoned. He plugged the coach in for power and all systems seemed to be working. I hooked up the car and beat a hasty retreat.

THE NEWS FROM ARKANSAS

I dropped the coach off at Don's. He called and wanted to know if the "Guys" had checked the tire pressure or the fluids. My "I sincerely doubt it." was followed by his "Don't worry Mom, I'll take care of it."

This is one of the reasons I thank God, each night for my wonderful children.

Another call from **Don...** "Mom, what do you have to do to get the lights to turn on in the coach?" **Me** "there's a switch just inside the side door you have to turn on." **Don** "I tried that." **Me** "Oh dear." **Don** "Don't worry Mom, I'll take care of it."

The next day I got a text. A picture of the inside of the coach. The lights were on and the note said, "Good news!" —*Love, Valerie.*

Its official, the house on Variel Ave., that I have owned for 40 years and where I raised my family now belongs to someone else. I'm here to help Larry and Kalyn move and start their new adventure.

The escrow process has been a nightmare. For some reason, the people buying this house couldn't get their funding taken care of in a timely manner. Since the monies from Variel were going to the new house, that process was held up also. The end of last week was a nightmare of phone calls and Emails saying it'll fund tomorrow, sorry it didn't fund, maybe tomorrow, and so on and so forth all week. I saved most of the emails and last night deleted the rest. There were 59 of them!

Our property finally did fund, on Thursday. It couldn't be recorded until Friday. It had to be recorded before the monies could be funded to the new escrow. If anyone had the misguided notion that Government offices did any kind of recording on the weekend, put them to rest. They don't! Our real estate agent said "possibly", if we went down to Torrance and got the papers from escrow, we could go to the courthouse ourselves and have it recorded in a special recording.

After many, many phone calls Larry, Kalyn, and I got in the car and drove over the hill to see if we could get that accomplished. The traffic was terrible because it was almost 3 o'clock. When we finally got there and called the escrow company they said "Sorry, the funds didn't get here in time. It's not possible to record today." Golf words! I had made a deal with Larry that when the escrow on Variel closed I would take us all out to a nice dinner and when Dominguez closed, he would do the same. He made some snide remark about hoping I liked Jack-in-the-Box, but he wasn't quite close enough for me to reach him with the back of my hand, so I let that pass.

We headed for the Red Lobster. Larry said he wasn't sure he liked the Red Lobster, but I told him my mouth was ready for some of their cheesy garlic biscuits and I didn't want to hear another word about it. We had a nice meal, with drinks, and checked in to Facebook to share our good news.

We spent the rest of the weekend packing what little was still left to pack. On February 1st Luz had moved out. Larry had told her she could have all the furniture that she wanted so she took everything, including the refrigerator and the washer and dryer. She's been doing Larry and Kalyn's laundry for them and I have been doing my laundry at my friend Charlotte's house. The only things left were a mattress on the floor in the guest room for me, Kalyn's soon to be replaced bedroom set and Larry's, also to be replaced, bed. Larry called for large item pick up and the just mentioned furniture was put on the curb for morning pick up.

Donald came to help take the mattresses and Kalyn's furniture to the curb and brought a blow-up mattress. Luz had their blow-up mattress. When Larry left to go get it he asked me if there was anything I needed. I told him *YES!* Please bring back the wine opener. Luz had taken all of those too and I was feeling quite a desperate need for my favorite alcohol.

When Larry was packing up the mattress, he threw the wine opener in the bag with it and put two holes in the bottom. After he and I had spent the better part of a half hour trying to blow it up we finally figured that out. The duct tape that was used to fix it only lasted three quarters of the night. Therefore, we were down to just one blowup mattress... he had also ordered a big trash bin to deposit all last minute "What the heck is this?" or "How long has it been since we used that?" items from the garage. —*Tired but hopeful, Valerie.*

It's 3 o'clock in the afternoon and I have just had my 1st cup of coffee. It took a while to find the pot. Kalyn took pity on me and went to the garage in search of it.

Larry and Kalyn are now in their new home. We got the truck unloaded last night around 10:30 PM, with a BIG help from Don. After looking over what needed to be moved Don had looked at his brother and said, "Larry how come you don't have a U-Haul truck?" They were soon on their way to get one.

We got everything safely tucked into the garage. The problem with that, we are now carrying those boxes up the stairs from the garage and then up more stairs to the bedrooms. My legs are done. I can still go up and down, but I can't carry anything that weighs much more than a feather.

Debbie, bless her heart, made a pot of homemade soup, and sent a big bowl of it with Don. Yum Yum Yum!

Larry and Kalyn stopped at McDonald's last night and had hamburgers and chicken tenders. Kalyn was kind enough to offer me some chicken tenders and they were very good. I had one.

Today around 2 o'clock after many, many, trips up and down the stairs I came down and smelled the chicken. I looked at her and said "I smell chicken! Smells good!" Her answer then was "Step away! These are all mine!" Humph. Well, I do have some homemade soup.

We have no water. Larry left the transfer of important items up to me. I mistakenly thought that water and power came in one package here in Torrance like they do in Canoga Park. However, they don't. The water lady on the phone must've taken pity on Larry when he called today. After saying "sorry no service until tomorrow" and then listening to our predicament said, "Okay I'll try to get somebody out there today." It's now almost 4 o'clock and still there is no water. We are washing our hands with bottled water. We won't want to meet any of the new neighbors until after we have been able to shower. :)

Good news, this morning, as promised, we got Larry's bedroom set delivered. No mattress, that's coming Friday. We got the pictures for the walls and the rug delivered. We got the dining room table delivered. And, hallelujah the refrigerator arrived! The even better news! DirecTV is here installing their service. I don't think Larry would've made it through the whole process without being able to watch his TV in the evenings. The whole system will be wireless, so Kalyn and Larry have scurried out to buy a TV for Kalyn's room. There is only the one TV and DirecTV couldn't get the channels to unscramble until we had at least 2 TVs to work with.

We have the dining room table now, so I have challenged them to a game of Sequence tonight. Larry somehow has the notion that he's going to kick our butts. We'll see about that!

One part of my missing memory has been restored! It is abundantly clear why I said, after moving into 9 Bella Lane, that I would never, ever, move again. It's not for sissies or for old folks. —*Keep praying, Valerie*

April. The last few weeks have been spent furnishing this new abode. As I mentioned before, Luz took everything, which Larry was fine with, so everything now had to be purchased. Larry, Kalyn, and I were on the search. A new couch was ordered. Larry was having it made to fit both the shape of the condo and a comfy place right under the ceiling fan for Larry to enjoy his

TV. New beds, bedroom furnishings, refrigerator, washer, drier, linens, kitchen gadgets, etc. etc. had to be shopped for. The three of us shopped for the large items together. Kalyn and I shopped for the rest with a continual stream of text messages, with pictures, to Larry for his OK. We were getting settled.

Larry's sister Denise and brother Don are happy for his move on several levels. They are happy that he and Kalyn will have a more peaceful life and that the new home is in the middle distance between their homes. Easter is coming, Mom is here, and has talked it over with Larry. We will host an Easter/Housewarming event. —*Love to all, Valerie*

Easter is tomorrow, and we are not quite ready. We are still putting things away and putting things together. Kalyn needs some new shoes which apparently must be purchased today. The new Fast and Furious movie is coming out today and must be also seen today. *And,* once again I have had it with my hair!

Larry and Kalyn flee the scene and go in search of shoes. I head for the drug store to buy some new hair trimmers. I purchase the only set they have. It has about 18 different blades.

Showered with clean dry hair I tackle the job. Then I notice that this handy dandy set has a special tip that is tapered to cut the sides. "Wow", I think, "This is going to make this so much easier!" I run it over the right side of my head, just above the ear and my hair is far from great. It is almost gone! "Oh dear." I decide not to try it on the other side and finish *trimming* the rest.

When Larry and Kalyn return and start making noise about going out to dinner and to the movie I suggest we wait for the movie as the TV stand is still not put together and we are just not ready for company. It turns out this is not an option as tickets have already been purchased via the phone.

Now, I had been careful to make sure they didn't see the right side of my hair and off we went for Mexican food and

Margaritas. We decided to have the waiter take our picture to check in on Facebook. When I said I needed to move to the other side of the table for the pictures they looked puzzled but said OK. Then I showed them what I had done to my hair. Larry just shook his head and laughed. Kalyn looked stunned and said, "Oh no Grandma!" They still took me to the show with them and did not say I needed to put a paper bag on my head.

The next day Denise said something about my hair getting shorter and shorter. When I explained what I had done she said she just thought I was trying the new style of shaving one side of the head and letting the rest grow. —*Love, Valerie.*

It was time to take the Minnie on the road. I would drive to Mesa, Arizona, pick up my sister Martha and head for home.

As it turns out, the electrical outlets on the driver's side of the coach are still not working, the generator won't stay running, we don't seem to have house batteries, and still no hot water. But the black tank seal actually was fixed.

So, not having the generator or house batteries we had no interior lights after dark. We parked under the lights in Walmart parking lots. North West Arkansas has a Camping World. I will be visiting them soon. Martha has been a very good sport about this turn of events. —*Love to all, Valerie*

April 10. On this day in 1996 I lost my son David. I dreamt about him last night. —*Valerie*

HOME! We're here and first things first. Bring in the stuff from the refrigerator. Check the plants. Feed the birds. Pour the wine! Martha has a job and can only stay for a few days, but it was so nice traveling with her again.

We took the Minnie to our local CW. Armed with paperwork stating that the repairs had been made in CA. We told a very nice young man our plight. As he was filling out our new paperwork, I informed him that I most certainly was *not* intending to pay for those repairs again. That was why I had gone to CW Valencia in the first place. Just for this type of thing. He promised to call Valencia and take the matter up with them. Believe it or not, CW Valencia did not answer their phone! But he promised to keep trying and would send them a FAX. He promised to get it all straightened out. We went home.

They did get it straightened out. We have the Minnie and our wallets are no less full. —*Love to all, Valerie*

May. I had been home from California for about two weeks. Bob said something had happened while I was gone, and he wanted to tell me about it. He said he had gotten home from golf one afternoon and was relaxing in his chair when his heart started beating terribly fast. He tried to get his blood pressure without any luck. My first question was "Did you call 911?" "No" he said "I just sat there for about an hour and waited for it to go away." Then a week or so later he had another event, but it wasn't nearly as bad. So, I asked the same question "Did you call 911?" and got the same answer "I just waited for it to go away."

On Tuesday I called him and told him there was high excitement at my house. It was the last night of Dancing with the Stars and they would be handing out the Mirror Ball Trophy! He is not a fan of that program but decided to come over to watch the big finish with me and spend the night. I got up at three in the morning to go to the bathroom and I heard his voice. "Valerie, are you awake?" My first thought was "No I must be sleep-walking", but I luckily managed to keep that to myself. Then he said "My hearts beating really fast and my pulse is really weak. I said I thought we should call 911. He wasn't too sure he wanted to do that. Right! I called 911!

The paramedics arrived and said they were going to take him to the Hospital. He wanted to know if he had to go. The paramedic said yes, the thing to do now was go to the hospital. They took him in, and I followed in my car. By then his heart rate had slowed down to 140! They ran some tests and said he had had a mild heart attack. They wanted him to spend the night. He got a room, I went home.

I went to pick him up the next day, but the doctor hadn't signed off on his release yet. I had a dental appt. in Joplin MO. so I told him I would be back to get him. He called me and told me they had found something else and he was to have surgery. One of his arteries was 90% blocked so they put in a stent. I got some pretty woozy phone calls that night. He told me several times that he was going to do better. He was going to start exercising again and cut back on the food, so he could lose some weight. They gave him a notebook about his care, what they had done, about a heart healthy diet, etc. and sent him home.

We stopped at Walmart to pick up his new meds and then headed for home. "Honey" he said, "Could we stop at El Publito and pick up some guacamole? Maybe have a bite to eat." My "New" man proceeded to order 3 tacos, a chili relleno, and a large order of guacamole. In his defense, he couldn't eat it all so enjoyed the rest for lunch today. He has been taking it easy all day and is feeling tired but better. He is on the mend. I am so glad I talked him into coming over to watch DWTS. If he had been home, he might not have called 911. When I got up this morning he was down on the treadmill! I gave him *what for* and sent him upstairs. He had a bowl of cereal and went home. It seems my bedside manner has not improved.—*Love, Valerie.*

August. I have had another trip to California... Flying in, transportation went without a hitch...leaving, not so much. I left Larry's house in what I thought was plenty of time. I plugged the address of the rental car depot into my GPS and took off. Apparently, my GPS thought that getting to Budget Rental car required a trip *through* the airport. I hate driving around LAX, dodging buses and cars. Trying to follow the detailed instructions that my GPS kept giving me was making things even more difficult! Lucky for her she didn't use that recalculating word that I hate.

After finally getting there, dropping off the car, and getting the shuttle bus *back* to the airport, I checked my one bag and went to the short line I always use, the one for pre-approved TSA passengers. I'm afraid I have been known to brag a little bit about the fact that I am TSA approved and don't have to stand in that long line at LAX.

Then I was told that I was *not* TSA approved and I would have to go to another line. I'm afraid I may have raised my voice when trying to explain to the gentleman that I was TSA approved!

He explained to me in a, "I've worked at the airport a long time and have already lost what little patience I may once have had" tone of voice, that I could go back to the terminal to lodge my complaint if I so desired.

So, the petite oriental girl who was standing behind me, and I, turned around and went back to the other line. I'm not sure which one of us looked more like a terrorist but we were both reassigned.

The GPS had put me behind schedule, and I did not want to miss my flight. I'm afraid I went under the barricade and just put myself, and her, in the front of the line. There was a gentleman that I let go ahead of us after he explained to me, in no uncertain terms, that most of the people in that line had been reassigned. He pointed behind him and informed me that the end of the line was down there! The rest of the people in line must've decided they didn't want to deal with the little terrorists and let us go ahead.

I'm afraid I was a little fidgety on the plane after all that but luckily it wasn't a full flight. The gentleman sitting next to me got up and went and sat someplace else. I guess he didn't want to deal with me either. I had two glasses of wine and a package of almond M&Ms and watched the movie Donald had helped me download onto my phone.

Bob picked me up, took me home, helped me unpack the car, and went home. In my defense, he had been sick most of the time I was gone and just wanted to go home and go to bed. Well that's what he said... I'm happily back in Bella Vista. — *Love to all, Valerie*

September. I am at the airport getting ready to take off to meet my friend Charlotte in New York for our cruise. I can't resist the gift shop. I just have to look at all the *Stuff*. I bought myself a selfie stick! I immediately took a picture of myself and sent it to my kids. Charlotte and I can be in all the pictures together! The selfie stick was marked $19.00. After it was rung up and tax added I paid $16.50 for it. My math is terrible, but I don't think that added up quite right.

There were some problems with the selfie stick. (Anyone who is thinking user error can stop right now!) It came with absolutely no instructions on how to put it together. There is an extra part. It is packed away with the stick for a future trip to CA so one of my children or grandchildren can show me what to do with it! Also, the trigger moves around. After taking my initial picture, I wanted to try again, and it just wouldn't cooperate! I was pressing on the raised button, but the trigger had moved to another location. OK, you get ready to shoot and then look for a lump in the handle. I can do that.

Next, my new iPhone is too slick and too narrow to stay in the holder and the plug is too short to make it through my Mophie charging case; Ah ha! Take the case off, thread the plug through the case and plug it in, place the case back on the phone. Now the phone will hold on to its new attachment. The extra "mystery part" may solve that problem. We will see. Time to board!

They just announced that we can't take off because something is broken. It just has to be *taped up* and only a "Qualified" someone from maintenance can do that. I hope they aren't talking about the wings. I don't know exactly *what* it is because my head was down by my feet. I was trying to get my earphones out of my carry-on bag, so I could watch the movie downloaded to my phone.

They just announced another 30 to 45 min. delay. The thing that has to be taped shut is a *hatch* and the guy who can do it is away from the airport. He must have taken the Duct Tape to lunch! Now I have to hope this hatch doesn't pop open and let my suitcase fall out!

I had gotten a good start on my movie when I notice the lady next to me had gotten her phone out to take a picture. When I looked up to see what she was pointing at I see the "Expert at hatch taping" has arrived and is busy fixing the problem. It was an overhead luggage bin. I'm pretty sure the plane could have flown safely with *that* hatch hanging open! I could have done that in much less than 45 min. And then we had to wait for the paperwork to be filled out!

Also, they had announced that since we would be sitting on the runway for such a long time anyone who wanted to could get off the plane and take a stroll. Now those folks had to be rounded up!

More good news, the announcement about missing connecting flights has been made. Charlotte and I were going to meet at the Hotel, have dinner at 7:30 and go to the top of the Empire State Building. I sent her a quick text telling her I wouldn't be there. I crossed my fingers. They announced we must go to airplane mode on our cellular devises. I hope this means lift off is imminent…

Is this starting to sound like a normal trip for me? Get your prayers ready.

Next stop, Charlotte NC. I have missed my connecting flight. I'm on standby for a 5:30 flight but it doesn't look promising. The next flight is at 8:20, also standby. There is a man in line in front of me who is raising hell and putting a block under it. Apparently, he doesn't know the young woman waiting on him is not the one who delayed our flight. Me? I have a place to plug in my phone and the cruise doesn't leave until tomorrow, so all is well...

As I was waiting to see if I would be one of the lucky few to make the 5:30 flight it occurred to me that for some completely unknown reason American Air had bumped me up to Gold status. Maybe that will put me on the top of the list! They loaded all the ticked passengers and called "Passenger Katz". I was up, and in what for me was a flash, hurried to answer the call. I got on and was bumped up to first class. Unfortunately, it was only a 1½ hour flight. They treat you really good in first class!

When I got to New York there was no waiting for my luggage. It had arrived many hours before me. After identifying myself and my luggage, I asked the lady where I could get a cab. She pointed me in the right direction. I walked out the door and a gentleman said, "You need a taxi?" I said "Yes". He said "I have a black town car over there. Where do you need to go?" When I told him he said, "That will be $75 and the tip is up to you". Right... We were off.

Charlotte was waiting for me. She said she was game if I still wanted to go to the Empire State Building. My "No" was followed by her "Oh thank God, I'm beat!"

Then I told her I had forgotten my luggage tags and all my cruise information. I'm pretty sure she threatened to kill me. Lucky for me she had brought both of her luggage tags and we were each only bringing one suitcase. All of her cruise information had both of our names on it, so I assured her all would be well the next day. She said she hoped so, otherwise she would be waving goodbye to me from the ship. It was 9:50 PM and we party animals were on the way to bed.

The next day, getting cleared to board the ship, I looked again at Charlotte's paperwork. There were 2 copies for Charlotte Afriat and daughter Valerie Katz. Ah ha! I told her not to worry, took one of the copies, and called her Mom until we were cleared and on board.

The first day was at sea. The highlight of the day was a Helicopter rescue. Someone had gotten hurt and had to be rescued. The ship did not have a helipad! First a man was lowered to the deck. Then the helicopter flew around the ship for about 20 min., came back, and dropped down a big basket. The injured party was loaded into the basket, drawn up to the helicopter, and off they went. Just like on TV!

We had dinner and went to the show. When getting ready for bed I was looking for the switch to turn off the overhead lights. I pressed one that immediately turned red. Uh Oh... An emergency switch? In less than 10 seconds our phone started ringing. It was someone wanting to know what our emergency was. "So sorry" I said. "I was looking for the light switch". Then instructions on how to cancel the alarm were conveyed but nothing on how to turn off the overhead lights. I eventually figured it out.

There is a large amount of excellent food on board a cruise ship. I started taking the stairs instead of the elevator on day 3. We discovered the cobbler bar at the buffet on day 4, warm cobbler with hot rum sauce and Ice cream IF you wanted the deluxe version. We did... Going up and down those stairs seemed to get a little harder by day 6. I think my purse must have been getting heavier. Thanks for joining me on my travels. —*Love, Valerie.*

September. For over a year I've wanted to do something with my front porch. It was all stained and the power washer didn't make a dent. Last year when shopping at Lowe's I had seen a product that I really liked. It put a really nice texture on cement or wood. The lady said it was very easy to use. You put the first coat on with a regular paint roller and the next day you put on a second coat with a different roller that looked like a round hairbrush. That's what gives it the textured finish. Let's do it now before it gets too cold! Fall is in the Air.

Two days to a beautiful porch!

I had made my decision on the product, so I was off to Lowe's. With my brochure in hand, I pointed at the picture and said, "This is what I want and that's the color I want it in". It was too late in the day to get started so I went to bed with pictures of a beautiful new red (Yes red!) porch dancing through my head.

Day 1, I played Mahjong in the morning. In the afternoon I put the first coat on. Hmm, It didn't look exactly like what I was hoping for but I figured the second coat would give it the texture I was counting on.

Day 2. There was an Altrusa meeting I needed to go to in the morning. I got home and put on the second coat. The porch was a beautiful color, but it still didn't look like it was supposed to. It was supposed to have a non-skid feel to it, and it was supposed to fill in those cracks.

When Bob came over, I said, "It doesn't look like I expected it to." He replied, "Don't worry honey it looks beautiful and you did a great job cutting in the trim." Still, it just did not look right.

Day 3, I got up and went out to look at the porch. Nope, didn't look right. I went to the garage to read the instructions one more time. It said for wood decks only! I compared my brochure to the front of the can. They had sold me the wrong thing!

Back to Lowe's... I went up to the return desk and asked to talk to the manager of the paint department. I remembered David's advice, "Ask for a supervisor!"

The lady asked me what my problem was. I told her. She said the manager of the paint department wasn't there, picked up the can, and walked me over to the paint department. The paint department lady took a look at the brochure and a look at the can and said, "That's not the same stuff." My "Yes I know that. Someone from this dept. sold me the wrong thing and there are two coats of it on my cement front porch now", was followed by her, "Yes, you're going to have to speak to a manager. She picked up the can and took me back to the help desk.

The help desk lady got a manager on the phone and after explaining my problem to him said, "You want me to give her back her money?" At that point I said, in what was no longer my indoor voice, "I don't want my money back. I want some help!"

The manager came out, picked up the can, and took me back to the paint department.

After a brief conversation on what products he thought I should use and telling the paint area lady to "Give her whatever she needs", he beat a hasty retreat. After he left the paint area the girl looked at me and said "He doesn't really know anything about paint. My paint manager will be in in about five minutes and... I held up my hand, gave her my "Stop right there" look, and said, "I'll wait."

I went through the whole story again with him and he was mortified. He went into action. He was going to help me fix the problem. He started bringing out products. "First you will have to strip the wrong stuff off the porch. Here's the stripper. It smells like oranges but does a great job. I use it here in the store all the time. Then you will need to scrape it off. Here's what you use for that. Then you have to scrub the rest of the stripper off. Here's some STP and a brush for that. Do you have a pole to put the brush on? Here's a pole. And here is a can of the correct product." I had grabbed 2 new liners for the paint pan, 2 new rollers, and made sure I got 2 more stir sticks and 2 new paint can openers. I went to get a cart to haul it all out to the car.

We were standing in the laundry room. As Bob was telling me I had done enough, I needed to take a break. I was busy taking my paint clothes out of the hamper and putting them back on.

The gentleman had said that unlike most striping agents, this orange stuff could stay on up to 24 hours. So, I started slathering it on. There wasn't enough!

Back to Lowe's... The looks on the faces of the paint department personnel said it all. They had hoped not to see me anymore that day, or possibly ever. I smiled, told them I just needed more of this stuff and raised my hand to show them my empty container. The manager said, "Oh yes, I wondered if that was going to be enough." I was way too tired to beat the crap out of him. Soon the rest of the porch smelled like oranges.

Bob and I had made plans to play 9 holes of golf and attend a bar-B-Que that day. I was thinking, "I can't go golfing, I need to stay home and tackle the front porch. My easy 2-day job has gotten out of control!"

But, since I didn't have anything on my schedule the next day, "Shocking!", I decided to let the orange stuff do its thing to the porch, play golf, relax and have a good time. I must admit, I had happy thoughts of Margarita's roaming around in my brain by then.

Day 4 In the morning Bob came over and we started scraping. The orange stuff had taken on a nice rosy hue from the paint but had had very little effect on the paint itself. That paint was not coming off the porch.

Bob was having his house painted and he went and talked to Glen, the gentleman who was working there. After hearing the tale of woe, he followed Bob to my house. There was much head shaking and commiserating. Then he left me his heavy-duty scraper and some brown paper to kneel on while I was scraping and went back to Bob's. We scrubbed! That paint was not coming off. We got out the power washer. It still wasn't coming off!

Bob had another talk with Glen who said he had some turbo tips that he used for his power washer that would take off anything! Bob went back home to get them. With great hope we attached them. No good. They had no more effect than mine! Glenn came back with his power washer. Still no luck.

Glen's next suggestion was to get some commercial grade stripper and a wire brush and go at it again.

Back to Lowe's. I explained my situation to, yet another manager of the paint department and she agreed to give me some more product. Wire brush and strong stripper in hand, I headed home. I had an appointment at 2 o'clock for a massage. I went.

When I returned home, Bob started talking about other things that might be done. I looked at him and said "Bob, I'm done. I'm going to hire someone to fix this porch. I am just done."

He went to put the power washer away and I said "No, don't put that away. I'm going to take out some of my frustration on the driveway." His "Honey are you sure?" was answered by *that look*.

And just to show you that Bob is a very smart man, he made sure that the gas was topped off, cranked the power washer over so it was running and went home. At 7:50 p.m., I'm sure the people on my cul-de-sac breathed a sigh relief and turned the volume to their TVs down. I had run out of gas and so had the power washer.

Days 5&6. Believe it or not, Bob came back. He had had an idea! There were some spots on the porch that we had managed to get down to the cement. We would put some of the new product there, let it dry overnight and see if it held up under the power washer in the morning. The next morning, we hooked up the power washer and gave it a try. The paint came flying off.

That was the day for the Altrusa annual spaghetti dinner to fund our dictionary project. We gave out over 1700 dictionaries to third graders in this area and they had to be paid for! I got busy, baked my two double batches of brownies, and went to help set up for and serve over 400 spaghetti dinners.

Day 7. Bob was back the next morning. Glenn and given him some ideas on what we could do to the porch. Since he was nice enough to come back, I figured the least (the very least) I could do was listen and nod my head.

The next thing I knew we were off to Sherman Williams paint. A very nice and very knowledgeable young man was able to help me with my problem. He said that the product we were using was probably as good any he had. The reason it came up with the power washer after an overnight rest was that it needed at least two weeks to properly cure. And best of all, there was no reason for more scraping. The area just needed to be clean and it sounded like we had cleaned it. Oh, yes, we had.

I was on my way home to try again. Bob's comment? "You are going to get this done come hell or high water, aren't you?" I had had a night's rest... I was ready to try again.

One of the things I got at Lowe's the day before when I was getting the new stripper and wire brush was a new yellow Mum for my yard. Bob was helping me put that in the flower bed and move one of the big rocks to make room for it when he said "Honey, how come every time I come over to your house I get dirty?" I said, "I don't know, I'm surprised you come over here anymore at all". He said he didn't know why he came over anymore either.

I put on the first coat of the new product and didn't like the color. When I told Bob, I was going to change it his reaction was disbelief. "What! And try to strip it again?!" "Oh no," I answered, "I can just paint right over it. The same brand has another product that will fill the cracks, and that is what I wanted in the first place!

Bob threw up his hands and proclaimed "That's it! I'm finished! You are on your own." He was no longer using his indoor voice either. With that he got in his car and went home.

I revved up the power washer again. I have a big driveway. At one time I had 2, 33-foot motor homes, slides out, with cars parked behind them in that driveway. I needed some more power washer therapy. I had pity on my neighbors. I only worked until 7:30 p.m.

Day 8. Brochure once again in hand I was off to Lowe's. I explained to the nice young lady that I wanted the heavy-duty stuff, the one that would fill up the cracks. I did not tell her my tale of woe. I picked up a new spiked roller and she said I would need one for each coat. I asked her if she was sure and she assured me she was. So, with more rollers, paint pan liners and stir sticks, I was headed home.

I applied the first coat with the spiked roller. That did not seem to be covering the last color very well at all. The paint is advertised as being 10 times thicker than regular paint, so I needed another can. I had my empty can with me. I was taking no chances. The gentleman who was helping me said he had used it on his deck before. As he handed me the paint he said "Yes, and in 2 months it all peeled right off." Oh dear... Well it's too late to turn back now.

Day 9. Bob, who was now speaking to me again, came over, looked at the job and asked me if I was satisfied. I told him no, but it did still need another coat. His plan for the day was to play golf so off he went. I told you he was a smart man. I had a nail appointment at 12:30 p.m. I figured I could give that porch a quick second coat and make my appointment, on time. (Still living in a dream world)

That spiked brush was not going to cover the old paint or the porch. It just left globs in its wake. My mind came back from one of its vacations and reminded me of my conversation, a year ago, with the first lady at Lowe's. Easy, first coat with regular roller, second coat with spiked roller.

I no longer had a regular roller in my arsenal, so I set about painting small sections of the porch with a brush and then rolling over them with the spiked roller. It was very slow going, but it was working! However, the paint was drying out and getting so thick it was extremely hard to use. I thought, "It is water-based paint, so I will just add some water."

That reminded me of when I was in Jr. High and was making some p-nut butter cookies. They came out very fluffy and quite tasteless. When my Mom asked what had happened I told her I didn't know but it might have been too much milk. Too much milk? The recipe said to cream the ingredients together and I didn't have any cream, so I added some milk and the recipe didn't really say how much I should use. Mom explained "cream together" for me. I was hoping adding water to the paint wouldn't have a similar effect.

I did have to call and delay my nail appointment. When I finally got there the manicurist wanted to know just what I had been doing with those hands!

I have kept the wet paint sign in front of the porch for a week now. I want it to have plenty of time to cure and bond with its new paint. —*Love to all, Valerie*

December. It looks like I will be spending my first Christmas in Arkansas. It was not what I had planned but as we all know, life is what happens while we are making other plans.

Bob has had another "Heart" episode and is back in the hospital. Last night he said he felt like his chest was in a vice. He would not hear of me calling 911. He said it would pass. This morning his night shirt was not damp but really wet from perspiration. He said his heart was beating really fast. He was sitting in his chair in the living room, *without* the TV on and he looked terrible. Again, he did not want me to call 911. Then he refused to go to ER. I said I would take him and if he *still* refused, I was, for sure, going to call the paramedics. Since I was supposed to be packing for my flight to CA that evening, he said he would go but he would drive himself. I said OK, but I was going to follow him to the hospital. I didn't trust him not to go straight home!

I grabbed a breakfast bar and my coffee and headed for my car. Today is trash day and when I started out of the driveway, he was pulling back in to take my trash to the curb. I assured him I could do it and that I would be right behind him.

I had to go back in the house to get my sunglasses. 5 min. later he called me. "Where are you honey? I don't see you behind me." When I told him, I had gone back for my glasses he said he was worried that I had, had car trouble. The man's heart was hammering away in his chest and he was worried about me. He called me again from his car to say we're going directly to the Dr.'s office. He had spoken to his heart Dr.'s assistant and she said to come straight there. They were waiting for him and took him right in.

She did an EKG. She tried several times to get his blood pressure. She finally got the top number, 90. She took a picture of his EKG on her phone and texted it to the hospital, put him in wheelchair, and walked him over to the ER. Then there were more tests. EKG, blood pressure, X-ray, blood, and urine samples.

They hooked him up to the monitors. Heart rate 80... Normal for him, 60. Blood pressure still low but climbing... blood test shows elevated white cells. Their "We would like to keep you overnight Mr. Edney" was followed quite quickly with his, "Oh No, I have to get this little lady to the airport so she can be with her family for Christmas. She has been planning this for a long time." All he could think about was getting *me* to the airport in time.

While all this was going on, I was busy tapping on my phone. "Just taking notes" I told him. "For your e-mails?" he wanted to know. When I said yes, he burst out laughing and said, "I finally made the News!"

It turns out he has pneumonia along with a heart that likes to scare us.

When I told him, I was going home to cancel my flights he was very distressed. I told him I wouldn't have a good time in CA worrying about him anyway and that would just have to be that.

When he finally accepted that news, he said "OK, will you bring me some things?" So now I have another list that I have tapped into my phone, not the least of which is a chicken sandwich from Sonic. Crispy with lettuce, mayo, pickles, and cheese. I hope they will let him eat it.

I guess we still need prayers. —*Love, Valerie.*

When talking to Bob last night he said they were going to wake him up at 4am to check his vitals. I asked him *not* to call me. ;) When talking to him this morning I asked him how he was feeling and what he was doing. He said he wanted to go home and when the nurse came in he was making up the bed. That's my guy. He hates to see an unmade bed. Bob is getting 2 doses of IV antibiotics today and so far, has not seen the Dr.

Yesterday on the way home I stopped by the hospitals gift shop. They have the best things in the gift shops at the Mercy clinics. Now, don't think that I was getting something for Bob. There was a pink sweater hanging by the door. It looked so soft and warm. I thought "When I go back to see Bob, he is going to love me in that sweater". Well, I guess it was partly for him. :)

We had lunch together. He was having turkey with mashed potatoes, dressing, and cranberry sauce. I had brought my chicken salad and crackers. His looked and smelled much better than mine. He was complaining about the lack of dessert and wanted me to call room service (Yes, our hospital has a room service menu.) and get him some. When I read his choices from the "Heart" menu he settled right down.

The nurse has been in to check on him. If he needs another round of IVs, he will have to spend another night here, if not he can go home. There may be more blood tests to determine that. We have our fingers crossed.

I have some baby blankets to make, so I'm off to get some yarn and snacks in case he must stay.

Yippee! I'm back and Bob has seen the doctor. His white blood cell count is good; the pneumonia is what caused the heart to go crazy. So, he is good to go. Next stop the Olive Garden. All those tests make my guy hungry!

Merry Christmas and Happy New Year y'all. —*Love to all, Valerie*

CHAPTER 10

Arkansas News 2016

January. It was time to get ready to go on the cruise. Belize was the stop that sold me on this trip. I picked up Bobbie and my new friend and roommate Roberta at 7:30 AM. These girls were definitely not thinking of a start time of 11:30.

We made several stops along the way and got into Houston after dark. Bobbie said she knew the way from there, so I didn't need to have my GPS on anymore. So, I turned it off. Apparently, inevitably that was *not* a good idea. We were soon lost. A telephone call was made to Suzanne, a very nice lady who lives in Houston and was nice enough to invite us to spend Thursday night, Friday night, and Saturday night before the cruise, so she and Bobbie could show Roberta and me around as we had never been to Houston before.

Suzanne started giving me instructions, which I didn't understand. She prefaced them with, go North, go south, go east or go west. I am directionally challenged so those things don't mean anything to me, even when I'm at home.

What I do know is turn right, turn left, make a U-turn, or recalculate. I turned my GPS back on.

VALERIE KATZ

Friday and Saturday, they showed us around Houston, and we went shopping. I shopped like I have an empty closet at home!

Sunday morning, we were up getting everything ready to head for the ship when we got a call from Katie, there was a delay. The ship wasn't in yet!

There was some talk about boarding passes. One of the girls said she folded hers and put it inside her passport. I thought "What a great idea. The two things I need to board ship will be together."

My passport was gone! I didn't have a boarding pass! I asked the girls if they were playing a joke on me. I knew I had brought them with me!

Suzanne went online to print me a boarding pass and the rest of us started to look for my passport. We went through my very small traveling purse, several times

I called Bob and asked him to take a picture, of the picture, of my passport that I had left with him. All he said was, "Just a minute Honey" and in minutes that picture was a text on my phone. That man has been listening when I was giving him instructions on how that phone works!

On Saturday we had been shopping at Sketchers and Stein Mart. Stein Mart wasn't open yet and Sketchers was a no. Never, ever have I waited and wished for a store to open like I did that day. At noon I called, and the answer was yes! Whoopee!

The cruise was very restful which was what both Roberta and I had wanted. We only got off the ship once. That was in Belize where I again forgot that I *did* have clothes at home and didn't have to fill an empty closet.

Happy Hour was every day from 3 to 4. All drinks... Buy one get one for 1.00. I was there every day enjoying the "Drink of the Day".

THE NEWS FROM ARKANSAS

We were having a great time. Then on Friday night I was headed for the bathroom and the door was locked. Now this was a communal bathroom. I couldn't figure out why anyone would lock the door, so I was making quite a production of shaking the handle around and pulling on the door when the girl inside opened the door and pushed out, hard. I went flying backwards landed on my back and hit my head pretty hard. My back felt a little uncomfortable that evening but the next day it seemed to be fine.

As we were getting off the ship and looking for our luggage, we discovered that Roberta's bag wasn't there. We had private transport home and didn't have to take the bus like the rest of the Bella Vista group did but Katie had arranged for us to take our luggage off at the same time the rest of the group did, and she had it expedited quite nicely. Suzanne's friend Randy had misunderstood her directions on when we were to be picked up, so he wasn't there. That was good news, sort of, as it took us another 40 minutes to find Roberta's bag. Apparently, someone had thought it was theirs, had taken it out of the terminal, and then had just abandoned it.

Randy did come to get us. We went back to Suzanne's and we got in my car for our 12 Hour Drive home.

I was driving the last phase of the journey as no one else wanted to drive after dark. About 15 minutes out of Bella Vista it started to snow. I have never driven in falling snow before and am not too keen on repeating the adventure.

During the night my back really started hurting. When I woke up in the morning, I had to roll out of my bed to get my feet under me. I sent Bob a text asking him to please, whenever he got up, call me. He called, and bless his heart, he came right over.

That brings us to today. I've been to the doctor and when I fell during the cruise, I dislodged one of my vertebrae. So, I have been stretched, had my back electrified, and I get to go back tomorrow and do it all over again. I am in a great deal of pain. But, if I don't move, try to take a deep breath, try to move my right arm, or horror of horrors, sneeze, I can remain somewhat comfortable. I think the poor girl that was trying to help me off the table in the doctor's office thought that I was going to break her arm when she tried to move me. Movement just takes my breath away.

Right now I'm sitting in the car in the parking lot of Walmart. I never really have a lot of food in the house but since I've been gone it is really depleted. So, if Bob is going to stay with me and help me get up and down and dressed and undressed etc. etc, I guess he thought he needed to stop and get some food.

The man is an angel....

It is now Sunday, I went to see my wonderful chiropractors Tuesday, Wednesday, Thursday, and Friday. The first thing they did was take x-rays and then the treatment began. That meant 20 minutes lying on this machine that stretches your back, 20 minutes lying on a table with electrodes attached to my back and laying on the ice pack. 10 minutes with my feet in water, also with electrodes, and of course a spinal adjustment. The adjustments have been necessary but very gentle due to the fact that I was in such pain.

This morning I got up out of bed without the excruciating pain. I have a way to go but the pain is definitely very manageable today. However, the treatment with my feet in water turned out to be a problem on Friday. All that time laying around and being treated could not have been tolerated without my trusty iPhone and earbuds to keep me company and entertained.

One minute into the foot and leg treatment you have to turn the velocity up to as much as you can stand. I usually turn it up until my feet are doing a little dance down there. ;) As I was reaching for those controls my phone took a nosedive right down into the water. Since it was tethered to the earbuds, I yanked it out in warp speed! Not fast enough...

So, on the way home a stop at the AT&T store was necessary. All things pertaining to my phone still are checked out with my son-in-law Kevin. I couldn't reach him, so I called Denise. "Mom" she said with a chuckle, "You know those phones can't swim". Yes, I do... I now have a new phone. Since the old one had taken a nosedive into the water it wouldn't come up and deliver any of my "Stuff" to the new phone.

I took it home and connected it to the Internet. No easy feat since the password is on the back of the router, which is on a short tether, under my desk, and my back was NOT happy about me trying to get down there! "Bob!"

The cloud brought back my calendar and my contacts but all the things that I need passwords for had to be downloaded from the App Store. Where do I faithfully store those passwords? Well on my trusty phone of course! The cloud, Netflix, Kindle, AOL, three banks, my credit card, Amazon, and Words with Friends were the ones I could remember. I have managed to find back doors on my computer to get to the "Forgot my password" area and am getting this business sorted out. Also, since I'm tangled up in my earbuds constantly, while I was getting a new phone I got a Bluetooth earbud gadget that should keep me out of trouble. (OK! Stop laughing!).

Bob has been here to get me in and out of the car, in and out of my clothes, in and out of my bed, in and out of my chair, and fix dinner with wonderful desserts. In answer to your queries, not he is not for hire.

So, the phone business is getting sorted out. My old phone is nestled in a bag of rice with the hope of getting it to summon up its memory. My back is doing better. And, I am *hanging on* to my sense of humor!

Thank you to all who have sent wishes for a speedy recovery. They are working! —*Love, Valerie.*

P.S. A big thank you to Siri. Not being able to spend much time in front of my computer, the news has been dictated to her. If you don't know who Siri is, ask a grandchild.

> *I drove myself for the first time today. I really needed to get my nails done! Bob would have taken me, but I cleared the driving possibilities with the Dr. He cautioned me to take it easy. Well, of course! God bless the Smith family chiropractic clinic. I'm 95% better!!* Love to all, Valerie
>
> **February.** *I have just returned from a weeklong trip to Branson MO. Except for lots of shopping, lots of laughing and way too much eating, I have nothing to report. I went with 7 of my Bridge (the card game) friends. I was invited to join this group last year and they are a fun bunch of gals. One of them brought all 6 years of Downton Abbey! Several of us had some late nights watching that. Love to all, Valerie*

April. So here I am, making plans to go to CA. Those are flight plans. My Minnie is sitting in her storage spot. When in CA I usually parked at the home on Variel. That is now no longer an option and Bob is not really interested in hitting the road in a coach. It looks like selling her may be in my future plans.

It is 75 degrees here today. My flowers are up, and blooming and North-West Arkansas is turning green again. Spring is in the air! Some of my friends here have warned me that it has showed here in April. I am trying not to listen.

I am still so happy to be here. I have made some wonderful friends (The ones who are threatening snow have not been scratched off that list) and I am, again, way too busy. Bob does seem to remind me of that from time to time. *Love to all, Valerie*

I have a new car. Did I need a new car? Was I looking for a new car? That would be a big NO. While I was in California, my honey, Bob, called me and said he was going to buy a new car.

Now that was new news about two years ago. He's always saying he's going to buy a new car but then remembers how much he loves the one he has and forgets about it for a while. I have a pat answer for him when he tells me this. "That's nice honey."

He called me a few days later telling me that he was going to put his car in the newspaper and sell it himself because those dealerships weren't going to give him what his car was worth. I figured that was just more talk… "That's nice honey."

Well, he did put his car in the paper and the first person who saw it realized its worth and bought it! It's a good thing there were several states in between us when he was delivering this news, so he couldn't see the startled look on my face! "Well honey" I told him "go over to my house, you know where the keys are, drive my car until you buy a new one". Again, it was a good thing there were several states between us because I knew every car on every lot in this area would have him looking through it. I had another week in California. He was on his own.

When I did finally arrive back in Bella Vista (It was midnight so there was no danger of immediate car shopping) he told me that he had narrowed the search. He no longer wanted a sedan. Now he wanted an SUV. Now you're talking! For me, a sedan is just transportation. A SUV is the bomb! We were off looking the next day.

Since we were in my car I told him that I was going home when he made his decision. I know how long this car shopping takes and I was sure my chatty guy was going to take at least twice that long. "Oh no honey" he said "I'm going to put the car in both of our names. I think you need to be here."

I was ready to take him to the Honda dealer because I am a Honda CRV girl. I have had two, my sister has one, and my granddaughter has one. We love them!

However, Hyundai had the color he was looking for, Sedona Sunset. So, *just* to be fair, we stopped by the Hyundai dealer first. This year Hyundai upgraded their Tucson which is the same size as the Honda CRV, and we took it for a drive. We made no commitment.

We then went across the street to the Honda dealership and drove the new CRV. The nice girl who took us around told us about a real nice Happy Hour a few streets away. We had that dialed in for later.

Afterward, when Bob said, "So honey, what do you think?" my immediate answer was "The Hyundai!"

I had fallen in love with that car. I couldn't tell him enough about what a good choice he had made and how much I liked it. His answer to that, "Well honey, if you like it so much you need to have one too. You need a new car anyway. You've been pretty hard on this one." (Only two small accidents and one of them wasn't my fault. I wasn't even in the car!) So, the next day we were back at the Hyundai dealership to purchase another car for me. I wanted all-wheel drive, so they had to send to Kansas City for mine. I decided to be *very* patient about the one day wait *and* about all the time the paperwork took.

So, the paperwork finally finished, and a 4 to 7 p.m. happy hour only a memory, the salesman took us out to the car to show us how all the bells and whistles worked. Now folks it has taken me almost 2 years to teach this man basic iPhone. Now he has Bluetooth, Serius Radio, navigation, Blue Link, and more. The Radio has an 82-page book titled the "Car Multimedia System", Blue Link has a 39-page book to introduce you to your "Genesis Intelligent Assistant".

Have you started praying for me yet?

There is a 38-page book titled "Quick Reference Guide". That book when into my glove box. All the other manuals went in that place in the back that holds the spare tire and a complementary first aid kit. I won't even try to describe the look on my honey's face when that happened.

So here we were with two brand-new cars and only one of us knowing how things worked. Our conversations went something like this. **Bob,** "we need to register for Serius radio." **Me,** "we don't have to do that now we have Sirius radio free for one year. We can do that later." **Bob,** "but I keep getting emails." **Me,** "Delete them. I'm not going to talk about this for a year." **Bob,** "but what if we're traveling across country and it goes out. (Oh no we might miss the end of the song)." **Me,** "Not for a year!" **Bob,** "It didn't used to be this complicated. Well what about "My Hyundai"? They want us to register for that also and you are going to need that for service reminders on the car." And he's right. I am going to need it. I'm going to need those reminders. But my man knows when all that stuff needs to be done. He won't need them. **Me,** "OK let's get breakfast, and a cup of coffee and go out on the deck. We're both getting the same emails. We'll go through them together, slowly."

Now most of you know, I hope, that everything in this world now needs a username and a password. My guy, not so much. But I am walking him through this with, what for me, is remarkable patients. I have him take notes and then I put the information in his iPhone. His phone is going to get even with me for that. I just know it.

He calls me from his car more often than is necessary. He doesn't complain any more about the poor service when I call him from mine. He says, "You see honey, you really did need a new car. I can hear you really well now." I love this guy. He's definitely a keeper!

Oh yes, Hyundai has great warranties and they plan on standing behind their cars. There's one more 16-page book. It's title is "A Consumer's Guide to the Arkansas Lemon Law". I put that one in my glove box too. —*Love to all, Valerie*

June. Bob is ready. He has put his house up for sale and will be moving in to 9 Bella Lane with me. We have been talking about it for a while but packing up the home he and Brenda had shared was just too daunting. I assured him I would be there to help him through the process. The idea was to sell the house, move the things Bob wanted to keep either to 9 Bella Lane or to a storage facility, and then have an Estate Sale to get rid of the rest.

I was very pleasantly surprised at how well he went through the process. When he asked me if there was anything, I might like to have I pointed to a small old-fashioned hutch and a clock hanging on the wall. He immediately picked them up and put them in the car. And so, it started. He was still living there, and on each visit, more things would end up in our cars.

Brenda and I had vastly different ideas on home décor and I kept thinking "What in the world would I do with this stuff at my house?" The downstairs of my home was pretty empty since Martha had moved out so there was room there.

I took my friend Bobbie to the Kenzie Lane house and she wanted to know why I was waiting. "Get a moving van and move all the stuff you want now." Bob was apprised of this plan and he agreed. Then the real decisions had to be made. Just what did Bob want to keep?

First the great room downstairs on Bella Lane had to be painted. I picked out a color from one of the pictures that was to be hung in that room, Bob hired Glen the painter who was fitting us into his schedule, and we were set to go. (Don't get nervous. It did not turn out to be the 7-day debacle the front porch turned into.) However, I was sent out for more paint that was going to be required for a second coat the next day and when I got back took one look at the paint already on the walls and said, "Oh dear!" Bob and the painter immediately stopped what they were doing and asked, "Don't you like the color?" It was bright! Bob looked at me and said softly, "Honey, this is the color that you picked out. Are you unhappy with it now?" I wasn't sure, but those two men were looking very distressed. Glen was, after all, fitting us in as a favor. So, I said it was just a little brighter than I thought it would be, but it would be OK. After the final coat was in place it was pretty bright, but that room is a little dark, so I figured all was well.

Brenda had "Stuff". There were many pictures on the walls at McKenzie Lane that we both liked but I kept asking Bob, "What will we do with them. I have no walls. There are 7 doors in the living room alone." However, there were two very big, newly painted, walls downstairs.

We needed to empty the bedrooms and clean out Brenda's closets and dresser drawers. Bob had never been able to tackle that job. I said just to bring three large bags to each room, one for Helping Hands and one for trash, and one for things to go to Bella Lane. Bob went to another part of the house to organize other areas and left me to take care of this business. He was handling the dismantling of this part of his life so well and I was more than ready to help and make it as easy for him as possible.

The kitchen was handled in the same manner. "Bring me 3 large bags". I must add here that the 3-bag rule was just a start. All rooms needed many more than three. When we finished the first weekend the front of the house was piled high with bags, boxes, and items that were not a good fit for Helping Hands. Monday was trash day and Bob got up early and waited for the trash man to arrive, so he could give him a very nice tip and help him load all that stuff into his truck.

Bobbie wanted to purchase some of the items from Bob's house so the things she and her husband Bill could not get into their car were to be moved by the truck. *Love to all, Valerie*

Moving Day... The truck was to come to Bella Lane first. All things being displaced by the addition of Bob's items were loaded. Then off to Kenzie Lane for those items to be unloaded and the furniture that had made the final cut to be loaded, along with the stuff for Bobbie. The movers were wonderful. They moved furniture from my top floor to the bottom floor and moved it around to my satisfaction. Then placed the new furniture in what we were hoping would be their final destination. We were pooped.

When Bob decided to take up residence on Bella Lane his first thought had been to not leave his home unattended but to stay there until the home was sold. I guess he decided he might as well move with the rest of his possessions, we could get his clothes when we were rested, and the two homes were only 5 minutes apart.

As Bob went back, almost daily, to check and see if the realtors had left any lights on or left the garage door open, I went with him and claimed more treasures. Soon his departures were announced with, "I'm going over to the house. Want to go shopping?" "Absolutely", I would say. "That place has the best no questions asked return policy. They will even come and pick the stuff up!"

Our home has quite a different look. Brenda was quite fond of a wild animal theme, so elephants, giraffes, lions, and tigers decorate both the upper and lower floors. I didn't think I would care for it but have decided I do like the many changes and Bob is happy with so many of his things around him.

This was a good move for us. We have settled in nicely and there was no need for a storage facility. We have turned the downstairs great-room into a cozy TV room and end most of our days there.

About Bob, **we** were introduced by Ron and Kay, Bob's neighbors, and my friends from church. In the twice monthly 9-hole golf matches the church folk partake in, I am usually matched up with various gents. The first time I drew Bob as my partner I was impressed by the care he took of me out on the course. Now, we *were* partners and there were prizes (a sleeve of golf balls) and *bragging rights* to be considered, but he took more notice of where my ball ended up, and helped with the reading of the greens etc. The group always goes for a meal after golf and he treated me. My "Oh no, you don't have to do that" was brushed aside with a smile and a "Yes please let me".

On another occasion Ron and Kay were getting a group together to go to the Moose Lodge for dinner and dancing. That was still bit emotional for me as we used to go there as a group with David, but with a little prodding I agreed to go.

When they came to pick me up, there was Bob sitting in the back seat. He bought my dinner and my drinks. It was a little more difficult to be there than I had anticipated and seemed to be made harder by the fact that Bob seemed to be treating it as a date. So, down went the drinks. Every time Bob asked if I wanted another, I said yes. It was a good thing we weren't driving. When we arrived at my house Bob said he would walk me to the door. I said that would not be necessary, so he planted a big kiss right on my mouth.

The next time I saw him he said he thought he owed me an apology. "For what?" I asked. "Well", he said, "The last time I saw you I planted a big wet kiss on you." Don't worry" I said, "No harm no foul."

We continued to be paired up for golf. I was a little suspicious as I had never had the same partner more than once before. About the third time we played together his daughter, Shelly, was in town and came to spend the afternoon on the course, visiting, not playing, she came up to me before the match and asked me if I wanted to ride with Bob. I said "No, I'm fine." She said she really wouldn't mind but I said, "No thank you, I'm fine too", and off we went. At dinner after the game Bob went to wash his hands and Shelly said, "I don't like a lot of people Valerie, but I really like you." I replied, "Well don't fall in love. I don't want a relationship with anyone, including your father." She said, "That's great, either does he! You can play golf, go dancing, and just be friends."

So that's how things went. We played golf, went dancing, *no kissing*, and were enjoying our time together. Then we started to have deeper feelings for each other. Neither one of us wanted to say anything as we had already made our positions *crystal* clear.

Then, after a golf outing, the meal being hosted by Ron & Kay at their home, they lived on the Scottsdale Golf Course right across the street from Bob, personal golf carts had been taken to the course, so we stopped at Bob's to drop his off. He invited me in for a drink which we took across the street to the party.

Later, Bob wanted to know if I wanted to go back to his house for a refresher of the drinks. I agreed and off we went. After the drinks were poured he told me he had purchased a new and quite expensive mattress and wanted me to see what I thought of it. I told him I was no expert, but he really seemed to want my opinion. He said to go ahead and sit on it which I did. Then he said to lie down and test it. At this point I burst out laughing and asked him "Did this line really work for you back in the day?" He laughed too, and we went back to the party.

Our feelings for each other grew and were acknowledged. Martha said her work here was done and moved to Mesa Arizona.

My children are happy for us and now when I am traveling there is someone else to share their concerns about my whereabouts and safety. Donald added an app to our phones, so my location could be pinpointed when I am on the road. He wanted to share the app with Bob to help allay his concerns too. I told him to wait. I would do it when I got home.

But Don called Bob anyway. After 30 min. of instructions Don was banging himself on the head and I was saying I told you so and now you know why! We got it sorted out when I got home. I am happy. —*Love to all, Valerie*

August. The Minnie has been sold and I have once again purchased a new motor home. It is a class B Road Trek. After much on-line looking I found exactly what I was looking for. Correct year, body style and price! When I called the owner, I told her I would meet her in Aug. with a cashier's check in hand. It was just 5 miles from Sister Martha's home in Mesa AZ!

We loaded the car up with what I decided would be the bare necessities for traveling in the new coach, and Bob drove me to Mesa. The next day we looked her over and took her to for a test drive. When we were pulling back into their driveway there was a man following us. He wanted to know if the Trek was still for sale. The owner said he thought I was going to take it but if I didn't he would have to get on a list. They had five people on a list to buy it if I changed my mind!

Bob went home, Martha and I went Trek'n to CA. It was time for the annual Birthday Bash!

My Granddaughter, Jennifer, drove back to Bella Vista with me. On the second day she asked me why everyone was so nervous about me traveling. It seems everyone, one at a time, had asked her to be sure to take care good of Grandma. I certainly can't complain that no one cares about me, but does she not read The News?! *Love to all, Valerie*

December. Martha has flown to Bella Vista. She will accompany me on my trip out to CA for Christmas. I will drop her off in Mesa and go on alone to CA. It only takes 1 day so no one is blowing too much sand over me driving alone.

I love my new Trek! I can park it in the driveway, no more storage site. We can drive it around town sometimes, so I don't have to worry about dead batteries and such. Dumping is ever so much easier, which is a BIG plus. But most of all, it is cozy and perfect for me. —*Love to all, Valerie*

CHAPTER 11

Arkansas News 2017

January. I have had a wonderful time in CA. I have been able to see all the family and many of my friends, but Bella Lane is calling. There have been many calls and texts to and from Bob. He has been keeping the home fires burning and sending me *stuff* I ordered before I left but had not arrived before Martha and I hit the road. Denise said now she knew why Bob had not come with me. He had chores!

Don took a few days off and drove home with me. A road trip with my boy always puts a smile on my face!

Before I left for CA, I had asked Bob to take the TV out of the Trek. Except for the time Martha and I wanted to watch Dancing with the Stars, I have never watched TV in any of my coaches. Don and Debbie bought me a projector that hooks up to my phone, so I can watch Netflix when I am on the road. It fits in the palm of my hand! The couch/bed in back is powered and will adjust to a nice reclining position and the large piece of heavy white cardboard that serves quite nicely as a screen, stores perfectly under one of the bed cushions. In the evening we poured ourselves a drink, put our feet up and watched a movie. Perfect...

VALERIE KATZ

I called Bob to tell him we were about 30 min. out. When we pulled into the driveway, he was waiting there for us. Since I had been gone for so long, I went up to him and said, "I would like to introduce myself. I'm your Sweetheart!" Then I threw my arms around him and gave him a big hug.

My Magnolia tree and I have grown, and our roots seem to be well established. This is home. —*Thanks for traveling with me. Valerie*